*The New York
Cruciform Lectionary*

Jeffrey C. Anderson

The New York Cruciform Lectionary

Published for
COLLEGE ART ASSOCIATION
by
THE PENNSYLVANIA STATE UNIVERSITY PRESS
UNIVERSITY PARK, PENNSYLVANIA 1992

Monographs on the Fine Arts
sponsored by
COLLEGE ART ASSOCIATION
Volume XLVIII
Editor, Nicholas Adams

Library of Congress Cataloging-in-Publication Data
Anderson, Jeffrey C.
　　The New York Cruciform Lectionary / Jeffrey C. Anderson.
　　　　p.　　　cm.—(Monographs on the fine arts ; v. 48)
　　Includes bibliographical references and index.
　　ISBN 0-271-00743-5
　　1. New York Cruciform Lectionary.　2. Evangeliaries
—Illustrations.　3. Illumination of books and manuscripts,
Byzantine.　4. Orthodox Eastern Church—Liturgy—Texts
—Illustrations.　5. Pierpont Morgan Library.　I. College Art
Association of America.　II. Title.　III. Series: Monographs on the
fine arts ; 48.
ND3359.N48A44 1992
745.6′7487—dc20　　　　　　　　　　　　　　　　　90-49687
　　　　　　　　　　　　　　　　　　　　　　　　　　　CIP

Copyright © 1992 College Art Association, Inc.
ALL RIGHTS RESERVED
Printed in the United States of America

*It is the policy of The Pennsylvania State University Press to use
acid-free paper for the first printing of all clothbound books.
Publications on uncoated stock satisfy the minimum requirements of
American National Standard for Information Sciences—Permanence of
Paper for Printed Library Materials, ANSI Z39.48–1984.*

In Honor of
Kurt Weitzmann

Contents

	LIST OF ILLUSTRATIONS	ix
	LIST OF ABBREVIATIONS	xi
	INTRODUCTION: THE BYZANTINE GOSPEL LECTIONARY	1
I	The Illustration and Decoration of the New York Lectionary	13
II	Making the New York Lectionary: Procedures and Techniques	31
III	Saints and Feasts Commemorated in the Menologion	41
IV	The Cruciform Lectionary in the Twelfth Century	75
V	Conclusion and Remarks on Style and Date	91
	INDEX	99
	ILLUSTRATIONS	103

List of Illustrations

Fig. A. Ruling pattern, Morgan MS 692
Fig. B. Ruling pattern to Evangelist portrait, Morgan MS 692
Fig. C. Ruling pattern, Lond. Add. 39,603
Fig. D. Ruling pattern, Dumbarton Oaks, MS 1 (double-column text)
Fig. E. Ruling pattern, Dumbarton Oaks, MS 1 (cruciform text)

New York, Pierpont Morgan Library, cod. M 692 (photos: Morgan Library):

1. Fol. 1v: Saint John the Evangelist
2. Fol. 2: Title page
3. Fol. 2v: John the Evangelist writing
4. Fol. 4: Saint Peter runs to Christ's tomb
5. Fol. 6: John the Baptist speaks of Christ to his disciples
6. Fol. 10v: Christ appears to the Disciples
7. Fol. 11: Christ speaks to Thomas and the Disciples
8. Fol. 22v: Miracle at the pool of Bethesda
9a. Fol. 23 (top): Christ and the Paralytic
9b. Fol. 23 (bottom): The Jews and the Paralytic
10. Fol. 25v: Christ in the temple at Capernaum
11. Fol. 29v: Christ and the Woman at the Well
12. Fol. 38: Christ and the Blind Youth
13. Fol. 56: Christ Teaching
14. Fol. 57: Christ, the Priests, and the Pharisees
15. Fol. 64v: The Healing at Gadara
16. Fol. 87: Title page: Beginning of the new year and the readings from Luke
17. Fol. 87v: Christ teaching at Capernaum, and the Man Possessed
18. Fol. 91: Christ heals the son of the Widow of Nain
19. Fol. 94v: Christ and the Rich Man
20. Fol. 123v: Saint Mark the Evangelist
21. Fol. 124: Title page of the first Sunday of Lent, and the beginning of the Mark readings; portrait of Saint Theodore Tiron
22. Fol. 135v: Christ on the Mount of Olives and Jerusalem
23. Fol. 136: The Disciples go to Jerusalem
24. Fol. 159v: Crowing rooster
25. Fol. 167v: Saint Peter weeps as rooster crows
26. Fol. 168: Portrait of Christ
27. Fol. 182v: Crowing rooster
28. Fol. 183: Saint Peter weeping
29. Fol. 214: Title page of the Menologion; portrait of Saint Symeon Stylites
30a. Fol. 221v (top): Christ kneels before the hand of God
30b. Fol. 221v (bottom): Christ explains the voice from heaven
31a. Fol. 222 (top): Crosses on Calvary
31b. Fol. 222 (bottom): Moses and cross with serpent
32. Fol. 222v: Priests plotting Christ's death
33. Fol. 223: Christ and Pilate
34. Fol. 224: The Crucifixion
35. Fol. 225: Saint Niketas
36. Fol. 235: Saint Luke
37. Fol. 238: Saint Demetrios
38. Fol. 260: The Baptism of Christ
39. Fol. 264: Presentation of Christ in the Temple
40. Fol. 284: The Transfiguration
41. Fol. 104: Initial *epsilon*
42. Fol. 160: Initial *epsilon*

London, British Library, Add. MS 39,603 (photos: British Library):

43. Fol. 1: Title page of the Easter and John readings
44. Fol. 1v: Initial *epsilon*
45. Fol. 42: Title page of the Matthew readings
46. Fol. 112: Title page of the Luke readings
47. Fol. 195v: Initial *epsilon*

List of Illustrations

Mount Athos, Iviron Monastery, unnumbered lectionary:
48. Fol. 1: Title page of the Easter and John readings
49. Fol. 100: Title page of the Luke readings
50. Fol. 135: Title page of the Lent and Mark readings
51. Fol. 281: Title page of the Menologion

Washington, Dumbarton Oaks Collection, MS 1 (photos: Dumbarton Oaks):
52. Fol. 22: Christ and the Woman at the Well
53. Fol. 65: Title page of the Luke readings
54. Fol. 122v: Saint Peter weeps as the rooster crows

Paris, Bibliothèque Nationale, gr. 189 (photos: Bibliothèque Nationale):
55. Fol. 315v: Saint Mark the Evangelist
56. Fol. 2: Beginning of the Gospel of John

Mount Athos, Panteleimon Monastery, cod. 2:
57. Fol. 115v: Saint Mark the Evangelist
58. Fol. 40v: Christ heals the Blind Youth
59. Fol. 63: The healing at Gadara

Athens, National Library, cod. 190 (photos: Kordouli, National Library):
60. Fol. 2v: Saint Peter
61. Fol. 56v: The healing at Gadara

62. Mount Athos, Gregoriou Monastery, cod. 157, fol. 79: Moses teaching
63. Istanbul, Topkapı Sarayı, cod. 8, fol. 203: Miracle of the Quail and Manna (photo: K. Weitzmann)
64. New York, Pierpont Morgan Library, cod. M 639, fol. 19v: Miracle at Bethesda (photo: Morgan Library)

List of Abbreviations

Aland, *Liste* — K. Aland, *Kurzegefasste Liste der griechischen Handschriften des Neuen Testaments,* Berlin, 1963.

Anderson, "Seraglio Octateuch" — J. Anderson, "The Seraglio Octateuch and the Kokkinobaphos Master," *DOP,* XXXVI, 1982, 83–114.

Colwell and Riddle, *Prolegomena* — E. Colwell and D. Riddle, *Prolegomena to the Study of the Lectionary Text of the Gospels,* Studies in the Lectionary Text of the Greek New Testament, I, Chicago, 1933.

DOP — *Dumbarton Oaks Papers*

Gregory, *Textkritik* — C. Gregory, *Textkritik des Neuen Testaments,* I, Leipzig, 1900.

Greek Manuscripts from American Collections — *Illuminated Greek Manuscripts from American Collections: An Exhibition in Honor of Kurt Weitzmann,* ed. G. Vikan, Princeton, 1973.

Huber, *Athos* — P. Huber, *Athos: Leben, Glaube, Kunst,* Zurich, 1969.

Lake, *Dated Greek MSS* — K. and S. Lake, *Dated Greek Minuscule Manuscripts to the Year 1200,* Monumenta Palaeographica Vetera, First Series, I–X, Boston, 1934–45.

Marava-Chatzinicolaou and Toufexi-Paschou, *Manuscripts of the National Library of Greece* — A. Marava-Chatzinicolaou and Ch. Toufexi-Paschou, *Catalogue of the Illuminated Byzantine Manuscripts of the National Library of Greece,* I, Athens, 1978.

Omont, *Evangiles* — H. Omont, *Evangiles avec peintures byzantines du XIe siècle,* Paris, n.d.

Omont, *Miniatures* — H. Omont, *Miniatures des plus anciens manuscrits grecs de la Bibliothèque Nationale du VIe au XIVe siècle,* 2d ed., Paris, 1929.

REB — *Revue des études byzantines*

Treasures of Athos — S. Pelekanides, M. Stylianos, P. Christou, Ch. Tsioumis and S. Kadas, *The Treasures of Mount Athos,* I–III, Athens, 1973–75.

Velmans, *Tétraévangile* — T. Velmans, *Le Tétraévangile de la Laurentienne,* Bibliothèque des Cahiers archéologiques, V, Paris, 1971.

Weitzmann, *Byz. Buchmalerei* — K. Weitzmann, *Die byzantinischen Buchmalerei des 9. und 10. Jahrhunderts,* Berlin, 1935.

Weitzmann, *Liturgical Gospels and Psalters* — K. Weitzmann, *Byzantine Liturgical Gospels and Psalters,* London, 1980.

Weitzmann, "Morgan 639" — K. Weitzmann, "The Constantinopolitan Lectionary, Morgan 639," *Studies in Art and Literature for Belle da Costa Greene,* ed. D. Miner, Princeton, 1954, 358–73; reprinted in *Liturgical Gospels and Psalters,* XIV.

Weitzmann, *Studies* — K. Weitzmann, *Studies in Classical and Byzantine Manuscript Illumination,* ed. H. Kessler, Chicago, 1971.

Introduction:
The Byzantine Gospel Lectionary

In his famous Letter 96 to Trajan,[1] the younger Pliny describes an early second-century Christian service. He tells of the congregation meeting before dawn and vowing to abstain from improper conduct. During the service the members chanted psalms in Christ's honor; then, after a recess, those who were baptized gathered for a meal. Around the middle of the century, Justin Martyr mentions the use of the writings of the prophets and what he calls the "memoirs of the Apostles" (ἀπομνημονεύματα τῶν ἀποστόλων) as part of the service.[2] Such sources reveal a liturgy that, although doubtless primitive, was structured in a familiar way, in two distinct parts. The first centered on a reading, which might serve as the basis of a sermon. In the private house converted for use by the Christian community of Dura Europos, Syria, exists some indication of the spaces in which these early rites were conducted. Later evidence casts an oblique light on the growth of the liturgy after the second century. The list of vessels and other objects confiscated during a raid on the North African church at Cirta Constantina in 303,[3] as well as church construction from Constantine to Justinian, speaks of cult practices requiring both a large, impressive stage[4] and substantial equipment in the form of patens, chalices, censors, and so on. But of the materials needed for the service, books are perhaps the most important. Books are what the authorities were searching for in the small North African church when they uncovered cups, plates, and garments. The importance books held for the early Church is attested by Constantine the Great's letter to Eusebius; in it he orders fifty well-made copies of the Holy Scripture to serve the needs of the various churches in the newly established capital.[5]

In the centuries after the death of Constantine, the liturgy became increasingly complex and richly ceremonial. As church feasts were added, passages from the Old and New Testaments were selected and assigned as more or less fixed readings. The Gospels, though, played a role beyond that of merely being the source for one set of lessons (and lessons of such importance that they were entrusted only to a deacon, never to a reader or chanter). By the early eighth century the Divine Liturgy began with the First (Little, Lesser) Entrance, which the Patriarch of Constantinople, Germanos I (715–30), described as a procession headed by the deacon carrying the Gospels,

---

1. *Pliny: Letters and Panegyricus,* II, trans. B. Radice, Loeb Classical Library, Cambridge, Mass., 1975, 288–89.

2. *Apology* 1.67: *Saint Justin: Apologies,* ed. and trans. A. Wartelle, Paris, 1987, 190–93.

3. We know this through quotations of the transcript of the bishop's trial in 320: C. Zwisa, *S. Optati Milevitani Libri VII,* Corpus scriptorum Ecclesiasticorum Latinorum, XXVI, Vienna, 1893, 187; on this matter, see also C. Lepelley, *Les cités de l'Afrique romaine au Bas-empire,* I, Paris, 1979, 336–38.

4. T. Mathews, *The Early Churches of Constantinople: Architecture and Liturgy,* University Park, Pa., and London, 1971, explores the relationship between the service and building forms.

5. Incorporated verbatim into Eusebius's *Life of Constantine,* 4.36: I. Heikel, *Eusebius Werke,* I, Die griechischen christlichen Schriftsteller der ersten drei Jahrhunderte, VII, Leipzig, 1902, 131–32.

Introduction

followed by the celebrant. To Germanos the entrance of the priest and deacon bearing the manuscript signified nothing less than the coming of the Son of God into this world.[6] A roughly contemporary Gospel book of the kind used in the service survives in the University Library at Basel.[7] The scribe who copied the text marked the beginnings and ends of the passages read in church, and in the margins he added the various phrases that served to introduce, as freestanding units, readings cut or pruned (*pericope*) from their narrative context. It is not difficult to find medieval manuscripts of the Greek Gospel text that include the liturgical apparatus: a set of tables to allow the reader to identify the passage for the day, the marginal or interlinear *arche* and *telos* signs that told him precisely where to begin and end the lesson, and the standard *incipits,* such as "At that time . . ." or "The Lord said to his disciples. . . ."[8] Such copies of the Gospels continued to be produced until the fall of Constantinople. Occasionally, the owner of a Gospel book made without the lectionary apparatus would have a scribe prepare it for use in the service. The Vienna Gospels (Vind. theol. gr. 154) was made around 1050, but its table of readings and the interlinear markings were added centuries later.[9]

However long and widespread the liturgical use of the Gospel book was, there also appeared at some time in early Byzantine history the kind of book known as the Gospel lectionary, the kind discussed here in a magnificent cruciform example in the Pierpont Morgan Library, New York. The New York Lectionary, along with most of the others I will use for comparison, is an invention of the Middle Ages. A Gospel passage is assigned to nearly every day on which a service might be held, and for important feasts readings are provided to cover morning and even hourly services. Owing to the nature of the calendar and the requirements of the church, the text was divided and subdivided into various parts. The basic division is twofold: the synaxarion and the menologion. The synaxarion contains the movable readings beginning with Easter Sunday and ending with the celebration of Christ's Passion. This first half is divided into four parts, which by the early eleventh century had come to be associated with the Evangelists: the John readings extend from Easter to Pentecost, those from Matthew from Pentecost to around mid-September and the Luke readings from mid-September to the beginning of Lent, and Mark supplies the Lenten pericopes. The menologion, the second major part of the lectionary, contains the fixed celebrations arranged daily and by month, beginning with September. So complete is the medieval calendar that the text of four Gospels was exhausted before the end of the lectionary. Some readings would be given more than once in the course of the year, and cross-references occur with increasing frequency toward the end of the menologion. Figure 31b, for example, contains one such reference. At the head of the pericope the scribe wrote two lines of gilt half-uncial, the first of which gives the day and then an instruction to the reader: "Saturday before the (Feast of the) Elevation (of the Holy Cross): see the seventh Saturday in Matthew." When preparing the service for that day, the deacon knew he would need to turn back to the synaxarion and find the Matthew readings, then select the passage for the

---

6. N. Borgia, *Il commentario liturgico di S. Germano patriarca Constantinopolitano,* Studi liturgici, I, Grottaferrata, 1912, 21 (sec. 24); see also his comments, 26 (sec. 31) and 27 (sec. 32), that relate the text to Christ and his Incarnation.

7. Universitätsbibliothek, cod. AN.3.12: W. Hatch, *The Principal Uncial Manuscripts of the New Testament,* Chicago, 1939, pl. XXXVIII; G. Cavallo, *Ricerche sulla maiuscola biblica,* Florence, 1967, 107; C. Nordenfalk, *Die spätantiken Buchstaben,* Stockholm, 1970, 189–94, figs. 52–56.

8. Eventually a set of six essentially standard incipits comes into use; the phrases are given in chapter III, note 10.

9. P. Buberl and H. Gerstinger, *Die byzantinischen Handschriften,* II, *Die Handschriften des X.–XVIII. Jahrhunderts,* Die illuminierten Handschriften und Inkunabeln der Nationalbibliothek in Wien, VIII/4, Leipzig, 1938, 21.

seventh Saturday. The reproduction shows another feature of the Gospel lectionary used in the Middle Ages; above the lines of text are the neumes, the markings of Greek ekphonetic notation. Generally written in carmine ink, they were added to enable the reader to chant the pericopes.

Although the structure of the medieval lectionary can be easily summarized, the historical circumstances surrounding its invention remain unclear. Who, for instance, ordered and supervised the arrangement of the calendar, and by what means were the manuscripts disseminated? What can be said about the lectionary prior to the ninth century? One finds that even basic issues, such as what the book was called, also remain unclear. The lectionary appears to have been known by a number of names. A scribe might refer to one he had written as the "book of readings" or a "collection of readings";[10] in the Typikon of Saint Sophia, which gives the pericopes and hymns used in the patriarchal service, the lectionary is called the *megaleion,* the "great book."[11] In fact, in trying to discover what the Byzantines normally called the lectionary, we encounter a linguistic confusion that seems to arise from their indifference to any need for a distinction between lectionary and Gospel book. Over centuries, both texts were identified by the same ancient name, *evangelion,* a name that stressed performance of the reading.[12] Yet there seems to come a time when it became either necessary or convenient to have separate designations, and the Byzantines then coined the term *tetraevangelion* to denote the Gospel book; the added prefix necessarily shifts the emphasis away from the performance of the reading to a book divided into four parts. The two terms regularly appear in the lists and inventories that survive in some number from the eleventh century onward,[13] just when the Gospel lectionary with a complete calendar of readings became popular. That the Byzantines would retain the ancient term for the new kind of book, or so often add lectionary tables to copies of the Gospels, should alert us to the potential difficulty of writing the history of the early lectionary. In addition, the centuries-long absence of clear language distinctions suggests that it is impossible to grasp the significance and purpose of the Gospels without at least having some working knowledge of the contemporary lectionary. Despite the amount of evidence available to us in the form of about 2,200 manuscripts,[14] the origin and history of the Gospel lectionary remain in considerable doubt.

Regarding the origin of the lectionary, we cannot determine with certainty whether we should speak of a process of development or perhaps something closer to an invention. According to a recent argument,[15] the Emperor Justinian (527–65) may have been instrumental in establishing the two-part structure of the service book; in the sixth century and after its development followed an organic process dictated by the growth of the liturgy, itself an expression of evolving doctrine acknowledged through corporate devotion. Unfortunately, no sixth-century lectionaries survive to confirm the origin. In fact, no lectionary, counting manuscript fragments, can be securely dated

10. That is, εὐαγγελικὴ βίβλος (Lake, *Dated Greek MSS,* IV, MS 173), and ἐκλογάδη τοῦ εὐαγγελίου (VI, MS 266).

11. J. Mateos, *Le typikon de la Grande Eglise,* II, *Le cycle des fêtes mobiles,* Orientalia Christiana analecta, CLXVI, Rome, 1963, 80, 82, 84.

12. G. Lampe, *A Patristic Greek Lectionary,* Oxford, 1968, s.v.

13. For the two terms used together, one turns to the inventories and donors' lists of the Middle Ages, to, for example, P. Gautier, "Le typikon du sébaste Grégoire Pakourianos," *REB,* XLII, 1984, 121, or C. Diehl, "Le trésor et la bibliothèque de Patmos au commencement du 13ᵉ siècle," *Byzantinische Zeitschrift,* 1, 1892, 514. These sources also provide us with the Byzantine terms for the Saturday-Sunday, σαββατοκυριακόν, and daily, καθημερινόν, lectionary types.

14. The estimate of K. and B. Aland, *The Text of the New Testament: An Introduction to the Critical Editions and to the Theory and Practice of Modern Criticism,* trans. E. Rhodes, Grand Rapids, Mich., and Leiden, 1987, 160.

15. Y. Burns, "The Historical Events that Occasioned the Inception of the Gospel Lectionary," *XVI. Internationaler Byzantinistenkongress, Akten,* II/4, Vienna, 1982, 119–27.

Introduction

before the eighth century.[16] It is not possible, in other words, to sift through a mass of surviving manuscripts, to place them in chronological order, and then, using these books as evidence, to trace the history of the lectionary and the Eastern church calendar. The early history of service books must be inferred from sources whose actual dates range from the eighth to fourteenth century and whose contents are far more restricted than those of most eleventh- and twelfth-century lectionaries. There exists a handful of manuscripts whose limited number of readings does not seem to satisfy what we could reasonably assume to be the church calendar as it was observed when the manuscripts were made. Some of the books with only a few readings may have been copied from much earlier manuscripts. The element of doubt that can always exist as to whether a manuscript is a fresh compilation or a copy of what happened to be available allows the surviving lectionaries to be studied by content rather than by their actual dates. Thus a fourteenth-century manuscript can be said to reveal seventh-century practices, whereas a tenth-century lectionary might reflect the liturgy of the ninth century. Although arranging the manuscripts according to content can create the appearance of an orderly evolution over time and can yield some truly important results,[17] one hesitates to consider this a wholly satisfactory way to study the surviving material because it demands that we ignore the provenance and chronology of the documents themselves.

Putting the problem into the starkest terms may be helpful: At what point did the number of readings become large enough to justify, in terms of opposing pressures, the production of a separate book? The cost of producing the lectionary for churches that had access to the readings in the form of the Gospel book or New Testament was undoubtedly a factor since the sixth to the ninth century in the East was often marked by economic uncertainty. In the Gospel book or New Testament, the user had a text that not only encompassed all possible readings but was written in a continuous narrative form that could be used for study and teaching. Outside the church service, the lectionary had no value. When we consider those lectionaries that seem to be out of date because their scribes copied only a small selection of readings, a number of explanations come to mind as ways to account for the apparent anachronism: the book that does not adequately represent the practices of its time because it contains fewer feasts than we know were then celebrated. But celebrated where, and by whom? For much of its history the Byzantine Empire covered a vast territory. Within it existed varying liturgical practices, some local in nature and others arising from differences between monastic and cathedral observances. The role of chanting may have some bearing on the growth of the lectionary.[18]

Differences in handwriting styles suggest that some of the early manuscripts and surviving

---

16. Ibid., 125, identifies the single-leaf Paris. suppl. gr. 1155, fol. 19, as the earliest lectionary fragment to survive and dates it in the seventh century. As Burns points out, the small amount of text we have suggests a kind of transition between a Gospel book and an actual lectionary of the medieval type. The script of the manuscript shows Western traits and has been associated, as an eighth-century work, with an Italian scriptorium: G. Cavallo, "Funzione e strutture della maiuscole greca tra i secoli VIII–XI," *La paléographie grecque et byzantine*, Paris, 1977, 106–7. For a leaf, see H. Omont, *Fac-similés des plus anciens manuscrits en onciale et en minuscule de la Bibliothèque Nationale du IVe au XIIe siècle*, Paris, 1892, pl. xx bis.

17. Burns (as in note 15), 124–26. Her analysis of the Vat. Ottob. gr. 175 yields important information on the patriarch's use of the lectionary in Constantinopolitan services prior to the tenth century: see Y. Burns, "The Lectionary of the Patriarch of Constantinople," *Studia Patristica*, xv/1, ed. E. Livingstone, Texte und Untersuchungen zur Geschichte der altchristlichen Literatur, cxxviii, Berlin, 1984, 515–20.

18. R. Devreesse, *Introduction à l'étude des manuscrits grecs*, Paris, 1954, 197–98, notes that texts were chanted from an early period; while generally true, the statement is too comprehensive. As late as the Middle Ages, one of the most important liturgical books, the psalter, was still not uniformly treated; see O. Strunk, "The Byzantine Office at Hagia Sophia," *DOP*, ix–x, 1956, 192.

fragments were produced over an area that stretched from Italy, through Constantinople, to Palestine.[19] Calendars may include—and illustration call attention to—celebrations of purely local significance; the handsome tenth-century lectionary at Saint Catherine's, Sinai. gr. 204, contains a full-page miniature of only one saint, the obscure Peter of Monabata.[20] It is also easy to lose sight of the fact that the Gospels were not the only source of readings in the Byzantine church. As Justin Martyr states, and as liturgical and direct evidence confirms,[21] Old Testament writings provided lessons as well, though we may have reason to believe that some began to fall into disuse between the eighth and tenth centuries, at least in the cathedral services of Constantinople.[22]

The practical argument fails because it cannot account for why lectionary manuscripts begin to appear in the eighth century. It actually leads one to wonder why any were ever made, since the owner of a Gospel book or New Testament could always add the apparatus and even update it when necessary.[23] Such notations are found in the famous *Codex Ephraemi Rescriptus*[24] and in the equally well-known *Codex Bezae*.[25] A ninth-century Gospel book in the Great Lavra, cod. B.52,[26] even has the ekphonetic notation to guide the reader in church. What we learn from considering the manuscript evidence is that the lectionary and Gospel book were not, in the stark way I have implied, somehow in competition. Practical considerations having proved to be largely irrelevant, one begins to think of the lectionary as an unusual kind of book. The care with which some of the early examples were written and decorated indicates that this may be so; Gospel lectionaries were apparently considered to be especially sacred collections produced for the most solemn times of the year. The Vatican lectionary gr. 351, which contains a mere sixteen lessons in addition to morning readings, must be counted among the finest manuscripts to have been made during the tenth century.[27] Its headpieces and initials bear a close resemblance to the ornament of two Gregory manuscripts written in minuscule: Paris. Coisl. 51[28] and Patmos cod. 40.[29] As an important manuscript of tenth-century Constantinople, the lectionary Vat. gr. 351 cannot be considered a provincial copy of an out-of-date service manual. The same claim can be made for other Constantinopolitan lectionaries of the late ninth and early tenth centuries, ones like Paris. gr. 278[30] and the related Vat. gr. 1522.[31]

19. For Italy, see Paris. suppl. gr. 1155, fol. 19: references in note 16 above; for Palestine, see the Sinai. gr. 210 and gr. NE Meg. Perg. 12, dated 861/62: D. Harlfinger, D. Reinsch, J. Sonderkamp, *Specimina Sinaitica: Die datierten griechischen Handschriften des Katharinen-Klosters auf dem Berg Sinai*, Berlin, 1988, 13–14.

20. K. Weitzmann, *Illustrated Manuscripts at St. Catherine's Monastery on Mount Sinai*, Collegeville, Minn., 1973, 14, fig. 14. The saint's name has various spellings: Monabata, Monobata, and Monabagou.

21. A. Rahlfs, *Verzeichnis der griechischen Handschriften des Alten Testaments*, Mitteilungen des Septuaginta-Unternehmens . . . , II, Berlin, 1914, xix–xx.

22. J. Mateos, *La célébration de la Parole dans la liturgie byzantine*, Orientalia Christiana analecta, CXCI, Rome, 1971, 131.

23. The requisite notes might not always appear where we expect; C. Nordenfalk, "Canon Tables on Papyrus," *DOP*, XXXVI, 1982, 36–37, has called attention to what appear to be lectionary markings on a set of canon table fragments dated to around the second half of the sixth century.

24. Paris. gr. 9: See the leaf published by Cavallo (as above note 7), pl. 82 (with comments on the date, 88–93).

25. Cambridge, University Library, cod. Nn.2.41: ibid., 75 n.4, pl. 60; Hatch (as in note 7), pl. XX, and *Codex Bezae Cantabrigiensis Quattuor Evangelia et Actis . . . phototypice repraesentatis*, Cambridge, 1899. J. Harris, *The Annotators of the Codex Bezae*, London, 1901, discusses some of its later history.

26. B. Metzger, *Manuscripts of the Greek Bible*, New York, 1981, pl. 24.

27. R. Devreesse, *Codices Vaticani graeci*, II, *Codices 330–603*, Vatican City, 1937, 32–33. Burns (as in note 15), 423; Cavallo (as in note 7), 118, dates the manuscript to the early eleventh century and compares its script to those of Bodl. Canon. gr. 92 and Paris. Coisl. 31; the scripts of all three are similar, but the decoration of Vat. gr. 351 cannot be compared with that of the two early eleventh-century manuscripts with which Cavallo draws specific comparison.

28. Weitzmann, *Byz. Buchmalerei*, 11, fig. 54.

29. Ibid., 7, figs. 30–32.

30. Ibid., 6–7, figs. 28–29.

31. Ibid., 6, figs. 25–27.

Introduction

One certainty is that the Gospels, regardless of their form, enjoyed a unique status among books. The evidence for this statement is mainly literary, but it can be supplemented by inferences made on the basis of book illumination. Early Christian and Byzantine authors tell us that the Gospels were an object of particular veneration. Cyril of Alexandria writes that at the Council of Ephesus, held in 431, the Gospels were placed on a throne to signify Christ's presence.[32] In the eighth century at Saint Sophia, the deacon incensed the Gospel text on the altar before he removed it to begin the reading;[33] and, as already noted, Germanos interpreted the opening procession into the church by the deacon, book, and celebrant as Christ's coming into the world. When, in 787, the Orthodox needed an illustration of the kind of reverence due to icons, they chose the veneration paid to the cross and to the Gospels.[34] It seems clear that the book from which the readings were taken was regarded with particular reverence over the fifth through the eighth centuries and, furthermore, that this reverence often arose from an identification of the manuscript with Christ. As the dogma of the Incarnation came to be a major issue in eighth- and ninth-century theology, the Gospels could provide the congregation with an objective analogue of impeccable orthodoxy, no matter what the beholder's point of view. In the passages cited, the vocabulary does not allow us to say with certainty whether a Gospel book or Gospel lectionary is the object understood, and it would not be appropriate to look for precise terminology in such writings; using the technical vocabulary of lists and inventories would not only be unnecessary in most literary contexts, it indeed would be graceless. Furthermore, we do not know exactly when the different terms came into widespread use.

The place of the liturgy in Byzantine life may be a factor in the development of the lectionary. In the sixth century, we are told, the people of Constantinople would gather enthusiastically around the ambo to touch or kiss the silver-covered Gospels used by the deacon.[35] The growing role of the liturgy in Byzantine piety can be documented in a variety of ways, beginning with the seventh- and eighth-century interpretative treatises of Maximos the Confessor[36] and Germanos. Popular enthusiasm for the Gospels and their role in the liturgy suggest that we consider the invention of the lectionary as part of the early Byzantine search for the holy within the mundane world. Unfolding over centuries, the sometimes painful debate tended to precise questions that directly or obliquely involved the Divine Liturgy: Did Christ appear in the elements? Did he appear in painted images? As late as the ninth century, the Iconoclast emperors could recall priests censured for mixing the paint from icons with the bread and wine of the service.[37] The content of some early lectionaries suggests an assembly of passages made to encourage a parallel between Christ and the book. The

---

32. *Apologeticus ad Theodosium:* ed. E. Schwartz, *Acta Conciliorum Oecumenicorum,* I/1.3, Berlin, 1927, 83. One's mental image of Cyril's description of the enthroned Gospels at the Council is inevitably shaped by the anachronistic depiction of the Council of Constantinople (381) in the late ninth-century Paris. gr. 510: Omont, *Miniatures,* pl. L. The view of J. Crehan, "Patristic Evidence for the Inspiration of Councils," *Studia Patristica,* IX/3, ed. F. Cross, Texte und Untersuchungen zur Geschichte der altchristlichen Literatur, XCIV, Berlin, 1966, 210–15, that the Gospels represented the Holy Spirit, is without foundation; see C. Walter, *L'iconographie des conciles dans la tradition byzantine,* Archives de l'Orient chrétien, XIII, Paris, 1970, 147–48.

33. As inferred from the order in which Germanos discusses the service: *Liturgy Commentary,* sec. 30: ed. Borgia (as note 6 above), 25; see Mateos (as in note 22), 135–36.

34. J. Mansi, *Sacrorum conciliorum nova et amplissima collectio,* XIII, Florence, 1767, 377D–E.

35. As reported by Paul the Silentiary: P. Friedländer, *Johannes von Gaza und Paulus Silentiarius, Kunstbeschreibungen justinianischer Zeit,* Berlin and Leipzig, 1912, 263, lines 247–48.

36. R. Cantarella, *S. Massimo Confessore, La Mistagogia ed altri scritti,* Florence, 1931, 122–215.

37. Michael II and Theophilos writing to Louis the Pious: *Monumenta Germaniae Historica: Leges,* sec. III: *Concilia,* II/2, ed. A. Werminghoff, Hannover and Leipzig, 1908, 479.

tenth-century Vat. gr. 351 tells the story of Christ's life in a handful of events: Easter, Ascension, Pentecost, Transfiguration, Dormition of the Virgin, New Year's Day, Birth of the Virgin, Exaltation of the Cross, Nativity, Baptism, Presentation, Annunciation, and Palm Sunday. The strength of the equation between the object and Christ was lost in the medieval compilation.

The tendency to relate the Four Gospels with Christ Incarnate took on particular significance in the seventh and eighth centuries. The parallel became unmistakable through the selection of events accepted as the most significant in Christ's life. The decoration of the lectionary tends to support the conclusion that the manuscript was of unique significance, though most ornament remains silent with regard to the precise nature of this significance. The evidence from manuscripts earlier than the ninth century is limited but rewards careful sifting and interpretation. Some of the evidence reflects the Byzantine indifference, encountered in the early literary sources, to a distinction between the Gospel book and lectionary. The Basel Gospels numbers among the most important illuminated manuscripts made prior to the late ninth century, perhaps because it was patterned on the contemporary lectionary. It contains painted headpieces that frame titles written in a style derived from that of monumental inscriptions. Beneath the frame, each Gospel begins with an initial filled with geometric decoration. The readings themselves are marked with elaborate uncial letters.[38] This system of decoration continues in Byzantine art, but in the lectionary, not in the Gospel book. There may be reason to believe that ornamental letters made with birds, fish, and human hands were used in Greek manuscripts before the ninth century. One of the most common initial types, the *epsilon*, whose cross-stroke is a hand gesturing in speech or holding a pen (Figs. 42, 44) may be of pre-Iconoclastic origin. One such letter is found in a mid-seventh-century Latin sacramentary that shows Greek influence.[39] When holding a pen, the *epsilon* could easily fall at the beginning of Luke's Gospel ("Inasmuch as many have undertaken to compile a narrative . . .") or be used in the context of authorship: the Evangelist writing the opening word of his Gospel (Fig. 3). The common lectionary *incipit* "The Lord said . . ." offers numerous instances, if not for the invention, then at least for the spread of the *epsilon* with gesturing hand. The design can be found in early lectionaries and throughout those made during the Middle Ages.[40] Rich ornament appears to have become a mark of sacred texts in the eighth and early ninth century, during the Iconoclast Controversy. Iconoclast patrons possibly considered book ornament, like the decoration of church buildings with plants and animals, a suitable way to express their piety. The evidence of surviving ninth-century manuscripts shows that decoration was considered especially appropriate to the lectionary, and it suggests a well-established base from which scribes and illuminators drew in making other kinds of texts in magnificent editions; the *epsilon* with gesturing hand appears in the Paris Gregory, gr. 510, made for the Emperor Basil I toward the end of the ninth century.[41]

Against the history of the early lectionary, which can only be pieced together from a number of sources, all incomplete, stands that of the medieval lectionary. In studying the manuscripts of the eleventh and twelfth centuries, the principal difficulty arises from the daunting amount of source material. The underlying questions posed by the manuscripts are, Why does the lectionary containing a full calendar of readings appear at this time? and What mechanism for the creation and

38. Nordenfalk (as in note 7), fig. 53.
39. St. Gall, Stiftsbibliothek, cod. 908: Nordenfalk (as in note 7), 126–28, pl. 53c.
40. For a ninth- or tenth-century example, see Mount Athos, Great Lavra, cod. A.86, fol. 114: Weitzmann, *Byz. Buchmalerei*, fig. 321 (also fig. 308, the writing Evangelist type).
41. Ibid., text fig. 1.

Introduction

dissemination of the medieval Gospel lectionary operated with such manifest efficiency? The movements and ideas that so charged the climate of the seventh through ninth centuries had either passed or had been discredited; by the eleventh century some were just taken for granted. The book would have had little value as an objective analogy for the Incarnation, since the image of the Virgin holding the infant Christ painted over the altar was far more effective in conveying this concept, particularly as it related to the liturgy. Finally, the book's unique role in the service had been eclipsed.

The early Byzantine liturgy began when the deacon, carrying the Gospels, led the priest and congregation into the church. After the completion of the first part of the ceremony (the Liturgy of the Word), the elements, which had been prepared beforehand offstage, were solemnly brought into the church and placed on the altar. By the tenth century the preparation of the bread and wine had become a nearly formal part of the service and had achieved a significance that tended to overshadow the First Entrance. At Saint Sophia, where the elements continued to be prepared in a smaller, flanking building, the changes might not have been so dramatic. The patriarch waited outside the central doors for the deacon, who came with the Gospels to lead him into the naos and signal the start of the public ceremony.[42] At other churches, where the bread and wine were prepared inside the church and not in a separate building, the First Entrance was reduced to the deacon and priest coming out of the sanctuary through a side door and processing briefly back to the central door.[43] Within the sanctuary, the Gospels were no longer the only object of censing; the clergy, the bema itself, and sometimes the icons were all incensed.[44] The book had become one of many sacred objects in a service whose emphasis had shifted to its second part, the eucharistic celebration.

The appearance of the medieval lectionary seems to respond to a powerful force felt in Constantinople near the end of the tenth century. Although generated within society as a whole, its point of expression was the rites of the Church, as has been recognized by Kurt Weitzmann.[45] Lectionaries of the kind presented here speak to a need for uniformity in what happened throughout the year. Each day's reading was specified, as was the method of its delivery in the chanted form. Whereas some Gospel books contain the musical notation, not all early lectionaries do.[46] Other expressions of the need to which the medieval lectionary responds can be found in the standardized edition of the lives of the saints produced under the leadership of Symeon Metaphrastes, or the many versions of the orations of Gregory of Nazianzus made to supply the priest with sermons for selected holy days throughout the year.

The emphasis on a full and regular calendar so central to the Middle Ages superannuated the earlier kind of manuscript that was brought out for use only on important occasions. The characterization "full and regular" means lessons for virtually every day of the year, for the early morning and evening services on important feast days as well as for offices at times when the Eucharist was not celebrated.[47] The liturgical calendar that the medieval lectionary reflects appears to be that of late tenth-century Constantinople, and specifically the calendar of the patriarchal church of Saint Sophia. The full medieval lectionary was created at a date that is perhaps just slightly later than the

42. R. Taft, "The Pontifical Liturgy of the Great Church according to a Twelfth-Century Diataxis in *Codex British Museum Add. 34,060*," *Orientalia Christiana periodica*, XLV, 1979, 284–87.

43. F. Brightman, *Liturgies Eastern and Western*, I, *Eastern Liturgies*, Oxford, 1896, 367.

44. Mateos (as in note 22), 135–36.

45. See his essay "Narrative and Liturgical Gospel Illustrations," *Studies*, 247–70, in which he speaks of the "liturgical" character of Byzantine art in the Middle Ages.

46. See the Sunday lectionary at Sinai: reference at note 19 above.

47. Later, in chapter III in regard to the calendar of the New York Lectionary, I will discuss in greater detail the questions surrounding the manuscript's use in the medieval service.

typikon of the Great Church in the form established by J. Mateos.[48] Over the eleventh and twelfth centuries the lectionary was reproduced in hundreds of manuscripts, yet the patriarch appears not to have had a department or office charged with the production or formal regulation of liturgical manuals. This is the judgment of J. Darrouzès,[49] who has studied the organization of the church, and the manuscript evidence tends to corroborate his view. The lectionary appears to have been widely disseminated through the initiative of many individual donors and the labor of nearly as many scribes.

The speed with which the medieval lectionary spread throughout the Empire must be in part attributed to a factor unrelated to the liturgy. The success of the eleventh-century Byzantine economy created wealth that found an outlet in pious foundations, monasteries, and churches. New and old foundations alike always needed icons, plate, lamps, and books. The records of three prominent Byzantines, one a Georgian, reflect the plans of those intent on founding monasteries. Gregory Pakourianos gave his monastery of the Virgin at Bačkovo two Gospel books and two Gospel lectionaries, in addition to other liturgical manuscripts.[50] For the monastery he intended to build on his property, Eustathios Boilas collected two Gospel lectionaries;[51] and Michael Attaliates, Boilas's eleventh-century contemporary, had assembled two Gospel lectionaries and one Gospel book.[52] The thirteenth-century inventory of the monastery of Saint John the Theologian on Patmos shows how holdings could quickly grow beyond the needs of a monastic community.[53]

Many donors required handsomely decorated and illustrated copies of the lectionary. Without question, some of the exceptional illustrated manuscripts of the eleventh and twelfth centuries are Gospel lectionaries. Standing in the first rank are: Mount Athos, Dionysiou Monastery, cod. 587;[54] New York, Morgan Library, cod. M 639[55] (and the related manuscript in the Société biblique française, Paris[56]) and cod. 692; Rome, Biblioteca Vaticana, gr. 1156;[57] and cod. 2 of the Greek Institute of Byzantine and Post-Byzantine Studies in Venice.[58] Of less distinction, but still important books for the history of Byzantine art, are: Athens, National Library, cod. 190[59] and cod. 2645;[60] Istanbul, Library of the Greek Ecumenical Patriarchate, cod. 8;[61] the Skevophylakion Lectionary of

---

48. J. Mateos, *Le typikon de la Grande Eglise*, I, *Le Cycle des douze mois*, Orientalia Christiana analecta, CLXIV, Rome, 1962 (x–xix on the date), and for the movable feasts, see his volume cited in note 11.

49. *Recherches sur les offikia de l'Eglise byzantine*, Archives de l'Orient chrétien, XI, Paris, 1970, 435–37.

50. The typikon, ed. P. Gautier (as in note 13), 121.

51. P. Lemerle, *Cinq études sur le XIe siècle byzantin*, Paris, 1977, 24–25.

52. P. Gautier, "La Diataxis de Michel Attaliate," *REB*, XXXIX, 1981, 93.

53. The thirteenth-century inventory records six lectionaries, five with richly decorated covers: see Diehl (as in note 13), 514–15.

54. *Treasures of Athos*, I, 434–46, figs. 189–277. C. Walter, "The Date and Content of the Dionysiou Lectionary," *Deltion tes Christianikes Archaiologikes Hetaireias*, XIII, 1988, 181–89. T. Masuda, *He eikonographese tou cheirographou arith. 587m tes Mones Dionysiou sto Hagio Horos*, Thessalonika, 1990.

55. Weitzmann, "Morgan 639."

56. *Byzance et la France médiévale*, Bibliothèque Nationale exhibition catalogue: Paris, 1958, 37 (no. 42). Yet a third work related to Morgan cod. M 639 may be the lectionary in the Historical and Regional Museum, Odessa: B. Fonkić, "Grečeskie rukopisi Odessy," *Vizantijskij Vremennik*, XLIII, 1982, 98–99, pls. 1–5.

57. Some leaves have been published by K. Weitzmann; see *Studies*, 209–10, 251–52, 256–57, 295–97, figs. 192, 235–38, 243–44, 297–99.

58. A. Xyngopoulos, "To historemenon euaggelion tou Hellenikou Institoutou Benetias," *Thesaurismata*, I, 1962, 63–88. This manuscript (Aland, *Liste*, 220 [l 279]) was formerly Gospel lectionary 1 in the church of San Giorgio dei Greci, Venice; it was part of the 1953 property transfer involved in the establishment of the Greek Institute of Byzantine and Post-Byzantine Studies in Venice: M. Manoussaacas, "The History of the Greek Confraternity (1498–1953) and the Activity of the Greek Institute of Venice (1966–1982)," *Modern Greek Studies Yearbook*, V, 1989, 333.

59. Marava-Chatzinicolaou and Toufexi-Paschou, *Byzantine Manuscripts of the National Library of Greece*, 154–61, figs. 349–81.

60. Ibid., 139–49, figs. 314–24.

61. G. Sotiriou, *Keimelia tou Oikoumenikou Patriarcheiou*, Athens, 1937, 86–92.

Introduction

the Great Lavra on Mount Athos;[62] Panteleimon monastery, cod. 2;[63] and Paris, Bibliothèque Nationale, suppl. gr. 27.[64] Of these books, only Morgan 639 can be called completely published; others, like the Vat. gr. 1156 and Morgan cod. 692, are hardly known at all. Here I present all the illustrations in the twelfth-century Morgan manuscript (cod. 692). When we survey this and other lectionaries of the medieval type, we find some completely isolated and others related by style of execution or method of illustration. In addition, questions arise from the Byzantines' approach to the illustration of this text and how it changes.

One common kind of lectionary illustration is the author portrait, which also may be one of the oldest forms of imagery in Byzantine books. Some lectionaries have Evangelist portraits as their only illustration.[65] In type and format, these portraits are identical to those used in contemporary Gospel books. Only their order differs—John, Matthew, Luke, and Mark. In itself, this fact has consequence only to the extent that it might bear on the dual use of a particular pose, one centered on the author slumped back in his chair in fatigue or deep reflection; in early illumination the composition was sometimes associated with Matthew,[66] but later it tended to be used more often for John (Fig. 1), one the first author in the Gospels, the other in the lectionary. The interleaving of Evangelist portraits in the synaxarion depends on a certain density of readings. Such images that strongly divide the text have no place in the early compilations. The creation of the medieval service book meant adding readings from the Gospels in long, nearly continuous runs. The synaxarion was given some of the character of the Gospels, and sections were named after Evangelists whose writings predominated. In the rubric quoted from Figure 31b, the reference is to the "seventh Saturday in Matthew." Although the use of Evangelist portraits within the synaxarion makes sense only in the medieval lectionary, portraits can be found in the early lectionary as well.

In some lectionaries author portraits occur in a manner that may reflect a practice with early Byzantine roots. In the late tenth-century Sinai. gr. 204, the miniatures all fall at the book's start and consist of Saint Peter of Monabata, the Four Evangelists, and, as the opening images, Christ and the Virgin.[67] The authors are prefatory to the Incarnation, implied by the sequence of Christ and his mother. Perhaps the best evidence for relating the manuscript type to the concept of the Incarnation is found in the late ninth- or early tenth-century lectionary in the Great Lavra of Mount Athos, cod. A.92.[68] It contains a frontispiece image in whose center stands Christ; next to him the illuminator has placed in two symmetrical rows six bust-length portraits in roundels; portrayed are the Virgin, John the Baptist, and the Four Evangelists, all represented at a slightly smaller scale than the image of Christ. Christ's mother and the last of the prophets and authors who wrote the divinely inspired

---

62. K. Weitzmann, "Das Evangelion im Skevophylakion zu Lawra," *Liturgical Gospels and Psalters*, XI.

63. *Treasures of Athos*, II, 348–51, figs. 272–95; and Huber, *Athos*, 187–98, figs. 84–111.

64. Omont, *Miniatures*, 48, pls. XCVII–C.

65. For instance, New York, Morgan Library, cod. M 647: *Manuscripts from American Collections*, 90–91; or the early example in the Vatican Library, cod. gr. 1522: Weitzmann, *Byz. Buchmalerei*, 6, figs. 21–24.

66. See the portrait of Matthew in Paris. Coisl. gr. 195: Omont, *Miniatures*, pl. LXXXI.

67. References in note 20 above. The full-page images of Christ, the Virgin, and Evangelists that have been bound into the Gospel book now at Princeton, University Library, Garrett MS 6 (*Manuscripts from American Collections*, 52–55; Weitzmann, *Byz. Buchmalerei*, figs. 374–78), may have come from an early lectionary. The Godescalc Gospel Lectionary, made in the West during the time of Charlemagne, also has the Evangelists grouped at the start of the manuscript: W. Koehler, *Die karolingischen Miniaturen*, II, *Die Hofschule Karls des Grossen*, Berlin, 1958, pls. 1, 2. As late as 1070 the illustrator of the lectionary that Peter of the Chalkoprateia School wrote for the Priest Constantine chose to place all four authors within a single prefatory image; Paris. suppl. gr. 1096: Lake, *Dated Greek Mss*, IV, pl. 299.

68. Weitzmann, *Byz. Buchmalerei*, fig. 179; *Treasures of Athos*, III, fig. 46.

Gospels are smaller, and each is incomplete: they have been subsumed into the grand figure in the center. Such images, which survive in any number of later Byzantine lectionaries[69] and in Gospel books as well,[70] may owe their invention to a time centuries before their first preserved examples. They appear to capture the concept of the Incarnation within the framework of the Four Gospels in the form of a liturgical manuscript that does not fully reproduce the writing of any one author.

The other form of illustration is the narrative imagery celebrating the important feasts of the Church. Examples of this type also appear as early as the ninth or tenth century; Leningrad cod. 21 is a lectionary with full-page Evangelist portraits and framed miniatures placed into breaks the scribe left in the text.[71] Lavra cod. A.86 and Patmos cod. 70 similarly are early manuscripts, though the images are scattered in the margins. By and large, the Lavra manuscript contains marginal portraits,[72] of Christ and the Evangelists, for example, but in addition has an image of Saint John Chrysostom and Christ revealing his wounds to Thomas. The Patmos manuscript contains more narrative scenes:[73] Christ healing the blind youth, Christ in the Garden, Christ washing the Disciples' feet, Peter denying Christ, and so on. In both manuscripts, which may not represent the best of tenth-century illumination, the initials are extensively decorated, a legacy that continues as an important aspect of the Byzantine lectionary. Some of the scenes illustrated in these three early manuscripts reappear in eleventh- and twelfth-century manuscripts; why this might be so is a question discussed in a later chapter.

By the end of the eleventh century many other kinds of books rivaled the lectionary for rich text illustration: psalters, the *Heavenly Ladder* of John Climacus, sermons of Gregory of Nazianzus, the Metaphrastic menologium, and manuscripts of *Barlaam and Joasaph,* to name just a few. In one regard the New York Lectionary proclaims its importance even in a world in which patrons vied to present churches and monasteries with ostentatiously handsome copies of various kinds of books; its text was written in the shape of a cross, an extraordinarily rare practice. Only Princeton. Garrett 1, a ninth-century Gospel book, readily comes to mind as an example made before the twelfth century.[74]

In the following chapters I will offer a description and analysis of the New York Lectionary, which contains an extensive cycle of narrative images and was executed by two craftsmen. The miniatures remain unfinished and therefore offer some particular insights into the making of illustrated manuscripts. Chapter 3 is devoted to the saints and feasts of the New York menologium. The chronology and dating of Western manuscripts have been vastly aided by studying calendars. Byzantine service books present us with much less variety, in part because many of the most

69. For example, the early twelfth-century Athens cod. 2645 (Marava-Chatzinicolaou and Toufexi-Paschou, *Manuscripts of the National Library of Greece,* 139–49, fig. 314); in the late eleventh-century Sinai cod. 208 (Weitzmann, *Manuscripts at Sinai* [as in note 20], 23, fig. 31); or the thirteenth-century Ann Arbor, University of Michigan, MS 171 (G. Galavaris, *The Illustrations of the Prefaces in Byzantine Gospels,* Byzantina Vindobonensia, XI, Vienna, 1979, 76, fig. 60), and in the lectionary in the Greek Institute of Byzantine and Post-Byzantine Studies in Venice (Xyngopoulos [as in note 58], pl. I.1).

70. The eleventh- or twelfth-century Vat. gr. 756 (Galavaris, as in note 69 above, 106, figs. 83, 84) and Venice, Bibl. Marciana, cod. Z 540 (ibid., 100–101, fig. 80). In the pages cited, Galavaris relates the images, but only generally, to Gospel prologues. Perhaps the presence of prologues only offered a hospitable environment for transplanting imagery developed for another context. On the relations between the headpieces in some manuscripts and the Byzantine liturgy, see especially the remarks of S. Tsuji, "The Headpiece Miniatures and Genealogy Pictures in Paris. Gr. 74," *DOP,* XXIX, 1975, 178–82.

71. V. Likhačova, *Byzantine Miniature,* Moscow, 1977, 5–10; see also C. Morey, "Notes on East Christian Miniatures," *Art Bulletin,* XI, 1929, figs. 63, 65, 71, 75, 83, 85, 90, 91, 94–96, 100, 101, 103.

72. Weitzmann, *Byz. Buchmalerei,* 46–47, figs. 305–23.

73. Ibid., 66–67, figs. 430–37, 440–47.

74. K. Clark, *A Descriptive Catalogue of Greek New Testament Manuscripts in America,* Chicago, 1937, 61–63, pl. VII; Hatch (as in note 7), pl. LX; *Manuscripts from American Collections,* 56–57, fig. 2.

Introduction

impressive lectionaries were made in eleventh- or twelfth-century Constantinople for use there. Minor variations do appear when the New York manuscript is compared with the printed calendars, and, in time, the slight differences among manuscripts whose dates and places of production have been established may prove useful to students in various fields of research. For now, the menologion can contribute to our understanding of how the lectionary text was copied and disseminated. The questions posed by the calendar and illustrations, like those greater ones surrounding the lectionary text, can be opened to serious discussion only by the publication of the monuments.

I

The Illustration and Decoration of the New York Lectionary

THE NEW YORK LECTIONARY, Pierpont Morgan Library, cod. M 692, contains the lectionary text of the Gospels written in the shape of a cross. With the exception of the full-page Evangelist portraits, the format was followed consistently throughout the manuscript; even the title pages were composed as crosses. In the history of manuscripts, such page design is extremely rare, largely because it left so much expensive parchment empty. In the case of the New York Lectionary, some of the quadrants contain miniatures, but not enough of them are filled to suggest that the decision to illustrate gave rise to or even influenced the unusual choice of format. Two other lectionaries with cruciform text survive from roughly the same period, and neither contains any miniatures. The combination of cross-shaped text and extensive illustration makes the New York manuscript unique in the history of Byzantine art. Although the nonfigural ornament was carried through to a uniformly finished state, the illustrations exist in several stages of completion, from quick sketches to delicately painted scenes. In this regard the manuscript affords an unusual, but not unique, opportunity for study. In the first part of this work I document and interpret three principal aspects of the New York manuscript. Chapter I is devoted to a description of the manuscript's content and the placement of the ornament and miniatures.[1] Chapter II has been given over to remarks on how the manuscript appears to have been made. In chapter III I reproduce and comment on the text of the calendar of saints. Other cruciform lectionaries survive; they and their possible relationship to the New York Lectionary are discussed in chapter IV. The manuscript's date (beyond a safe circa 1150) and the broad art-historical considerations, such as how the illustrations enrich our understanding of twelfth-century Byzantine painting, are discussed in chapter V.

I begin with an analytical catalogue of ornament and illustration and conclude with some prefatory remarks regarding provenance and the manuscript's makeup. A number of parallels are considered in the course of the catalogue, and as a conclusion I take up the questions that the many parallels inevitably raise: Who chose the scenes to be illustrated, and why were these subjects chosen and not others?

---

1. For having allowed me the opportunity to study the manuscript on more than one occasion, I wish to thank John Plummer, former curator of Medieval and Renaissance Manuscripts of the Pierpont Morgan Library. Photographs of the New York, London, and Athos lectionaries were obtained with the help of a grant from the Graduate School of Arts and Sciences, The George Washington University.

The New York Cruciform Lectionary

Provenance: In October 1925 the lectionary was purchased by the Morgan Library from the dealer Mitchell Kennerley.[2] Other indications of prior ownership exist in nonscribal notations, of which there are five. On fol. iv (the back of the author portrait) is the number 17, written in arabic numerals; beneath it is a faint two-line entry, followed by a third written in purple ink in a bold hand. This last note reads: ὁ ἱερατικῶς προϊστάμενος Οἰκονόμος πάπα Γεώργος Αδ Ρηγόπουλος Κωνσταντινουπόλει. Two more nonscribal notes appear on fol. 2 (Fig. 2). The first, in the upper right-hand corner, reads:

τὸ ἱερὸν τουτοὶ τεῦχος προ[σ]κλήρωται ἀναποαδάστως ἐν ὑψωμαθείοις ἀρχαιοτα[τη] ἱερῷ ἐκκλησίᾳ τοῦ μεγαλομ[αρτ]υρος Γεωργίου τοῦ ἐν Κυπαρ[ισσοις] ,αωλν^ῳ′ ἔτει κατὰ μῆνα απρ[ιλλίου. . .].

Ἀρχιερεὺς Κωνσταντινουπολέως Κωνστάντιος

The second one, at the bottom of the leaf, has been smudged and cancelled, but it too recorded the dedication of the manuscript—θεον κ(αὶ) ιερον ευαγγελιον—to the church of the Martyr George (ἀφιερωθα τοῦτο . . . τῷ τοῦ μεγαλομαρτυρος Γεωργίου ναῷ). The church of Saint George in the Cypresses is attested in the Byzantine literature as early as the ninth century. After the Turkish conquest the Christians continued to use it. In 1833 the Patriarch Konstantios II undertook to restore damage done by a fire in 1782.[3] The note on fol. 2, signed by the Patriarch[4] and dated April 1835, states that he assigned the manuscript as inalienable property to the church, no doubt in connection with his restoration campaign. The entry made by the Economos George Rigopoulos confirms Patriarchal control over the lectionary.

Contents: Gospel lectionary; fols. 1–213, synaxarion daily in John, remainder Saturday and Sunday only; menologion follows at fol. 214 and continues to fol. 289; the eleven morning readings of the Resurrection fall at the end of the manuscript, fols. 289v–293; fol. 293v is blank.

Description: The lectionary contains 293 leaves and has two lacunae; the leaves, which measure 34 by 24 cm, were ruled for the cross-shaped text in a pattern that appears drawn to scale (see Fig. A) (fol. 152, typical). The two-line title guides that appear at the top and bottom of each leaf were rarely used by the scribe (for an unusual example, see fol. 87v: Fig. 17). The vertical column of text measures 9 by 25.1 cm and the horizontal 16.8 by 7.9 cm. Seven lines appear in the top section, eight in the crossbar, and eight in the lower section. Pricking remains visible in the lower margin, but the top and fore-edge have been heavily trimmed. The text is written in dark brown ink in the bold minuscule associated with contemporary service books; ekphonetic notation is in carmine;[5] K. Clark has published a page of text (folio 146).[6] The parchment is of varying quality and has been

---

2. *The Pierpont Morgan Library. A Review of the Growth, Development and Activities of the Library during the Period between its Establishment as an Educational Institution in February 1924 and the Close of the Year 1929*, New York, 1930, 51–52.

3. R. Janin, *La géographie ecclésiastique de l'Empire byzantin*, I, *Le siège de Constantinople et le patriarchat oecuménique*, 3, *Les églises et les monastères*, Paris, 1953, 75.

4. As I read it, the title is not what we would expect; in contemporary documents the patriarch used the formula: ἐλέῳ θεοῦ ἀρχιεπίσκοπος Κωνσταντινουπόλεως νέας Ῥώμης, καὶ οἰκουμενικὸς πατριάρχης.

5. I here follow the usage of K. and S. Lake: "vermilion" denotes ink that tends to have an orange tint, and "carmine," which shades to blue.

6. K. Clark, *A Descriptive Catalogue of Greek New Testament Manuscripts in America*, Chicago, 1937, pl. XXXI.

Illustration and Decoration

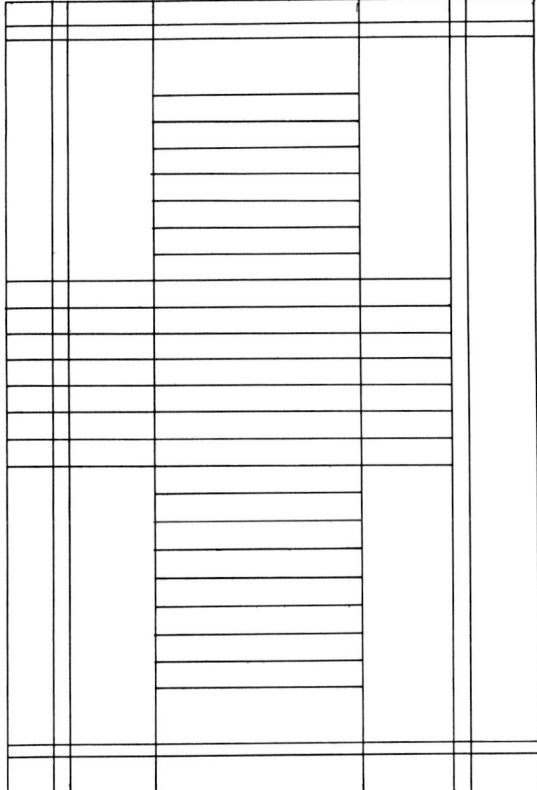

Fig. A. Ruling pattern, Morgan Library, MS 692

Fig. B. Ruling pattern to Evangelist portrait, Morgan Library, MS 692

gathered into thirty-eight quires as follows: I quaternion plus one single leaf added for portrait, II–VI quaternions, VII quaternion plus one single leaf (fol. 58, end of section), VIII originally a quaternion, but one leaf now missing at start, IX–X quaternions, XI binion with single leaf (fol. 82), XII–XV quaternions, XVI binion, XVII quaternion with single leaf added for portrait (fol. 123), XVIII–XXIV quaternions, XXV quaternion of three bifolia and two single leaves, XXVI and XXVII quaternions, XXVIII bifolio (end of synaxarion), XXIX–XXXII quaternions, XXXIII quaternion plus single leaf (fol. 249), XXXIV quaternion, XXXV ternion, XXXVI and XXXVII quaternions, XXXVIII originally quinion. The leaf between fols. 284 and 285 has been lost, leaving fol. 293 as a single leaf.

Illustration: The illustration consists of narrative images and Evangelist portraits. Only the portraits of John, fol. iv (Fig. 1), and Mark, fol. 123v (Fig. 20), survive. Both were painted on the hair side of single leaves cut wide enough to allow for binding; the stub ends appear after fols. 9 and 131, the last of quires I and XVII. The use of single leaves permitted the ruling pattern to be modified so as not to interfere with the portraits; the scheme for fol. 1 appears in Figure B. It shows the pairs of horizontal—and essentially vestigial—title guides, but no lines for text. The portraits of Matthew and Luke should appear at the beginning of the parts of the synaxarion whose readings are principally drawn from their Gospels. Thus the portrait of Luke would face the title on fol. 87 (Fig. 16). That of Matthew would fall after fol. 58v, a point at which a quire has been disturbed. One leaf was cut from the beginning of gathering VIII; it would have been decorated with the headpiece on its recto and the beginning of the first Matthew reading on its verso. This disturbance suggests that although the manuscript is unfinished in other ways it once had a complete set of portraits. The cruciform headpiece and Matthew portrait were probably removed at the same time.

The second category of illustration consists of the narrative miniatures, which I discuss in order of their appearance in the manuscript. Often it is worthwhile to note parallels with the two well-known Gospel books, Paris. gr. 74, made around the middle of the eleventh century, and Laur. 6.23, made early in the twelfth century. I also include references to five other lectionaries; three are eleventh-century manuscripts, whose cycles range from unusually dense, as in Mount Athos, Dionysiou monastery, cod. 587, to what might be called "average," at least in terms of length: New York, Morgan Library, cod. M 639, and Paris, Bibliothèque Nationale, suppl. gr. 27. The remaining two are roughly contemporary, twelfth-century lectionaries: Mount Athos, Panteleimon monastery, cod. 2, and Athens, National Library, cod. 190. Citations to published miniatures appear in the text rather than in a cumbersome series of notes.

Fol. 1v: Portrait of Saint John (Fig. 1). The background is gold leaf and the frame a blue border decorated with white crenellation and red t-shapes. John wears a pink himation and a gray-blue tunic, only a small portion of which is visible around his neck; the neck- and hemlines are outlined in black. The flesh tones are warm brown modeled with highlights and red shading; the red of the cheek is a prominent spot. In painting both flesh and garments, the illuminator used heavy layers of pigment and the result is a hard, shiny surface. The vermilion of the halo matches that of the inscription, of which survive only the words ὁ ἅγιος and the final *sigma* of John's name.

Fol. 2: Cruciform headpiece (Fig. 2); The holy and great Sunday of Easter, Gospel according to John. The decorative uncials are gold-dusted carmine.

Fol. 2v: Easter Sunday (Fig. 3); Jn 1:1–17. John writes the opening words of his Gospel, which begin the reading for Easter. The figure within the outlines of the *epsilon* wears a lavender himation, with white highlights and blue shadows, over a blue tunic. The portrait appears to lack detail, to be somewhat out of focus, but this may be the result of light abrasion. The colors, heavily applied and carefully modeled, match those of the rest of the initial letter. The design is hardly uncommon in Byzantine illumination,[7] and a similar initial appears in the Panteleimon Lectionary, fol. 1 (Huber, *Athos,* fig. 88).

Fol. 4: Tuesday of Easter week (Fig. 4); Lk 24:12–35. In the lower right quadrant Saint Peter is depicted running toward Christ's tomb. Peter holds a scroll and is dressed in a salmon-colored himation over a blue tunic; his hair is the same color as the tunic. The pigment layers, including the flesh tones, are a wash so thinly applied that the underdrawing can still be seen. The wash on Peter's face contains vermilion. (The nearby initial letter is painted in dense layers of polychrome.) Shown within the tomb are the grave clothes, the body wrapping, and napkin for covering the head. John (20:6–7) mentions these, but Luke does not. The fact that the reading from Luke is embedded in a sequence from John may have some bearing on this apparent borrowing; in fact, the first verse of the reading is probably a lectionary *incipit,* not a genuine part of Luke's Gospel, and one that was devised to give the reading some coherence within the sequence of Easter lections.[8] The reading is

---

7. Complete figures depicted within the initial occur as early as the tenth century; see Mount Athos, Great Lavra, cod. 86, fol. 94: Weitzmann, *Byz. Buchmalerei,* fig. 308.

8. See *Novum Testamentum graece,* ed. Eb. Nestle, E. Nestle, and K. Aland, Stuttgart, 1963, 226.

commonly illustrated in lectionaries of the eleventh century, for example, Morgan MS 639 (Weitzmann, "Morgan 639," fig. 296), Dionysiou cod. 587 (*Treasures of Athos*, I, fig. 192), and Paris, suppl. gr. 27 (Omont, *Miniatures*, pl. XCVIII, 6), all of which show Peter in some relationship to Christ's tomb. In the illustration of the Athens Lectionary (Fig. 60), Peter is posed against the initial *tau*.

Fol. 6: Wednesday of Easter Week (Fig. 5); Jn 1:35–52. John the Baptist speaks of Christ to his two disciples. John is depicted wearing a green himation over a tunic in a warm tone of tan; his disciple at the left wears a dusty green himation over a dull red tunic; the one at the right a gray-blue tunic and a tan himation the same tone as John's tunic. The drapery troughs are simply denser mixtures of these few colors. The flesh of all figures has received a layer of wash, but the portrait of John has been more densely painted. Against a background of vermilion wash, Christ is depicted wearing a purple tunic and blue himation; his face remains only lightly washed in a dilute mixture of the brown used for the drawings. The miniature appears to be finished. The passage is illustrated in Morgan 639 (Weitzmann, "Morgan 369," fig. 297), Dionysiou cod. 587 (*Treasures of Athos*, I, figs. 193, 194), and Paris. suppl. gr. 27 (Omont, *Miniatures*, pl. XCVIII [8]). It also appears, in a similar form, in Panteleimon cod. 2 (Huber, *Athos*, fig. 84). The miniature has been previously published.[9]

Fols. 10v and 11: Sunday after Easter (second Sunday of readings from John) (Figs. 6, 7); Jn 20:19–31. There is considerable flaking, but no underdrawing has been revealed. In the lower left quadrant stands a compact group of disciples, at the head of which appears Andrew, dressed in a brown tunic and green himation; the others wear combinations of deep blue and pale dull pink. In the opposite quadrant, Christ stands in a doorway. He wears a deep blue tunic with scarlet bands; the halo is red with blue bars. The faces of all figures are modeled with great delicacy and plasticity. At the bottom of the facing leaf appear the other disciples, most of whom look toward Christ, here wearing a blue tunic and dull tan himation; his face has completely flaked away to reveal only a faint outline. On fol. 11 the disciples wear garments painted light green, dull pink, tan, or blue. The two leaves appear to have been painted together since the colors match precisely. The portraits are all well modeled with light rouging of the cheeks and subtle shading of the eye sockets. The text near the second image is John 20:25, Christ's words to Thomas. The compositional arrangement is based on a natural division of the story into two episodes: first Christ appears through the doors to his disciples (fol. 10v), and then a second time eight days later, in which he invites Thomas to test the wounds (fol. 11). In the illustration on fol. 11 Thomas stands at the right of a less compact group as he gestures forcefully toward Christ, who appears without the door at his back. In the first instance, Christ holds his hand outward in a simple greeting, whereas in the second he addresses Thomas. Though the illuminator created two distinct episodes, he in a sense portrayed the disciples only once, in two complementary groups. The choice of Andrew and Peter as the principals of the respective groups may be noteworthy. The reading is illustrated, although not as a two-part sequence, in other representative lectionaries: Dionysiou cod. 587 (*Treasures of Athos*, I, figs. 199, 200) and Morgan 639 (Weitzmann, "Morgan 639," fig. 298). For a similar division into episodes, the Florence (Velmans, *Tétraévangile*, fig. 300) and Paris Gospels (Omont, *Evangiles*, pls. 183, 184) offer parallels.

Fol. 22v and 23: Fourth Sunday in John (Figs. 8, 9); Jn 5:1–15. Again, a sequence has been

---

9. *Greek Manuscripts from American Collections*, fig. 62.

devised. In the first scene, a group of four invalids is shown lying around the pool at Bethesda, whose waters are stirred by an angel; in the right quadrant are the five porticoes mentioned in the text (Jn 5:2). The two parts of the miniature have been painted, but it can hardly be considered complete. The colors are pink, blue, brown, and tan. In painting the garments, pallets, and porticoes, the illuminator varied colors for the sake of change and tried to alter the juxtapositions. The face of the angel is drawn in carmine, and what outlines appear around the face of the invalids were done at the time the garments were painted. At the top of the facing leaf (Fig. 9a), Christ stands in the left margin gesturing to the paralytic lying on his bed with the blanket pulled to his waist. In the lower quadrants of this leaf (Fig. 9b), the paralytic walks off the page, away from the Jews, shown at the left, who had questioned him to discover the identity of the healer working on the Sabbath. The miniatures, which are unfinished, were drawn in carmine ink essentially the same as that used for the ekphonetic notation. Christ's halo on fol. 23 has been painted carmine but not gilt. A complicated illustration of this reading occurs in Morgan MS 639 (Fig. 64); it includes Christ standing before the city of Jerusalem, the infirm beside the pool, and the healed man, his bed on his back, confronting three figures inscribed "pharisee," "Jew," and "scribe." In terms of composition, the scene of the angel stirring the waters finds a parallel in Dionysiou cod. 587 (*Treasures of Athos,* I, fig. 202). In light of some equally strong compositional similarities with the Paris (Omont, *Evangiles,* pl. 152) and Florence Gospels (Velmans, *Tétraévangile,* fig. 277), particular ties to any distinctive tradition of representation would require considerably more knowledge of the history of this subject than is now available. The depiction of the pool within a lobed enclosure and the grouping of those lying around it seem to be relatively fixed in Byzantine art of the general period.

Fol. 25v: Wednesday of the fourth week in John (Fig. 10); Jn 7:14–30. Although flaked, the miniature is finished. Its subject is Christ teaching in the temple at Capernaum. Christ is posed against the initial *tau,* flanked by two groups presumably intended to represent the Jews who marvel at his words; in each group men gesture in astonishment. The temple is represented below as a centrally planned structure within the city walls. Christ wears a purple tunic and a gray-blue himation. The red detailing of his face on a tan base tone makes the portrait stand out from the others, which are executed in a deep shade of tan. Noteworthy are the density of the pigment layers used for the portraits, the garments, and the city, and the amount of fine linear detail that articulates all the miniature's parts. The reading is illustrated with Christ teaching in Morgan MS 639 (Weitzmann, "Morgan 639," fig. 302) and Dionysiou cod. 587 (*Treasures of Athos,* I, fig. 203); in Paris. suppl. gr. 27 (Omont, *Miniatures,* pl. XCVIII), only his portrait is represented. In the Athens Lectionary, Christ stands against the initial *tau* and holds a book (Marava-Chatzinicolaou and Toufexi-Paschou, *Manuscripts of the National Library of Greece,* fig. 357).

Fol. 29v: The fifth Sunday in John, the Sunday of the Woman of Samaria (Fig. 11); Jn 4:5–42. The miniature is a finished drawing that includes details of the faces. No washes have been applied. In the left quadrant Christ sits on a hillock speaking to the woman, who holds a ewer in one hand and what appears to be a towel in the other; standing next to the well, she gently inclines her head toward Christ. This reading is commonly illustrated in the Byzantine lectionary; Dionysiou cod. 587 (*Treasures of Athos,* I, fig. 204), Morgan MS 639 (Weitzmann, "Morgan 639," fig. 303), and Paris, suppl. gr. 27 (Omont, *Miniatures,* pl. XCIX, 1) offer parallels.

Fol. 38: The sixth Sunday in John, the Sunday of the Blind Man (Fig. 12); Jn 9:1–38. The miniature is unfinished, as is the initial, the outlines of which have been drawn in carmine and

Illustration and Decoration

dusted with gold. Christ stands against the *tau* and gestures toward the blind youth in the opposite quadrant. He wears a blue tunic and gray himation; the youth wears a short vermilion tunic. The youth's purse, staff, and hair are washed in gray-blue, as is Christ's hair. The faces have not been painted, although a wavy gray-blue ground line was added. The text is illustrated with the same subject in Dionysiou cod. 587 (*Treasures of Athos,* I, fig. 205), Morgan MS 639 (Weitzmann, "Morgan 639," fig. 304), and Paris. suppl. gr. 27 (Omont, *Miniatures,* pl. XCIX, 5). The scene is also illustrated in Panteleimon cod. 2, folio 40v, where Christ stands against the *tau* and touches the eyes of the blind youth (Fig. 58). In the Athens Lectionary the initial is historiated with the blind youth walking, slightly bent and using a staff (Marava-Chatzinicolaou and Toufexi-Paschou, *Manuscripts of the National Library of Greece,* fig. 359).

Fols. 56 and 57: Pentecost Sunday (Figs. 13, 14); Jn 7:37–52, 8:12. In the first illustration Christ stands against the *tau,* his right arm pulled away from the body and his hand held in a gesture of speech as he delivers the famous words of John 7:37ff. The initial has been meticulously finished and shows Christ wearing a tan tunic with white and vermilion articulation and an unusually light blue himation. The shade of blue is more common to the finials and initials than to the miniatures. On the recto of the next leaf the text continues with the fifty-first verse of chapter seven. Next to the half-length portrait of Christ is the only inscription to accompany a miniature, "I am the light of the world," the culmination of the lection (Jn 8:12). In the upper quadrants are figures whom we may assume to be the chief priests and pharisees; all are seated in judgment, and one in the group at the left has his head covered, a common way of distinguishing the Jews (see fol. 23; Fig. 9b). Here, though, the man wears what looks like a white turban with red linear details. Christ is portrayed wearing a red tunic with blue and white articulation; his himation is blue. There is some flaking on his forehead. For the group of seated figures at the left, the illuminator has alternated blue and olive tunics and himations; those to the right are in blue and dull green. The colors are set apart from those of Christ's garments by the extensive use of white articulation. All the portraits are carefully modeled in white and dark brown.

The passage illustrated by this miniature dramatically intercuts one of Christ's sermons with the actions of the officers sent by the priests to arrest him and the deliberations of the priests themselves. The figures portrayed are not actually together, and the illuminator has captured the long-distance drama between Christ and the authorities by showing him in their midst but not in fact fully present. The reading is otherwise illustrated: in Morgan MS 639 (Weitzmann, "Morgan 639," fig. 308) with Christ in the *tau* holding a codex. The Pentecost, celebrated on the day the text is sung, was represented in Dionysiou cod. 587 (*Treasures of Athos,* I, fig. 213) and Paris. suppl. gr. 27 (Omont, *Miniatures,* pl. XCVIII, 1). In contrast with the scenes in the Florence Gospels (Velmans, *Tétraévangile,* fig. 281), the composition in the New York Lectionary finds some interesting parallels in Paris. gr. 74 (Omont, *Evangiles,* fig. 157). In the Athens Lectionary, Christ stands against the *tau* holding a scroll (Marava-Chatzinicolaou and Toufexi-Paschou, *Manuscripts of the National Library of Greece,* fig. 360). The miniature on fol. 57 has been published.[10]

Fol. 64v: The fifth Sunday in Matthew (Fig. 15); Mt 8:28–9:1. The depiction of the healing at Gadara is unfinished. A brown wash has been applied to all the figures' flesh. Christ wears a purple

---

10. Belle da Costa Greene, *Exhibition of Illuminated Manuscripts Held at the New York Public Library,* New York, 1934, pl. 36; *Greek Manuscripts from American Collections,* fig. 61.

tunic and blue himation, the same tone used for the loincloths of the possessed. The dense layers of wash have received no articulation; they are just flat tones. The miracle is represented in the Paris (Omont, *Evangiles*, pl. 17) and Florence (Velmans, *Tétraévangile*, fig. 26) Gospels but is not common in the lectionaries. It is, however, similarly represented in Paris. suppl. gr. 27 (Omont, *Miniatures*, pl. XCIX, 9) and the Panteleimon (Fig. 59) and Athens lectionaries (Fig. 61).

Fol. 87: Headpiece; First Saturday in Luke, Beginning of the New Year (Fig. 16). This headpiece has been painted with a relatively broad palette. The lower ornament is particularly striking; the bottom leaves, or calyxes, are blue on the outside and a strong, dense shade of orange inside. Green stems rise to carry pink flowers.

Fol. 87v: First Saturday of the New Year (Fig. 17); Lk 4:31–36. Christ is posed against the initial *tau;* he wears a brown tunic and blue himation. The shade of blue is not the same as that of the initial itself. In the right quadrant is the city of Capernaum with its temple shown inside as a domed building, handsomely drawn and painstakingly shaded and detailed. The illuminator has finished both figure and city. In the lower right quadrant is a very faint drawing lightly washed. It shows the possessed man whom Christ heals; a light green wash has been applied to the man's loincloth and used to indicate the strip of ground on which he stands. The reading is not often illustrated. It is in the Athens Lectionary, where the initial has been historiated with an author portrait (Marava-Chatzinicolaou and Toufexi-Paschou, *Manuscripts of the National Library of Greece,* fig. 351). The miniature has been published.[11]

Fol. 91: Third Sunday in Luke (Fig. 18); Lk 7:11–16. The miniature is sketched in carmine and shows little detail in the faces. In the left quadrant Christ stands with two figures, presumably disciples, as the widow of Nain kneels in supplication before him. In the right quadrant is the second part of the story: Christ leans from a tower in the city wall toward the widow's dead son, lying at the foot of the wall on a bier. The illustration does not accord with a literal reading of the text. Most significantly, Luke does not write that the widow implored Christ to raise her son from the dead, as the sequence of miniatures seems to suggest. Versions closer to the text are found in the Paris (Omont, *Evangiles*, pl. 107) and Florence (Velmans, *Tétraévangile,* fig. 204) Gospels. The composition in the Lectionary clearly shows elements of the more common healing of the woman with the issue of blood: Paris. gr. 74, fol. 73v (Omont, *Evangiles*, pl. 67) and Laur. 6.23, fol. 71v (Velmans, *Tétraévangile,* fig. 142). The episodic treatment of supplication and healing also occurs in conjunction with the depiction of the story of Christ's healing the daughter of the Syrophoenician woman (Mk 7:25–30) in Paris. gr. 74 (Omont, *Evangiles*, pl. 71).

Fol. 94v: The fifth Sunday in Luke (Fig. 19) Lk 16:19–31. In the lower portion of the leaf is an unfinished illustration. Christ stands at the left, gesturing in speech toward the right quadrant. Depicted here is the palace of the rich man, shown in the upper story looking out of the unshuttered window. At the doors below stands Lazarus. The drawing was done in red ink; Christ wears a purple tunic and a blue himation. The colors, applied as heavy washes, remain unarticulated. Christ's halo has been gilt, but its crossbars and Christ's flesh remain unpainted. Flat tones of ocher, green, pink, and blue have been applied to the palace and the grassy strip around it. In painting this strip the illuminator covered Lazarus's feet and legs; his long tunic is pink and he wears what appears

---

11. *The First Quarter Century of the Pierpont Morgan Library: A Retrospective Exhibition in Honor of Belle da Costa Greene,* New York, 1949, pl. 7.

to be a wide lavender belt or apron. The rich man is dressed in purple. The reading is illustrated in the Panteleimon Lectionary, fol. 90v, where the rich man appears in the *epsilon,* his palace immediately below it and Lazarus walking with canes in the margin; in the Athens Lectionary the initial contains a bust-length portrait of Christ (Marava-Chatzinicolaou and Toufexi-Paschou, *Manuscripts of the National Library of Greece,* fig. 365). The reading is not illustrated in the other three lectionaries surveyed.

Fol. 123v: Portrait of Saint Mark (Fig. 20). The format and framing pattern are the same as those used for the portrait of John, but Mark wears a blue tunic and a creamy tan himation. Edges of the garments are outlined in black. His flesh is heavily painted with green shadows and touches of red. Again the line for the halo is the same vermilion that was used for the inscription, of which only a few letters survive: ὁ αγ . . . κος. The miniature has been published.[12]

Fol. 124: Cross headpiece with portrait of Saint Theodore Tiron (Fig. 21); First Saturday of Lent and the Commemoration of the Great Martyr, Saint Theodore Tiron. The headpiece frame, containing animals with expressive faces, is finished. The bust-length portrait of the saint is simply sketched, and of it only the head and neckline, a round fibula, and the hand clenched as if holding a cross. The beginning of the readings drawn mainly from Mark coincides with Lent. Though technically not the feast of Saint Theodore, it is the day with which he was customarily associated because of his effort to save fourth-century Christians from eating food that had been secretly polluted with the blood of pagan sacrifices.[13] He illustrates the first reading in Dionysiou cod. 587 (*Treasures of Athos,* I, fig. 216) and Morgan MS 639 (Weitzmann, "Morgan 639," fig. 314). In the Athens Lectionary the first reading in Lent opens with a *tau* historiated with a portrait of Saint Theodore (Marava-Chatzinicolaou and Toufexi-Paschou, *Manuscripts of the National Library of Greece,* fig. 353).

Fols. 135v and 136: Palm Sunday, morning service (Figs. 22, 23); Mt 21:1–11, 15–17. In the lower quadrants of fol. 135v, next to the start of the reading, Christ stands on the Mount of Olives and gestures toward the city of Jerusalem in the opposite quadrant. At the top of the facing leaf two of the disciples vigorously walk toward another representation of the city, in this instance with its gates thrown open. The drawings are relatively finished ones, and the foliage of the Mount of Olives has been painted green. This reading is not illustrated in Morgan MS 639, but it is in Paris. suppl. gr. 27, where the Entry into Jerusalem has been depicted (Omont, *Miniatures,* pl. C, 3). Dionysiou cod. 587 is missing a leaf at this point (C. Walter, "The Date and Content of the Dionysiou Lectionary," *Deltion tes Christianikes Archaiologikes Hetaireias,* XIII, 1988, 184).

Fol. 159v: (continuation of) Morning reading for Holy Thursday (Fig. 24); Lk 22:1–39 (which begins on fol. 157). A rooster is painted in the bottom right quadrant near Luke 22:35, Christ's prediction of Peter's betrayal. The bird is densely painted in unnatural colors.

Fol. 167v: (continuation of reading for) Holy Thursday (Fig. 25); Mt 26:1–20, Jn 13:3–17, Mt 26:21–39, Lk 22:43–45, Mt 26:40–27:2 (which begins on fol. 160). The illustration appears at the end of this lengthy reading. The proximate text is that of Matthew 26:74ff., in which Peter, having denied Christ and heard the cock crow, breaks down and weeps. An oversize rooster stands in the left quadrant; at the right Peter sits dejectedly on the ground, his head inclined, as he wipes tears

---

12. *Greek Manuscripts from American Collections,* fig. 60.

13. Weitzmann, "Morgan 639," 371–72, recalls the sources and story in detail.

from his eyes with the left hand. He wears a blue tunic with fine linear detail and a creamy tan himation articulated with wide strokes; his halo is painted light blue. The ground beneath him is a rocky brown landscape. The reading is illustrated in Dionysiou cod. 587 (*Treasures of Athos,* I, fig. 225), although with different subjects, ones appropriate to the location of the miniatures at the start of the text. Peter's denial is shown as a framed scene on fol. 271v of Morgan MS 639, but to a different reading (fourth Passion reading; Weitzmann, "Morgan 639," fig. 317). A nearly identical illustration appears in the lectionary in the Greek Institute of Byzantine and Post-Byzantine Studies in Venice.[14] The illustration tends to call to mind the Byzantine psalters. A similar image illustrates Psalm 38:12 ("O Lord, . . . attend to my tears . . .") in a number of the psalters from the late ninth or early tenth century to the eleventh century.[15] The Psalm verse is not specified for this celebration by the Typikon of Saint Sophia; on the verse and the liturgy, see C. Walter.[16]

Fol 168: First Passion reading (Fig. 26); Jn 13:31–18.2. A bar of ornament sets off these, the last illustrated lections in the synaxarion. Christ is depicted in the initial *epsilon* in essentially the Pantocrator type. He is shown all in blue; the object he holds in his right hand is scarlet. The face is a dusty, somewhat cool tan; the eye sockets are brown. Other shadows and highlights are done in scarlet and white, with an overall effect that is impressively subtle. The reading is often illustrated: in Dionysiou cod. 587 with Christ in Gethsemane and Christ teaching (*Treasures of Athos,* I, fig. 226) and in Paris. suppl. gr. 27 with the arrest of Christ (Omont, *Miniatures,* pl. XCVIII, 2). Representations of Christ in the initial also occur in the Athens (Marava-Chatzinicolaou and Toufexi-Paschou, *Manuscripts of the National Library of Greece,* fig. 352) and Panteleimon (fol. 140) lectionaries.

Fols. 182v and 183: (continuation of) Third Passion reading (Figs. 27, 28); Mt 26:57–75 (which begins on fol. 181). A rooster appears in the lower left quadrant of fol. 182v and is depicted in tones markedly more naturalistic than those used in the previous examples; he has tan and brown feathers, carefully articulated, and a red comb and wattles. In the upper right quadrant of fol. 183, Saint Peter is depicted seated on a rocky landscape and using his himation to wipe away tears. The tunic is blue, the himation brown, and the halo a dense vermilion. The garments are articulated extensively in white, and his face is carefully drawn and shaded.

Folio 214: Beginning of the second part of the lectionary (menologion), the fixed readings (Fig. 29). The cruciform headpiece encloses an inscribed portrait of Saint Symeon Stylites, above whom appears the Hand of God. The frame is complete, as are the column and its base and capital. The colors used are approximately the same for frame and architecture, but the lines of the capital are carmine, whereas those of the flowers in the frame are vermilion and more finely drawn. The inscription ("The blessed Symeon Stylites") was not dusted with gold powder. Saint Symeon's is the first life commemorated in the year, which begins on 1 September, and he is often portrayed at this point in the lectionary: Dionysiou cod. 587 (*Treasures of Athos,* I, fig. 237), Morgan MS 639 (Weitzmann, "Morgan 639," fig. 319), and Paris. suppl. gr. 27 (Omont, *Miniatures,* pl. XCVIII, 3).

---

14. A. Xyngopoulos, "To historemenon euaggelion tou Hellenikou Instioutou Benetias," *Thesaurismata,* I, 1962, 67.

15. See the Chludov (M. Ščepkina, *Miniatiury Khludovskoi Psaltyri,* Moscow, 1977, fol. 38v) and Pantocrator psalters (S. Dufrenne, *L'illustration des psautiers grecs du Moyen âge,* I, *Pantocrator 61, Paris grec 20, British Museum 40731.* Bibliothèque des Cahiers archéologiques, I, Paris, 1966, pl. 7). Peter weeping before the cock also appears in the eleventh-century Theodore (S. Der Nersessian, *L'illustration des psautiers grecs du Moyen âge,* II, *Londres, Add. 19.352,* Bibliothèque des Cahiers archéologiques, V, Paris, 1970, fig. 81) and Barberini (J. Anderson, P. Canart, C. Walter, *The Barberini Psalter: Codex Vaticanus Barberinianus Graecus 372,* Zurich, 1989) psalters.

16. "Christological Themes in the Byzantine Marginal Psalters from the Ninth to the Eleventh Century," *REB,* XLIV, 1986, 278–79.

Fol. 221v: September 13 (Figs. 30a, b); Jn 12:25–36. In the top left quadrant Christ is shown prostrate, and at the right the Hand of God extends from heaven to signify the words quoted in John 12:28. At the bottom of the leaf Christ appears opposite a group of men, to whom he explains the meaning of the voice from heaven. The scroll Christ holds is open, an image unique among his portraits in the lectionary; the illuminator apparently intends the beholder to draw a parallel between Christ and Moses, who holds an open scroll on the facing leaf (Fig. 31b). These drawings are in tan ink. The lower hand of God was drawn in what appears to be pencil, and at the very bottom of the leaf is a sketch in dilute red ink; both of these are doubtless much later additions. The upper scene reflects the composition associated with the Agony in the Garden, and Christ's words to his disciples at this moment after the triumphal entry into Jerusalem foreshadow those spoken in Gethsemane. Christ speaking of his death to a crowd is depicted in the Florence Gospels (Velmans, *Tétraévangile,* fig. 290); the passage is somewhat differently illustrated in Paris. gr. 74 (Omont, *Evangiles,* pl. 167). For the feast celebrated, see below on fols. 222v–224.

Fol. 222: Sunday before the Exaltation (of the Holy Cross) (Figs. 31a, b); Jn 3:13–17. The illustration to the reading fills all four quadrants. At the bottom left stands Moses pointing across the page to the opposite margin, where the cross on Golgotha is represented. A serpent wraps around it, in illustration of the text (Jn 3:14): "And as Moses lifted up the serpent in the wilderness, so must the son of man be lifted up." In the top quadrants are the crosses on which the two thieves were crucified. The typological image in the New York Lectionary recalls the illustration of the same passage in Paris. gr. 74, fol. 171 (Omont, *Evangiles,* pl. 148): Moses pointing to the serpent raised on the pole is contrasted with Christ and the cross of crucifixion.

Fols. 222v, 223, and 224: 14 September, Liturgy for the Feast of the Exaltation of the Holy Cross (Figs. 32–34); Jn 19:6, 9b–11, 13–20, 25–28a, 30–35. Colwell and Riddle give the long lectionary *incipit,*[17] which is the source of the first miniature (Fig. 32). In the lower left quadrant sits the council of priests and officers (elders), who plot Christ's destruction and then go to Pilate with the order to crucify him. The illuminator has depicted the transmission of their verdict in the opposite quadrant. The miniature has been previously published.[18] Next, on fol. 223 (Fig. 33), Christ is depicted in the lower left margin speaking (Jn 19:11); at the right the illuminator has shown Pilate seated. The proximate text is Jn 19:13, which records Pilate's reaction to Christ's words and the demands of the Jews: he went and took the seat of judgment. The reading continues on fol. 224, the illustration of which flanks Jn 19:25 (Fig. 34). In the left quadrant stand the two Marys; at the right is the crucifixion. Mary and John flank the cross; Christ's head slumps markedly, and above are the sun and the moon, shown as profile heads in circles. The feast of the Exaltation of the Holy Cross, held on 14 September, was an important one in Byzantium and its celebration began well before the fourteenth of the month. Miniatures pertaining to the feast appear in the menologium sections of Dionysiou cod. 587 (*Treasures of Athos,* I, figs. 239, 240) and in the eleventh-century Vatican lectionary, gr. 1156,[19] both of which show elements of a commemorative service; that is, they do not actually illustrate the readings associated with the feast. In the long sequence in the New York Lectionary the illustration is narrative in character. The typology of the first miniature arises

17. *Prolegomena,* 130.
18. K. Weitzmann, "Narrative and Liturgical Gospel Illustrations," *New Testament Manuscript Studies,* ed. M. Parvis and A. Wikgren, Chicago, 1950, pl. xv.
19. K. Weitzmann, "Byzantine Miniature and Icon Painting in the Eleventh Century," *Studies,* figs. 297–99.

The New York Cruciform Lectionary

from Christ's own words, which were also illustrated in Paris. gr. 74. In the New York Lectionary, though, the format invited the illuminator to fill each of three quadrants with a cross; he sketched the outlines of an impressive, balanced composition. The remainder of the illustration follows important moments in the story of the Passion and culminates in the Crucifixion. The council of the priests and officials also appears in Dionysiou cod. 587 (*Treasures of Athos*, I, fig. 240), though in a different way: the figures stand facing one another in discussion.

Fol. 225: September 15 (Fig. 35); Mt. 10:16–22. Portrait of Saint Niketas, whose memory is celebrated on this day. He is dressed in a chlamys and is nimbate; his right hand is held to his chest and clenched, but the object he would grasp (a cross) has not been drawn.

Fol. 230: *Pi*-shaped headpiece to mark the beginning of the October readings.

Fol. 235: October 18 (Fig. 36); Lk 10:16–21. In the bottom right quadrant Saint Luke has been drawn togate, holding a book. His eyes look sharply toward the text.

Fol. 238: October 26 (Fig. 37); Mt 8:23–27. Saint Demetrios is drawn in military dress, including a cape, and is armed with a shield and spear.

Fol. 238v: Headpiece to mark the beginning of the November readings.

Fol. 241v: Headpiece to mark the beginning of the December readings.

Fol. 254v: Headpiece to mark the beginning of the January readings.

Fol. 260: January 6: Liturgy of the Feast of the Lights; Mt 3:13–17. In the lower right quadrant is the Baptism of Christ (Fig. 38), sketched according to contemporary custom. The Baptism of Christ appears in Dionysiou cod. 587 (*Treasures of Athos*, I, fig. 255) and Morgan MS 639 (Weitzmann, "Morgan 639," fig. 326). It also appears as part of an initial letter in the Paris. suppl. gr. 27, but to the reading for 3 January (Omont, *Miniatures*, pl. C, 12).

Fol. 263v: Rinceau to mark the beginning of the February readings.

Fol. 264: February 2: Presentation of Christ in the Temple (Fig. 39); Lk 2:22–40. In the left quadrant stand Anna and Symeon, the latter stepping forward to reach for Christ; in the opposite margin the Virgin holds out the child as Joseph stands behind her with the offering of doves. The Presentation also appears in Dionysiou cod. 587 (*Treasures of Athos*, I, fig. 260) and Morgan MS 639 (Weitzmann, "Morgan 639," fig. 328), in both cases as a framed miniature.

Fol. 267: Headpiece to mark the beginning of the March readings.

Fol. 271: Rinceau to mark the beginning of the April readings.

Fol. 272v: Headpiece to mark the beginning of the May readings.

Fol. 274v: Headpiece to mark the beginning of the June readings.

Fol. 281v: Rinceau to mark the beginning of the July readings.

Fol. 284: Headpiece to mark the beginning of the August readings.

Fol. 284: August 6: morning service in commemoration of the Transfiguration (Fig. 40); Lk 9:28–36. Using red ink, the illuminator has sketched only the figures of Christ and, to his left, Moses. The initial *tau* has not even been drawn. Perhaps the plan was to make use of the initial in the illustration. The illuminator, however, proceeded in a way that suggests he decided otherwise. It is difficult to imagine Elijah or the disciples somehow having been worked into the letter. This is the only miniature that is truly unfinished, and it is the last one in the manuscript. The Transfiguration appears in Dionysiou cod. 587 (*Treasures of Athos*, I, fig. 271).

Fol. 289v: Headpiece at the start of the morning Resurrection readings. This is the final decoration and it marks the last series of readings.

Illustration and Decoration

The New York Lectionary is a highly decorated book; its various parts, most traditional by the twelfth century, combine to facilitate the book's use in church and to make it a donation of particular richness, even in this time of exceptional opulence in manuscript illumination. From the description of the manuscript one can begin to explore the sources and use of the initials, headpieces, and miniatures. In addition to the miniatures, the lectionary contains an unusually wide selection of nonfigural ornament in the form of headpieces and initials. The initials are of two sorts: either simple gold or a polychrome essentially the same as that of the miniatures, headpieces, and finials. In general, but not with much regard for consistency, the illuminators began the Sunday readings and those for great feasts with a painted initial, whereas other days open with a letter in plain gold. By about 1150 this essentially hierarchical system had been in widespread use in lectionary decoration for well over a century. The headpieces were also designed and located according to a pattern that relates to the manuscript's use. But here too, by the twelfth century the placement of headpieces had so long a tradition that the illuminators would have reacted nearly instinctively to the structure of the text. Creative or innovative planning is not an issue in the design or placement of the ornament. The first part of the manuscript, the synaxarion, was treated like a Gospel book, with full-page Evangelist portraits facing title pages (for example Figs. 1, 2). This system almost certainly emerged in the 900s, when the primitive lectionary was expanded to cover a full year of celebrations; the expansion relied on runs of readings taken from individual Gospels, with the result that the lectionary became more like a Gospel book, a fact revealed and reinforced by rubrics like the "third Sunday in Luke" (Fig. 18). In the New York manuscript the pages opposite the Evangelist portraits (Figs. 2, 16, 21) do not contain text along with the title, as is so often the case;[20] only the titles, handsomely framed within crosses, are painted. That such headpieces have few forerunners[21] can probably be attributed to the rarity of cruciform manuscripts generally and specifically to the amount of parchment that has been used for fewer than a dozen words. The use of material is conspicuous. In addition to the four cruciform titles painted to mark the divisions of the synaxarion, another separates the synaxarion from the menologion (Fig. 29). The secondary divisions of any section (the Passion readings at the end of the synaxarion and the months of the menologion, Fig. 26) are set off by bars of ornament or lines with a few decorative flourishes.

In the Middle Ages, book ornament functioned in several ways. Primarily it served to facilitate movement among chapters or other divisions. The *skevophylax* or *ekklesiarch* charged with preparing the books, or the deacon who read the passage, could move quickly from one section of the synaxarion to another, as well as between the months of the menologion, by paying attention to the titles strikingly framed by the headpieces; because of their decoration, the beginnings of the pericopes likewise jump off the page to meet the eye. Bold section markers would have been especially helpful in using the menologion since it relies on an elaborate cross-reference system. The decoration, with five major headpieces and a series of smaller bars and one *pi*-shaped frame, combined with its many painted and gilt initials, also gave the lectionary a richness rarely paralleled. The decorative designs—flowers and leaves set in a variety of geometric frameworks—were traditional by the twelfth century. In type and in their execution with thick layers of dense color, the

---

20. For examples, see the original placement of Saint Mark and the beginning of the Lenten readings in Serres, Prodromos Monastery, cod. 17: *Greek Manuscripts from American Collections*, 73, fig. 13; or the headpieces of London, British Library, Harley 5598: Weitzmann, *Byz. Buchmalerei*, figs. 200–203.

21. The early Patmos Gregory (Monastery of Saint John the Theologian, cod. 33) contains some of the few, but even they are not exactly title frames: Lake, *Dated Greek MSS*, I, MS 15.

The New York Cruciform Lectionary

headpieces intentionally parallel the gold and enamelwork of reliquaries and icon revetments. It is its lush ornament that placed the lectionary at the level of the icon, chalice, or paten. The quality and extent of the ornament would have met what one might reasonably surmise was a donor's wish to offer a gift of extraordinary cost and beauty. This now-forgotten Byzantine donor's satisfaction may not have been limited to the moment of presentation. The phrases most commonly inscribed in manuscripts tend toward one sentiment: they ask the reader to pause and remember to God the donor of the book that he or she is holding. The extremely rare and costly format of the New York Lectionary may reflect the donor's hope to set his or her gift apart from all others and thus ensure the fulfillment of this basic wish.

The illustration of the lectionary is more difficult to evaluate in terms of use. The miniatures do not help the reader move efficiently through the text; the red and gold titles serve that function. We can also eliminate from consideration any polemic role for the imagery. As the medieval psalters more than amply demonstrate, the Byzantines were adept at forging pictures and words into powerful arguments. Nothing in the lectionary cycle as we have it or in the individual miniatures suggests that either the patron or illuminators intended for the miniatures to convey some particular meaning to the reader. The many parallels with other lectionaries tend to confirm this conclusion. To both patron and user, the miniatures served to increase the book's value. Any further evaluation of the cycle founders on one problem—our natural reticence in the face of the cycle's state of completion. The use of ornament was essentially standardized by the twelfth century, but illustration had never become so common as to be equally predictable. One cannot say that some particular subject is missing, and the comparisons made with the Athens and Dionysiou lectionaries reveal the range of possibilities in medieval illustration. The illuminators may have executed only a fraction of the originally intended narrative miniatures. The logical possibility cannot be eliminated, but close study of the comparisons shows that even if the illuminators did not complete the cycle, neither did they leave it obviously truncated. There is a pattern to lectionary illustration and the New York manuscript follows it.

The miniatures in the New York Lectionary can be studied as an essentially complete set. The scenes are familiar ones that reflect medieval interests shaped by the unique requirements of the manuscript type. The medieval lectionary served as a source of public readings; to this end it was almost invariably written in bold letters, usually in double columns (for example, Fig. 61) and with few interruptions apart from the internal references and guides. Illustrations were placed between readings, in the initials or in the margins, where they would not interfere with a book's use. Illuminators often had to be concise in serving the requirements of format, and contemporaries would likely meet exigencies in similar ways, thus creating apparent similarities between unrelated images. Furthermore, for much of the eleventh and twelfth centuries, patrons and artists favored modes of illustration other than the grandly pictorial; the images in psalters, collections of sermons, or Gospel books are often historiated initials, marginal figures, or miniatures with little more than a green brush stroke beneath figures' feet to suggest spatial context. Utterly unrelated versions of subjects like the Baptism or Crucifixion will have much in common once the artists have eliminated the story's background and all but its principal actors. What I actually have in mind in speaking of patterns in lectionary illustration is the medieval illuminators' tendency to favor certain passages in the text.

The miniature cycle of the New York Lectionary, like those of most other medieval lectionaries,

Illustration and Decoration

is highly selective. Illustrated are major events from Christ's life, the Baptism, the Presentation in the Temple, the Transfiguration, and the Crucifixion (Figs. 38–40, 34). The cycle contains a proportionately large selection of healing scenes, including the Miracle at the Pool of Bethesda, Christ and the Blind Youth, the Healing at Gadara, and Christ and the Son of the Widow of Nain (Figs. 8, 12, 15, 18). But Christ's role as teacher (Figs. 10, 13, 30b) is also included. In some regards, then, the cycle presents a balanced picture of Christ's life. In other ways, though, the selection seems perplexing. Some fascinating passages have no miniatures when others of somewhat less interest, like Peter rushing to the tomb or John speaking to his two disciples, are illustrated (Figs. 4, 5). The medieval selection of twelve feasts that appears on icons can serve as an index of important moments in the liturgical year;[22] of the feasts, the Presentation in the Temple, the Baptism, the Transfiguration, and the Crucifixion are depicted, whereas the Annunciation, the Nativity, the Raising of Lazarus, the Anastasis, the Ascension, Pentecost, and the Dormition of the Virgin are not. Also noteworthy is the uneven distribution of scenes; eight of the John readings are illustrated, whereas only one in Matthew, three each in Luke and Mark, and two in the Passion readings are illustrated. The menologion was illustrated with portraits of four saints (Symeon Stylites, Niketas, Luke, and Demetrios: Figs. 29, 35, 36, 37), three feasts from Christ's life (the Baptism, the Presentation in the Temple, and the Transfiguration: Figs. 38–40), and the typological and narrative scenes relating to the Feast of the Exaltation of the Holy Cross, which includes the Crucifixion (Figs. 30–34).

The shape of the cycle of images in the New York Lectionary, both the clustering of subjects and the inclusion of minor subjects and the omission of some major ones, generally accords with that of other lectionaries of the period. The running comparisons reveal almost nothing in the narrative cycle of the New York manuscript that cannot be found elsewhere. At the same time, no other book is so very nearly the same as to suggest that the cycle is the copy of another or that it is the product of a group of craftsmen who essentially repeated the same images from commission to commission. The exact choice of scenes is unique, but unique within a certain type of picture cycle. This fact, if we can account for it, has important implications: something other than the explicit directions of the patron or idiosyncratic choices of the illuminators shaped the illustration of the New York Lectionary. In attempting an explanation, I will concentrate on the illustrations in the synaxarion.[23]

A lectionary illustration has two significant attributes: one is its relationship to the content of the text and the other is its relationship to the liturgical celebration on the day the text was sung. Sometimes the two coincide; other times they do not. Since the consideration of the images by subject matter led to questions, then we should pass on to their position within the liturgical text. Of the passages illustrated in the New York Lectionary, all but three are also illustrated in one or more of the other lectionaries used for comparison (Dionysiou cod. 587, Morgan MS 639, Paris. suppl. gr. 27, and the Athens and Panteleimon lectionaries). The three readings are those for the third Sunday in Luke (fol. 91), the morning reading for Holy Thursday (fol. 157), and the third Passion reading (fol. 181). Although not found in members of the group surveyed here, two of these passages were illustrated in other lectionaries. The lectionary in the Greek Institute of Byzantine and Post-Byzantine Studies in Venice has a similar illustration for Holy Thursday.[24] The illustration of

---

22. Most recently, see E. Kitzinger, "Reflections on the Feast Cycle in Byzantine Art," *Cahiers archéologiques,* XXXVI, 1988, 51–58.

23. The problem of the menologion in all its aspects—illustration, rubrics, content—will be taken up separately in chapter III.

24. Xyngopoulos (as in note 14), 67.

27

The New York Cruciform Lectionary

the third Passion reading more or less repeats the same illustration, which happens to be similar to the miniature on fol. 122v of the Dumbarton Oaks Lectionary, cod. 1 (Fig. 54). The Dumbarton Oaks manuscript was written in part in the shape of a cross; if, as seems possible, it is somehow related to the New York manuscript, then the evidence of its parallel at this point would be of little value to my ultimate argument. In any event, only one illustrated lection (fol. 91) is unique to the New York Lectionary. I should also point out that several readings, though illustrated elsewhere, are not common to all or a large number of the medieval lectionaries: the fifth Sunday in Matthew (fol. 64v), the first Saturday of the New Year (fol. 87v), and the fifth Sunday in Luke (fol. 94v). As potentially important as unusual parallels may be, dwelling on them at this stage only distracts from the most important point. Of the one hundred and fifty or so readings in the synaxarion of a Saturday-Sunday lectionary, an astonishingly small number of them turn out to be illustrated again and again during the Middle Ages. This cannot be accidental. Furthermore, the variations that might seem to compromise this assessment tend to follow their own pattern in that they occur toward the end of the synaxarion, not within its first parts; they appear mostly in the Passion readings.

That structure governs the distribution of the scenes in the medieval lectionary can be confirmed through subject matter. A number of subjects tend to be common to the lectionaries surveyed (as well as to the others to which only occasional reference has been made): Peter going to Christ's tomb (fol. 4), the story of Thomas's doubt (fols. 10v, 11), the Miracle at Bethesda (fols. 22v, 23), the Woman of Samaria (fol. 29v), and the healing of the blind man (fol. 38). In other instances, though, a different subject will illustrate the same reading for the same day. The illustrator of the New York Lectionary showed Christ standing against the initial *tau* as illustration of the pericope (Jn 7:37–52, 8:12) read on Pentecost Sunday (fol. 56; Fig. 13); at this same place in the lectionary, the illuminators of Dionysiou cod. 587 and Paris. suppl. gr. 27 depicted the descent of the Holy Spirit related in Acts 2. The first of the Passion readings (fol. 214) is generally illustrated but in any number of ways. It is the other instances, such as the different subjects at the same locations, that reveal the importance of structure in the illustration of the medieval lectionary. It was the use of the pericope for the feast of the Pentecost that prompted illustrators; some chose to show the standard image of the descent of the Spirit on the Apostles, others chose to show Christ teaching, an illustration of the opening verse (" . . . Jesus stood up and proclaimed, 'If any one thirst . . . ' "). Study of the titles written above readings, the manuscripts' rubrics, reveals what guided illuminators.

The titles that gave the day on which a passage was read clarify some issues of manuscript illustration, but they also raise a particular question in the case of the New York Lectionary. Most of the days in the lectionary are given simply by count: "the third Sunday in Luke," for instance.[25] A handful of others go by nicknames: the "Sunday of the Women at the Tomb" (literally, of the *myrophoron*), ". . . of the Paralytic," ". . . of the Woman of Samaria," ". . . of the Blind Man," "Assumption Thursday," "Sunday of the Holy Fathers of Nicaea," the readings of Pentecost week, the new year, and the various days of Cheese Week, Lent, and Holy Week. These days that bear distinctively precise rubrics form the core of the illustrated lessons; often they were illustrated in a way directly related to the title. In addition, the week after Easter (διακαινήσιμος, Renewal Week)

---

25. The titles in medieval lectionaries are enumerated in Colwell and Riddle, *Prolegomena*, 85–127.

and following Sunday (ἀντίπασχα) are often illustrated. Thus, in the way the text is laid out and the various readings titled, we have the forces that shaped the decoration and illustration of the medieval lectionary. Turning specifically to the New York Lectionary, one finds that throughout most of the synaxarion, including its early parts, the scribe numbered the readings. He used the nicknames only for the "Sunday of the Woman of Samaria" and the "Sunday of the Blind Man" (Figs. 11, 12). The illuminators added images that relate to other lectionaries and to the structure of the text itself. In some ways, of course, the rubrics simply focus attention on the most important feasts. The level of consistency in the placement of illustrations in manuscripts made over several centuries would not, I think, have been possible without this part of the lectionary text as an internal guide. That most of the precise rubrics are absent yet the manuscript is illustrated as if they were present leads to a hypothesis: the illuminators of the New York manuscript had prior experience with the lectionary.

Testing the hypothesis of the illuminators' prior experience with the lectionary forms part of the next stage in the study of the manuscript. Along with this one must also consider what is unusual, including the menologion illustrations, which seem to be more a matter of the illuminator's individual taste. Why in some cases did the illuminators depart from what appears to be a kind of tradition of illustration shaped by common reactions to format and text structure? As with the formation of the core of illustrations, our understanding ultimately depends on having some knowledge of those who were responsible for the manuscript. These are the scribe and illuminators, and, standing behind them, the patron.

II

Making the New York Lectionary: Procedures and Techniques

WE CANNOT CLAIM to be particularly well informed on the subject of how manuscripts were made in Byzantium. No compelling models of production exist to help us in organizing our impressions when leafing through a book. In publishing the New York Lectionary, it seems worthwhile to draw attention to evidence that might bear on how the manuscript was made. Our language happens to particularize the medieval world into one of scribes, illuminators, and binders, and our analytical method encourages us to envision the work as carried out in stages. The parchment was prepared and sold to the scribe, who folded the sheets, then cut, pricked, and ruled them to receive the Gospel text, which he wrote in brown ink. The rubrics—red and gold titles and instructions—were probably executed by the scribe at the same time. Once the text was finished, the finials, initials, and headpieces could be executed. Then the manuscript was illuminated as the last step before the binder sewed the quires and affixed the cords to the wooden support for the covers.[1] Without question, some parts of the book had to have been executed before others, yet is one justified in breaking the work down into a series of craft specialties? Alone, the decorated pages challenge our resources. Were they the result of a coordinated effort of a team of specialists, or were they the work of an individual? Perhaps the manuscript was executed methodically by one person, who worked leaf by leaf.

We can say unequivocally that at least two craftsmen worked on the New York Lectionary. The assertion is proved by the manuscript's illustration, which was done by two painters. Other elements of the staged execution I have sketched can be demonstrated as plausible. What little we know of parchment suggests that scribes did not begin with raw hides but bought the parchment already prepared.[2] That scribes executed text and rubrics simultaneously may be inferred from Evangelist portraits. Many of these portraits (see, for example, Fig. 52) show the author with both brown and red ink ready on the desk; likely this reflects medieval scribal practice. Titles in the Lectionary were often dusted with gold. Does this mean that the scribe may have had a hand in other parts of the manuscript in which the use of gold is prominent? Perhaps he was one of the illuminators. The

---

1. Judging from contemporary sources, the binding was quite possibly more than leather over wood (C. Diehl, "Le trésor et la bibliothèque de Patmos au commencement du 13ᵉ siècle," *Byzantinische Zeitschrift,* I, 1892, 514; P. Gautier, "La diataxis de Michel Attaliate," *REB,* XXXIX, 1981, 93; idem, "Le typikon du Sébaste Grégoire Pakourianos," *REB,* XLII, 1984, 121); it may have been silver and decorated with figures and enamels whose execution demanded another specialist. Since we no longer have the original cover of the New York Lectionary, speculation is useless.

2. N. Wilson, "Books and Readers in Byzantium," in *Byzantine Books and Bookmen,* Washington, D.C., 1975, 1–3, offers a good discussion.

The New York Cruciform Lectionary

relationship of the illuminators to the other ornament in the manuscript also needs to be explored, even if attributions are difficult to make. I will begin with the scribe and the two illuminators and conclude with remarks on how technique contributes to our knowledge of lectionary illustration.

The text of the New York Lectionary was copied by one scribe, who wrote in a highly controlled hand using letter forms that had evolved for large books used in the church service. By the twelfth century, the manner had long been traditional and no attribution could be based on it; such handwriting is not even easy to date.[3] The scribe appears generally, but not always, to have ruled the leaves on the hair side one at a time and to have made up the quires as he went along. It was the scribe's habit to begin each major division of the manuscript on a regular quaternion; to do so meant composing irregular quires at the ends of the John, Matthew, and Luke sections as well as at the end of the synaxarion. For two reasons I speak of this makeup as the result of habit and not as proof that the manuscript was planned from the start to receive full-page portraits on separate leaves. First, no full-page image would have been placed between the synaxarion and the menologion. Though a celebrated figure, Saint Symeon Stylites could be accommodated in a headpiece; he did not command a portrait at the level of those of the Four Evangelists. Second, other manuscripts similarly composed and without illustration are known; a pertinent example is the cruciform lectionary in the British Library, London (Figs. 43–47).

As he wrote the text, the scribe of the New York manuscript left indentations of differing sizes depending on the initial letter omitted. For the *tau,* usually only one (fols. 4, 25v, 91, 222v, 260, 264: figs. 4, 10, 18, 32, 38, 39) or two (fols. 29v, 64v, 87v: figs. 11, 15, 17) lines were indented, the space being equivalent to that of two or three letters. As these examples show (and others could be added from leaves lacking illustration), the decision to historiate an initial did not influence the size of the offset. Yet when writing the passages on fols. 38 and 56 (Figs. 12, 13), the scribe strongly indented four entire lines of text. One can only assume that he shaped the lines knowing that historiated initials would be added. These indentations are perhaps our only certain evidence that illustration was planned from the outset. Because the two indentations are quite large, we may also suggest that the scribe had in mind specific illustrations; the survey in chapter I shows that both readings were illustrated in lectionaries of the time.

After the text was written, the next step appears to have been painting the eight finials on each page, all carefully executed according to a pattern. The pairs at the top and bottom of the cross are blue throughout (though the colors range from light to dark blue). The finials at the crossbar are diagonally paired in red and green. In at least two instances,[4] on fols. 18v and 19, finials had to be scraped away and repositioned to allow for initials. On fols. 74, 81v, 122, and 244v, the finials are complete but the initials only drawn in carmine and dusted with gold. The initial *tau* is absent from fol. 284 (Fig. 40). Of course, this last case is special because the reading is illustrated. On fol. 81 is another space for a *tau;* the pericope, read on the fifteenth Sunday in Matthew (Mt 22:35–46, the lawyer examines Christ on the Commandments), was not illustrated in any of the lectionaries against which the New York manuscript was compared. The absence of the initial is unlikely due to the scribe's having left the work to an illuminator, as might be true of the letter missing on fol. 284 (Fig. 40). The initials were drawn in carmine, dusted with gold (see Fig. 12), and, finally, their

---

3. Some comparisons are given in chapter V.

4. In other cases, for example, fol. 67, rubbing and flaking make conclusions difficult.

Procedures and Techniques

segments painted. The carmine underdrawing is in the same ink as the ekphonetic notation, which was presumably written by the scribe at the time he wrote the sheets of Gospel text. The unfinished initials suggest that he or another craftsman did not draw and paint the initials immediately after the sheets with text had been finished; they were done as another stage in the process. The few scraps of evidence we have thus suggest that after the text was written the finials and initials were added to the leaves in two more or less separate stages of work.

The variously designed headpieces form the last of the nonfigural ornament. Where their execution fits into this schematic picture is difficult to say, although the examples on fols. 124 and 214 (Figs. 21, 29) show that they were done before the miniatures and, in a sense, as a separate step. Especially noteworthy is the unfinished state of the headpiece portraits. Both were sketched but not painted, and the uncial title was carefully composed with the portrait in mind. What my survey suggests is that the manuscript was planned as an illustrated one and that the scribe and other craftsmen cooperated closely. The juxtaposition of finished ornament and sketched portraits may offer evidence for the apportionment of work; to interpret it, though, requires turning to the illuminators.

Without question, two painters executed the miniatures in the New York Lectionary. I will refer to the two as illuminators A and B. An initial division of labor can be established on the basis of manifest differences in style. Illuminator A did the scenes on fols. 2v, 10v, 11, 22v, 23, 25v, 56, 57, 87v, 91, 94v, 159v, 167v, 168, and 284. To Illuminator B may be attributed the illustrations on fols. 4, 6, 29v, 38, 64v, 135v, 136, 214, 221v, 222, 222v, 223, 224, 235, 238, 260, and 264. Both left work in varying stages of execution, although I should stress that only the Transfiguration (Fig. 40) lacks figures; it alone can be considered unfinished by medieval standards. The individual drawing styles of the two illuminators serve to divide the work between them as surely as do the fully painted scenes, for the illuminators drew in fundamentally different ways, each in a style closely related to his finished work. Illuminator A sketched rapidly and without detail; his miniatures are painted with heavy layers of polychrome that cover all traces of underdrawing. Illuminator B, on the other hand, was far more careful in his sketching, preferring to use thin layers of polychrome, which allow the underdrawing to play an active role in the finished image.

When making his sketches, Illuminator A drew uneven outlines (Figs. 9, 18, 40). His brush strokes are short and quick and he varied the pressure on the brush. Most of the drawing in the manuscript was done in brown ink, which seems to be a dilute mixture of the ink used by the scribe. But some sketches were made in carmine (Figs. 8, 9, 10, 18, 19, 40), and all of them were done by Illuminator A.[5] When indicating the profile of the foot, Illuminator A drew only two lines, one for the inside of the leg, the other for the sole; hands and fingers are just a few short strokes. He might represent the facial features with dashes, a set for the eyes, and another for the mouth and shadow under the nose (Fig. 9). He might draw only the brow ridge (Fig. 18) or not indicate the features at all (Figs. 8, 18, 40). In only one instance did he correct a drawing: in the bottom right quadrant of fol. 91 (Fig. 18), the cornice of the city wall runs through the arm of one of the miracle's two witnesses. The illuminator was an expert, and for him, as for the other artists whose drawings we know because of severe flaking or because they remained unpainted, the preliminary sketch was

---

5. Sketches in both brown and red also can be found in Sinai. gr. 48: K. Weitzmann, "The Sinai Psalter Cod. 48 with Marginal Illustrations and Three Leaves in Leningrad," *Byzantine Liturgical Psalters and Gospels*, VII, 2–8.

almost never the place to work out new ideas; instead it was a practical first step that every artist was trained to make decisively and with precision. The fact that the scene of Christ performing the miracle from inside the city is so rare may explain why Illuminator A made a change;[6] it was not a subject firmly engraved in his repertory. Some elements of composition may in this case have been worked out on the parchment. Illuminator A painted with such heavy layers of pigment that all traces of underdrawing soon disappeared. Good examples of his finished miniatures appear on fols. 25v, 56, and 57 (Figs. 10, 13, 14). In each instance the layers are dense and heavily worked; sometimes the articulation of the garments is by wide areas of highlight and in others with a mixture of fine and thick lines. The way in which his style tends toward broken outlines reflects not a hesitancy in draftsmanship but a sensibility carried throughout the work. It can be seen in the breaking folds and loops that interrupt the contours, especially in the moving images of Saint Peter (Figs. 25, 28). The drawings of architecture on fols. 25v and 87v (Figs. 10, 17) are complementary because they too reveal a gift for the interaction of complex shapes that conforms to his vision of the single figure. The portraits executed by Illuminator A are also richly plastic. Flesh was heavily painted and articulated with white highlights and brown shadows, including sharp triangles that rake down the cheeks of the figures on fol. 57 (Fig. 14). In some cases the final treatment of the eyes was with thin lines in black or dark brown. Illuminator A's work is most effective, and most easily recognizable, at the tiny figure scale of the miniatures on fols. 2v (slightly abraded), 23, 25v, 56, 57, 87v (top portion), 167v, 168, and 183 (Figs. 3, 9, 10, 13, 14, 17, 25, 26, 28).

Illuminator B's draftsmanship differs from that of his colleague; his preliminary drawings are invariably more finished in character (Figs. 11, 12, 22, 23, 30–39). He always sketched in brown ink and his outlines are steady in both flow and width. He outlined feet, hands, and faces with particular care and then drew the details of the portraits. The question of degree of completion (if understood mostly as an issue of connoisseurship) becomes especially acute when evaluating his style. The scenes on fols. 4 and 6 (Figs. 4, 5) can, I believe, be taken as finished, whereas that on fol. 38 (Fig. 12) seems to have received only a partial wash. In this last scene, Christ and the Blind Youth, the pigment layer on the garments is relatively thin and allows the underdrawing to show through clearly. In the two finished miniatures the areas of flesh are done in a highly dilute mixture of the brown used for the drawing itself. The face of Saint Peter on fol. 4 and that of John on fol. 6 (Figs. 4, 5) have a further wash of dilute vermilion added over the thin ink. In this way the illuminator calls attention to the central actor in the composition. Illuminator B takes the trouble to draw the faces and hands carefully because the lines are part of the final work; they were not lost, as was the case with Illuminator A's miniatures. In fact, at no point are the final layers of color by Illuminator B as thick as those of his colleague. Moreover, they have a dull surface, in contrast with the dense sheen of the miniatures completed by A.

For the most part the division of labor can be easily ascertained, but some miniatures resist easy attribution. The articulation of the garments of the disciples on fols. 10v and 11 (Figs. 6, 7) lacks the energetic quality of Illuminator A's other work, although the portraits are certainly by his hand. The preliminary layers of color on fols. 22v and 94v (Figs. 8, 19) also strike a discordant note. What sets these miniatures apart from the others are their scale and degree of execution: all are large and possibly unfinished. Again the problem of scale complicates the attribution of the author portraits

---

6. See the comments on this miniature (fol. 91) in chapter I.

Procedures and Techniques

(Figs. 1, 20). Judging by the plasticity of the faces, the articulation with carefully worked highlights, shadows, and touches of pure line, an attribution to Illuminator A seems entirely reasonable. The dense pigment layers and the portraits' hard and somewhat glossy surface help confirm the hypothesis. I should also point out that in one instance the two illuminators worked on the same leaf, fol. 87v (Fig. 17). Illuminator A did the portrait of Christ and cityscape in the top half; the unfinished drawing in the bottom right was added by Illuminator B. The proportions and drawing style of the possessed man are his, as is the method of coloring the flesh with a thin wash of brown ink. The portrait of Christ in the initial relates across the page to the city of Capernaum. The top half, in other words, is a self-sufficient unit that illustrates the opening sentences of the pericope (Lk 4:31–36). The figure of the possessed man forms an intrusion stylistically and compositionally, since Christ takes no note of him. The purpose of the addition was to heighten the dramatic moment of the passage: the healing of the demoniac. After Illuminator A had finished, his colleague apparently decided to draw and apply a wash to the small figure in the lower quadrant.

When we weigh the compositional parallels given in chapter I, they reveal no work to which the New York Lectionary is related by a process of copying. From the way in which the second illuminator chose to add a figure to a reading Illuminator A had already illustrated, one might again infer that the illuminators were not actually copying another book. Just how they went about illustrating the text is not immediately apparent. The state of completion of any miniature often relates to its place within the cycle; those at the front are more likely to be finished than those at the end. But too many exceptions exist for us to conclude that essentially finished quires were divided between A and B, who then went to work drawing and painting the miniatures seriatim. Illuminator A's drawing on fol. 23 falls earlier than his finished miniature on fol. 25v (Figs. 9, 10); Illuminator B's sketch of Christ and the Woman of Samaria comes before the partly washed scene of the healing of the Blind Youth (Figs. 11, 12). The problems we face seem somewhat bewildering, but by looking at other unfinished manuscripts it is possible to make some sense of how the illuminators have approached the illustration of the lectionary. How they left their work permits a broad yet important conclusion.

One manuscript contemporary with the New York Lectionary offers a contrasting method of illumination. The work is the Seraglio Octateuch,[7] whose unfinished state suggests rigid organization. Miniatures are finished up to the point at which the cycle abruptly stops, with the exception of the illustrations in one quire, which contains an outline drawing and scenes in various stages of completion. The impression left by the state of completion is that of a highly organized project, and this is surely an accurate assessment. The illustration of the Octateuch had to be painstakingly planned and executed because the illuminators' commission was to make an exact duplicate of an older book containing hundreds of pictures. Three separate artists went to work copying the model, which we have reason to believe was divided into two volumes. The illuminators of the Octateuch, unlike the two working on the Lectionary, could not scatter work throughout the manuscript. The Octateuch commission dictated careful organization to prevent any mistakes that would simply be compounded throughout the cycle.

---

7. Istanbul, Topkapı Sarayı, cod. 8: published by Th. Uspenskij, "L'Octateuque de la Bibliothèque du Sérail à Constantinople," *Izvestija Russkogo Arheologicheskogo Instituta v Konstantinople,* XII, 1907; see Anderson, "Seraglio Octateuch," 83–114, esp. 88–89, for remarks on the method of production.

A second unfinished manuscript is the eleventh-century psalter preserved at Mount Sinai, cod. gr. 48.[8] One illuminator drew and painted all its miniatures, which exist in several states: sketches, drawings with wash, and one completely finished scene. Although the drawings are finished to Psalm 56, the process of painting them did not follow a clear system. The one completed miniature, the illustration for Psalm 53, comes late in the book. Unlike the Octateuch, one of a number of closely related copies of a single source, the Psalter has no clear relatives. In this regard, it and the New York Lectionary are similar. Both may reflect the way in which experienced craftsmen sometimes illustrated books they were familiar with; the drawings were made and then painted, several at a time and not necessarily in order from front to back. An illustrator might have second thoughts and make an addition, as seems to have been the case when Illuminator B sketched the man possessed on fol. 87v (Fig. 17). If this inference is correct, then it seems that Illuminator A was far more willing to exploit the opportunities created by the cruciform text. His scenes of the Doubting Thomas, the pool at Bethesda, Christ at Capernaum, Christ and the council, or the raising of the son of the widow of Nain (Figs. 6, 7, 9, 10, 14, 18) expand to fill the spaces around the text and create a pictorial quality foreign to the work of Illuminator B, whose scenes find closer counterparts among the works surveyed in chapter I.

Beyond the two illuminators, how many craftsmen did it take to make the manuscript, and what was their working relationship? Might one of the two also have transcribed the text? And who did the ornament? In formulating hypotheses to organize and interpret the evidence, we may again find outside sources helpful. In addition to other manuscripts made as collaborative efforts, inscriptions and anecdotes can offer guidance. In the eleventh and twelfth centuries, patrons might sometimes turn to organized scriptoria. Places like the monastery of Saint John Studios[9] and the Prodromos-Petra monastery[10] met the demands of one part of the market; the Studios in particular was equipped to make books with illustration, which were no doubt sold to provide income for the monks. But there may have been few comparable producers.

The concept of a monastic scriptorium organized as a kind of factory to produce luxury goods may not accord with the social and economic realities of medieval Byzantium. Monks could be skilled in many trades, and be recompensed for their work,[11] yet surviving manuscripts (and icons) do not suggest methods of production that relied on the coordination of highly specialized craftsmen; collaborative projects like the New York Lectionary or Seraglio Octateuch do not make up a large proportion of the manuscript production. Furthermore, they are more than balanced by large projects, like the Theodore Psalter[12] or Paris Gospels, gr. 74,[13] whose illustrations were done by a single painter—in these two examples, by monks of the Studios monastery.

Some of the literary evidence shows that the creation of large monastic scriptoria was not actively encouraged. Christodoulos, the eleventh-century founder of the monastery of Saint John the Theologian on Mount Patmos, warns his monks that any money they receive from copying books

---

8. As in note 5.

9. A comprehensive study is not available, but some of the evidence has been collected by N. Eleopoulos, *He bibliotheke kai to bibliographikon ergasterion tes mones ton Stoudiou*, Athens, 1967.

10. H. Kakoulide, "He bibliotheke tes mones Prodromou-Petras sten Konstantinoupole," *Hellenika*, XXI, 1968, 3–38.

11. See the skills and duties listed in the Athos document published by P. Lemerle, A. Guillou, and N. Svoronos, *Actes de Lavra, I, Des origines à 1204*, Archives de l'Athos, V, Paris, 1970, 361.

12. London, British Library, Add. MS 19,352: S. Der Nersessian, *L'illustration des psautiers grecs du Moyen âge, II, Londres, Add. 19.352*, Bibliothèque des Cahiers archéologiques, V, Paris, 1970.

13. H. Omont, *Evangiles avec peintures byzantines du XI*^e *siècle*, Paris, n.d.

must be turned over to the monastery:[14] making books thus appears to have been left to individual enterprise. Theodore the Studite orders monks engaged in copying texts to keep to their own materials;[15] he refers to parchment prepared by one monk being used by another. Nevertheless, active shops as we imagine them in modern times require cooperation at every stage of work. Although study of the subscriptions published by the Lakes shows that monks were the most active force in the book market,[16] most of them probably operated alone. An inscription giving a monk as scribe does not entail a monastic scriptorium. In some instances, the appearance of a thriving monastic center may simply reflect the period of activity required to furnish a new foundation. Two decades after the start of the Great Lavra on Mount Athos, John, a student of the founder, Saint Athanasios, still makes and decorates liturgical books for the monks' use, but the tradition seems to die out with him.[17] The same may hold true of production at the monastery of Saint George Manganes.[18]

Manuscript production in monasteries appears to reflect a pattern found throughout society: books were more often made by single craftsmen than by large collaborative efforts. Inscriptions suggest that often those who required books made them themselves or paid someone else to make them. When Strategos, a priest appointed to the Patriarchal Oratory, needed a copy of a new prayer book, he transcribed it himself;[19] the priest John Kaloploïmos commissioned the reader Niphon to copy a *stichararion*,[20] or the priest Constantine had a teacher at the Chalkoprateia school make him a Gospel lectionary.[21] Most who used books were likely trained in the writing styles necessary to make them, as suggested by the role that copying plays in the correspondence of a tenth-century Byzantine schoolteacher.[22] Those who proved especially adept might style themselves calligraphers and supplement their modest incomes from other sources; the priest Basil, copyist of Paris. gr. 784, calls himself a calligrapher "by trade."[23] To a person of high social standing, like the late tenth-century Admiral of the Fleet, Niketas, the writing of a book for donation could be a pious act.[24] For most Byzantines who wrote their own books or paid an acquaintance to do the work, there was no need for decoration beyond simple initials or headpieces done in ink. Occasionally some sought illuminated and even illustrated texts: additions that required uncommon materials and, if they were to be passably handsome, rare skill. For them it was possible to turn to illuminators. Theodore, abbot of the Galakrenai monastery, followed a common practice in having his student and fellow monk Symeon make a copy of the selected sermons of Gregory of Nazianzus in 1062. The Abbot then took the manuscript to a pair of illuminators who added the headpieces and gold titles and initials, most historiated with simple and common subjects; as the subscription tells us, Theodore

14. F. Miklosich and J. Müller, *Acta et diplomata graeca medii aevi*, v, Vienna, 1890, 75; that Patmos monks were paid for making books is confirmed by the inscription in cod. 245: A. Komines, *Facsimilies of Dated Patmian Codices*, Athens, 1970, 21.

15. J.-P Migne, *Patrologiae cursus completus, Series graeca*, IC, Paris, 1903, 1740C.

16. *Dated Greek MSS*; see also A. Cutler, "The Social Status of Byzantine Scribes, 800–1500: A Statistical Survey Based on Vogel-Gardthausen," *Byzantinische Zeitschrift*, LXXIV, 1981, 328–34.

17. Weitzmann, *Byz. Buchmalerei*, 34–39; J. Irigoin, "Pour une étude des centres de copie byzantins, II, Quelques groupes de manuscrits," *Scriptorium*, XIII, 1959, 196–200.

18. See the subscription of Mount Athos, Stauronikita, cod. 15: G. Galavaris, *The Illustrations of the Liturgical Homilies of Gregory Nazianzenus*, Studies in Manuscript Illumination, VI, Princeton, 1969, 214–15.

19. Paris. gr. Coisl. gr. 213: Lake, *Dated Greek MSS*, v, pl. 258.

20. Patmos cod. 221: Komines (as in note 14), 25.

21. Paris. suppl. gr. 1096: Lake, *Dated Greek MSS*, IV, pl. 300.

22. R. Browning, "The Correspondence of a Tenth-Century Byzantine Scholar," *Byzantion*, XXIV, 1954, 438–39, collects the passages.

23. Lake, *Dated Greek MSS*, IV, pl. 250.

24. So I interpret the circumstances suggested by the subscription to Paris. gr. 479, Sermons of Saint Basil finished by Niketas four years before he gave it to the church of Saint George; Niketas worked under unusual conditions: Lake, *Dated Greek MSS*, IV, pl. 240.

paid to have the work done.²⁵ The inclusion in the Basil Menologium of its illuminators' names suggests that they too were working on a piecemeal basis. The copy of Saint Basil written by the Admiral of the Fleet has fine polychrome decoration that he, like Theodore, surely paid someone to execute for him.

The illumination of manuscripts in Byzantium often seems to have been carried out by professionals, who were prepared to finish books written by others. A scribe might leave blanks for decoration;²⁶ if the spaces were to be filled with gold or polychrome initials, sometimes the scribe would discreetly cue the illuminator by writing the omitted letters in the gutter and fore-edge margins.²⁷ The premium placed on illumination during the Middle Ages gave rise to craftsmen who called themselves "illuminators," taking the old word "chrysographer" and attaching a slightly new significance to it.²⁸ Although some well-known cases of illustration involve collaboration, most illuminators seem to have worked alone. Much of the evidence thus points away from a book market dominated and stabilized by a handful of large producers. The need for decorated manuscripts appears to have been met through something closer to a network of individuals who devoted their time more or less to book crafts. Collaborations between scribes and illuminators might then have been ephemeral relationships, formed to execute a commission and dissolved upon its completion. Some painters did not receive their entire income from books, for they were competent at panel painting as well as illumination.²⁹

In light of the many possible combinations of scribes, illuminators, and panel painters, writing the history of medieval illumination is daunting. One further surmise, though, may offer some welcome stability. I would guess that in the Middle Ages illuminators were men who began as scribes and who happened to show skill at designing headpieces, initials, and miniatures. Rarely, if ever, would a boy have been trained as a book illuminator. The work of an illuminator will tend to appear with the same style of handwriting throughout his career. In considering the New York Lectionary, we should therefore begin with the scribe and the possibility that he was responsible for other parts of the manuscript. The only ground on which skills in writing and illustration come together are miniatures with inscriptions. Known cases warn against the simple conclusion that the handwriting of the inscription is that of the illuminator. In the Seraglio Octateuch, the Smyrna Octateuch, and the Madrid Skylitzes, the scribes, not the illuminators, wrote the inscriptions.³⁰ In the Basil Menologium it was the scribe who wrote the names of the artists next to the miniatures.³¹

Few periods in the history of Byzantine art find both scribes and illuminators exercising such idiosyncratic styles that it is possible to base trustworthy attributions on style alone.³² The New York Lectionary does not belong to such a period. Sometimes the way work was divided may lead

---

25. J. Anderson, "Cod. Vat. Gr. 463 and an Eleventh-Century Byzantine Painting Center," *DOP*, XXXII, 1978, 177–83.

26. See Washington, Dumbarton Oaks, acc. no. 79.31: G. Vikan, *Gifts from the Byzantine Court*, Washington, D.C., 1980, back cover illustration.

27. Found in two manuscripts of the sermons of Gregory Nazianzus: Sinai. gr. 339 and Turin, Bibl. Univ. C.I.6.

28. J. Anderson, "On the Nature of the Theodore Psalter," *Art Bulletin*, LXX, 1988, 558–59.

29. In some cases, icon painters may have illuminated manuscripts, as suggested by I. Ševčenko, "On Pantoleon the Painter," *Jahrbuch der österreichischen Byzantinistik*, XXI, 1972, 241–49.

30. For the Octateuchs, see Anderson, "Seraglio Octateuch," 99–101; and for the Skylitzes, I. Ševčenko, "The Madrid Manuscript of the Chronicle of Skylitzes in Light of its New Dating," *Byzanz und der Westen*, Österreichische Akademie der Wissenschaften: Philosophisch-historische Klasse, Sitzungsberichte, CCCCXXXII, ed. I. Hutter, Vienna, 1984, 118.

31. I. Ševčenko, "The Illuminators of the Menologium of Basil II," *DOP*, XVI, 1962, 245.

32. For one example, see S. Madigan, "Three Manuscripts by the 'Chrysostom Initialer': The Scribe as Artist in Tenth-Century Constantinople," *Scriptorium*, XLI, 1987, 210–13.

one to infer that a scribe was also an illuminator.[33] In the case of the New York Lectionary, nothing in style, inscriptions, or the division of labor can serve to connect the scribe unequivocally with the ornament or miniatures. The relatively even width and flow of the letters and words suggest that Illuminator A, who tends to favor a broken outline for his sketches, did not write the text. By this token, Illuminator B, who draws with so even and controlled an outline, would seem to present a promising candidate, but only if we actually knew that one of the illuminators wrote the text, and this we do not know. I am inclined to think that the scribe was responsible for other parts of the manuscript, but I can find no truly solid evidence on which to identify those other parts. Material evidence cannot be considered trustworthy; both illuminators sketch using the same ink as that of the text. The pigments are far more complicated but still are of little help. When comparing color schemes used on individual pages, one finds that sometimes all parts match and other times they do not. All this proves is that colors were mixed in batches and that a run of finials would be painted, or a series of letters filled, until the colors ran out. Although this suggests that parts were done individually, it does not mean they were done by different artisans. Naturally when an illustration was to be part of an initial, the outlines of the letter were left for the illustrator to draw and paint; the initial on fol. 38 and the absence of one on fol. 284 (Figs. 12, 40) demonstrate this.

The bulk of the initials in the manuscript may not have been the province of either illuminator. Someone else may have done them, quite possibly the scribe. If so, then neither illuminator was the scribe. The proof will require looking at initials done by the illuminators. On fol. 160 (Fig. 42) an *epsilon* with gesturing hand begins the reading for the liturgy of Holy Thursday. The scribe left the usual curved indentation for a painted *epsilon*, since the lesson was a major one that would be set out with a decorated initial. The style in which the hand was painted is unique among such letters, for it is carefully painted and shaded in dense, dusky tones. Without doubt, this initial was done by Illuminator A. Its style of rendering matches that of the portrait on fol. 168 (Fig. 26). The pericope (Mt 26:1–20; Jn 13:3–17; Mt 26:21–39; Lk 22:43–45; Mt 26:40–27:2) relates Christ's movements on the days before Passover. When the scribe left a space for the initial, did he assume that this reading would be illustrated? We cannot know what was on the scribe's mind, but presumably he foresaw illustration of the reading and was correct in his presumption. Illuminator A did illustrate this lection, though a later part of it, not its beginning (Fig. 25).[34]

Let us turn to one last letter. The eleventh Sunday of Luke begins with an *epsilon* containing both a hand and a grazing lamb (Fig. 41). The reading opens on the words: "The Lord said, 'Fear not, little flock, for it is your Father's good pleasure to give you the kingdom.'" The painter of the initial has shown the hand holding out a piece of foliage and the sheep chewing on the vine pendant from the *epsilon*. The initial was crudely done by someone other than Illuminator A, whose style of letters we know from the *epsilon* on fol. 160 (Fig. 42). The drawing of the hand and sheep is as flat as their painting. If one compares the draftsmanship with that of Illuminator B (for example, Figs. 4, 5, 11, 12), it seems likely that he did not draw the hand holding the foliage, or, or course, the lamb below. A third hand can thus be detected in the illumination of the manuscript. Just how much of the decoration

---

33. See, for example, the Seraglio Octateuch (Anderson, "Seraglio Octateuch," 98) or the change in miniature frames accompanying the change of scribe in the twelfth-century Athens, National Library, cod. 93: E. Constantinides, "The Tetraevangelion, Manuscript 93 of the Athens National Library," *Deltion tes Christianikes Archaiologikes Hetaireias*, IX, 1979, 186, 188.

34. The beginning is illustrated in Dionysiou cod. 587 with the figure of Christ in the *epsilon* gesturing in speech to his disciples in the opposite margin: *Treasures of Athos*, I, fig. 225.

The New York Cruciform Lectionary

he might have been responsible for is difficult to say; the basic framework of his initial is competent enough. He may well have done others in the manuscript as well as finials. The unfinished headpieces on fols. 124 and 214 (Figs. 21, 29) suggest some breakdown in responsibility, perhaps dictated by individual skills, areas in which scribes were thought to excel.[35] It is possible that the third hand was that of the scribe, and that the number of craftsmen required to make the lectionary was no more than three.

Examining techniques and procedures, though in some ways inconclusive (and intended mainly to contribute to the body of such evidence), does sharpen our image of the manuscript and its illustration. By virtue of the number of craftsmen involved, the New York Lectionary is an unusual manuscript. Perhaps the collaboration was ad hoc, a team assembled quickly to execute one commission; that the miniature cycle remains without its final touches could be taken as relatively unambiguous evidence of time constraints. An alternative does exist: the makers of the lectionary enjoyed a long-standing relationship. In chapter I it was shown that the illuminators likely had some experience with this kind of manuscript. They drew and painted images in the absence of the text cues generally associated with the lectionary. As it turns out, the manuscript was to be illuminated from the start, and the scribe, who probably did not paint any miniatures, was himself familiar with illustration; he left two large indentations for readings to receive miniatures or historiated initials. The order in which the images were drawn and painted indicates that no model was being copied. In fact, one can interpret the evidence to suggest a somewhat informal approach to the illustration. The spaces left by the scribe were not always used; Illuminator A's miniature on fol. 87v was supplemented by Illuminator B, who apparently felt that the point of illustrating the pericope was to show the healing of the demoniac, not Christ teaching in the temple (Fig. 17). The miniatures give other indications of the illuminator taking individual initiative. Illuminator A felt free to expand compositions and take advantage of the large quadrants (for example, Figs. 8–10), whereas Illuminator B remained more closely bound with the kind of simple initials and marginal groups so often found in eleventh- and twelfth-century lectionary illumination.

Together, the observations suggest that the New York Lectionary was the work of an unusual group that had made such books before. We would legitimately look for other manuscripts made by its members or done in imitation of their work. One such book may be the twelfth-century Dumbarton Oaks Lectionary, cod. 1. Fol. 122v (Fig. 62) of this lectionary is one of the few leaves that is both cruciform and illuminated; the cross format was taken up only after the John section, which contains most of the miniatures. In the two quadrants are Peter and the cock, an illustration similar to that found for the same reading in the New York Lectionary (Figs. 28, 54). The London and Mount Athos cruciform lectionaries may represent work of the group and not just that of followers. (This argument I will take up later.) What technique in conjunction with the extent of the miniature cycle finally suggests is the control the artists exerted. Some patron initiated the process and may have gone to the craftsmen specifically because of their reputation for such rich lectionaries. But once work on the commission began, the choice of subjects and how they would be executed appears to have been completely under the artists' control; the design and placement of the ornament would naturally have been their responsibility, too. In this light, we should examine the text of the manuscript to see just how much latitude existed and how it was exploited.

---

35. The slightly unequal division of labor in the decoration of Vat. gr. 463 may indicate that one artist was better at decoration and the other at figures; see Anderson (as in note 25), 183.

III

Saints and Feasts Commemorated in the Menologion

THE RITES OF THE medieval Byzantine church were varied and complex. Services in which the Eucharist was celebrated were held not only on Sundays and major feast days but on Saturdays and sometimes even daily. Depending on the time of year, the lay public might attend morning services, vespers, and vigils. On some days two Gospel passages would be sung and on others none. Occasionally the congregation might only meet in the narthex of Saint Sophia for psalms and hymns, but on great feast days complex stational services had the patriarch, clergy, and faithful traveling through the city, stopping at churches and public squares for readings and commemorations. Since laymen rarely received the sacraments, they were interested mainly in the readings and hymns and the sermon. The passages sung usually related to the day's celebration, which in turn had a seasonal significance. For the laymen, attendance at every service throughout the year would have surely proved difficult, whereas for monks attendance at each office and service was mandatory. At the eleventh-century monastery of the Theotokos Evergetis, Constantinople, the Eucharist was celebrated every day,[1] which means that the Gospel readings likewise were daily. We tend to think of the monasteries as following a rite uniformly different from that of the patriarch, but the reality seems to have been somewhat more complicated. The monk Timothy, who composed the liturgical prescriptions for the Evergetis monastery, used as models the rite of Saint Sophia, which he combined with those of other monasteries.[2] Founders could dictate how and when services were celebrated, and some foresaw services outside the range they had specified, realizing that commemorations might be added to the liturgical calendar.[3] Perhaps the major unifying force of the Byzantine liturgy was the prestige of the patriarchate and a handful of respected monasteries.

The complexity of the liturgical year is not just a matter of modern perception, the result of working from imperfect records to reconstruct changing celebrations of different kinds. For the Byzantines themselves the proper observance of the services often required the supervision of a kind of master of ceremonies. At the Cathedral the *skevophylax* was in charge not only of the vessels and books but also of some personnel active in the performance of the service.[4] In the monasteries it might be an *ekklesiarch* who ensured that all involved were properly arranged and aware of the day's

---

1. P. Gautier, "Le typikon de la Théotokos Evergétis," *REB*, LX, 1982, 23.
2. Ibid., 8, where Gautier collects the references in Timothy's text.
3. See the *typikon* of Gregory Pakourianos's monastery, P. Gautier, "Le typikon du sébaste Grégoire Pakourianos," *REB*, XLII, 1984, 63, where the *ekklesiarch* and abbot are given responsibility for services outside those normally specified.
4. J. Darrouzès, *Recherches sur les offikia de l'Eglise byzantine*, Archives de l'Orient chrétien, XI, Paris, 1979, 315.

order of service.⁵ These officials had their own handbooks, called *typika,* and in them the various readings were meticulously specified. The Gospel lectionary was just one of the books, scrolls, and diptychs handed back and forth by the clergy as the service unfolded within the church. In isolation, a lectionary's use seems straightforward: the readings were sequential through both movable and fixed sections. Generally, not all the pericopes would be read in any year, although at a monastery like the Theotokos Evergetis more readings than are found in the New York manuscript would have been required.⁶ Liturgical differences, though, seem not to be reflected in the lectionaries. And one other factor needs to be taken into account: like other manuscript books of its time, the New York Lectionary was commissioned by a patron who doubtless had a recipient in mind. A disparity exists between our legitimate expectation and received opinion regarding lectionary content. Books were made for specific places, each with perhaps its own variation on the rite, yet the current view holds that the manuscripts do not vary in content. In the belief that small but significant differences may well exist, I here publish the list of fixed feasts and saints,⁷ which is likely to be the one part of the manuscript sensitive to change and reflective of small institutional differences.

From the calendar of the New York Lectionary we learn something about the manuscript, though not for whom it was made. Its calendar tends to follow the lectionary type but does not conform precisely to those established by C. Gregory⁸ or by Colwell and Riddle;⁹ for these authors, the aim was to gather a group of manuscripts, compare their calendars, and arrive at a kind of ideal composite. Their lists have proved invaluable in determining what is noteworthy in the New York manuscript as well as identifying those cases in which the scribe may have been paying less than full attention to his work.

I begin with the text of the menologion, which I render in English. In publishing it I have attempted not to intervene, even in some instances of scribal error. Square brackets enclose additions and comments, and the words in parentheses are expansions taken from liturgical sources to help the modern reader; for example, where the scribe simply wrote Saint Gregory, I expand the name to Saint Gregory (of Agrigentum), Saint Gregory (the Wonderworker), and so forth. Rather than impose English versions of Latin spellings, I transcribe the original, departing only in the cases of the Apostles, the Old Testament Prophets, and a few others. The text is sometimes rather compressed, and I have silently expanded all abbreviations, though much of the flavor of the original should come through. The scribe's use of the term *hieromartyros,* as well as his titulature, is retained throughout, even when it is confusing. Following the day is the name(s) of the saint(s) or the feast, followed by either the scribe's reference to the day where the reading can be found, or, if he wrote out a Gospel passage, what he wrote, which is printed in italics. The *incipit* designations given in roman numerals follow the usage of Colwell and Riddle, *Prolegomena,* 84;¹⁰ Psalm refer-

---

5. In some cases the *ekklesiarch* is mentioned handing things to the priest in the course of the service. See the citations in the editions of P. Gautier, "Le typikon du Christ Sauveur Pantocrator," *REB,* XXXII, 1974, 33, 35, 55; the Evergetis Monastery *typikon* (as in note 1), 19; and that of Bačkovo (as in note 3), 59.

6. The London Lectionary, discussed and illustrated below (Figs. 43–47), has readings for every day of the movable year.

7. In addition to those saints and prophets commemorated in the menologion, the synaxarion contains rubrics for Isaiah (sixth week of John: Jn 12:36–47) and the Fathers of Nicaea (seventh Sunday in John: Jn 17:1–13).

8. *Textkritik,* 330, gives the earlier, difficult-to-locate lists, which he used in establishing the calendar he publishes.

9. Based on a comparison of four manuscripts, which they describe, *Prolegomena,* 81–83.

10. I = τῷ καιρῷ ἐκείνῳ; II = εἶπεν ὁ κύριος τοῖς ἑαυτοῦ μαθηταῖς; III = εἶπεν ὁ κύριος πρὸς τοὺς ἐληλυθότας πρὸς αὐτὸν Ἰουδαίους; IV = εἶπεν ὁ κύριος πρὸς τοὺς πεπιστευκότας αὐτῷ Ἰουδαίους; V = εἶπεν ὁ κύριος; VI = εἶπεν ὁ κύριος τὴν παραβολὴν ταύτην.

ences are after A. Rahlfs, *Septuaginta,* Stuttgart, 1935. Notes follow some of the readings; a few are historical, but most point out questionable or unusual assignments. In the notes I refer to several sources, which I cite in abbreviated form:

BHG   J. Halkin, *Bibliotheca hagiographica graeca,* 3d ed., Subsidia hagiographica, VIIIa, Brussels, 1957: a general index of writings devoted to the saints of the Orthodox Church.
L(C-R)   menologion table in Colwell and Riddle, *Prolegomena,* 128–56.
L(Greg)   menologion table in Gregory, *Textkritik,* 365–84.
SynaxCP   H. Delehaye, *Synaxarium Ecclesiae Constantinopolitanae,* Propylaeum ad Acta sanctorum Novembris, Brussels, 1902: Synaxarium, which gives brief biographical sketches; the edition uses the TypkSS as one of its sources.
TypkSS   J. Mateos, *Le typikon de la Grande Eglise,* I, *Le Cycle des douze mois,* Orientalia Christiana analecta, CLXV, Rome, 1962: publication of the calendar and partial order of services of the Patriarchal church around the tenth century.

At the end of the menologion I have appended an index of the saints and feasts and an index of the biblical passages reproduced or cited through cross-reference. In compiling the indices I have tried to render faithfully what the scribe of the New York Lectionary set down; the assignments and associated texts may in some instances be idiosyncratic by design or, in others, by mistake. Following the indices are remarks on how the calendar might have been made and used.

SEPTEMBER

1   Beginning of the indiction, and commemoration of the blessed Symeon Stylites, and of the Great Fire: *I + Lk 4:16–22a.*
    Note: the reference is to the fire that occurred on this day in 461.
2   The holy martyr Mamas: cf. Friday of the first week of Lent.
    The same day, the holy patriarchs John the Faster and Paul the Younger: *II + Mt 5:14–19.*
    Note: John is again celebrated on 19 February.
3   The holy hieromartyr Anthemios, bishop of Nicomedia: *V + Jn 10:9–16.*
4   Martyrdom of the holy hieromartyr Babylas and the (Eighty-four Holy) Children: cf. the tenth Saturday in Luke.
    The same day, the holy martyr Hermione: cf. the seventeenth Saturday in Matthew.
5   The holy prophet Zachariah: cf. the end of the menologion.
    Note: The reference is to a reading reproduced separately at the end of the menologion.
6   The archangel Michael at Chonae: cf. 18 October.
    The same day, the holy martyr Eudoxios and his companions: *I + Mk 12:28–38a.*
7   The holy martyr Sozon: cf. the third Saturday in Easter.
    Note: Rubric in gold. The scribe wrote in gold each title that either began a month or fell before a pericope written in full. I call attention only to the titles whose gilding is unrelated to the manuscript format.
8   Birth of the All-holy Virgin, morning service of adoration. [In the upper margin the scribe has

added:] In the second plagal mode: *Ps 44:18a* [first two words in a variant typical of Byzantine psalters], the verse: *Ps 44:11a* [first two words]; + *Lk 1:39–49, 56*.

Note: Here and in five other instances (6 January, 25 March, 25 and 29 June, and 6 August), the scribe gave direct references for the Psalm antiphons used in morning services.

[Same day and feast] For the liturgy: *I + Lk 10:38–42, 11:27–28*.

9   The holy and just Joachim and Anne: cf. the sixth Saturday in Luke.
    Note: Rubric in gold.

[10] Adoration of the Venerable Wood (of the Holy Cross): cf. Monday of the sixth week in Easter.
    The same day, the holy martyrs Menodora, Metrodora, and Nymphodora: cf. the seventeenth Saturday in Matthew.

11 Adoration of the Venerable Wood: cf. Friday of the fourth week in Easter.
    The same day, the blessed Theodora (of Alexandria): cf. 8 October.

12 Adoration of the Venerable Wood: cf. the fourth Saturday in Easter.
    The same day, the holy martyr Julian of Ankyra: cf. the third Saturday in Easter.

13 On the adoration of the Venerable Wood: *V + Jn 12:25–28a* [scribe inserts] Beginning of Morning Reading, *incipit* V [then continues:] *28b–36*.
    Saturday before the adoration: cf. the seventh Saturday in Matthew.
    Sunday before the adoration: *V + Jn 3:13–17*.

14 Elevation of the Holy Cross, morning service: cf. the great Wednesday (of Holy Week), in the middle (of the reading).
    [Same day and feast] For the liturgy: *I + Jn 19:6, 9b–11a, 13–20, 25b–26a, 30b–35a*.
    Saturday following the Elevation: cf. Friday of the fourth week in John.
    Sunday following the Elevation: cf. the third Sunday of Lent.

15 The holy and great martyr Niketas: *II + Mt 10:16–22*.

16 Saint Euphemia, [daughter?] of Paneuphemos: *I + Lk 7:36–50*.
    Note: It is unclear to me precisely what the scribe had in mind when writing this entry; his source may have characterized Euphemia with the epithet "wholly blessed." The scribe wrote a masculine article that disturbs the grammatical relationship, so that *paneuphemos* now reads like the name of a parent (Euphemia's father was actually named Philophron).

17 Saints Sophia, Pistes, Elpes, and Agape: cf. the seventeenth Saturday in Matthew.

18 Saint Eumenios (bishop of Gortyna): cf. the first Sunday in Matthew.

19 Saint Trophimos: cf. 15 September.

20 Saint Eustathios and his companions, lection: *V + Lk 21:12–19*.
    Note: The scribe has identified the reading as from Matthew.

21 The holy prophet Jonah: *I + Lk 11:29–33*.

22 Saint Phokas: cf. 24 September.

23 The conception of the Forerunner: cf. 24 June.

24 Saint Thekla: cf. the seventeenth Saturday in Matthew.

25 Procession to the Campus: cf. 14 December.
    Note: For this day the SynaxCP celebrates the procession of Emperor Theodosius and Patriarch Proklos to the Campus of the Hebdomon at the time of an earthquake. Other processions under similar circumstances are attested; according to the *Paschal Chronicle* (ed. J.-P. Migne, *Patrologiae cursus completus, Series graeca prior*, XCII, Paris, 1865, 984B), an earthquake

in 611 prompted another procession to the Campus, where the *Trisagion* was chanted. The entry here probably refers to a historical event commemorated by a service within the church, although the TypkSS notes that the terrors that will accompany the end of the world are recalled on this day by a procession through the city, stopping at one point in the Campus.

26 The death of (Saint John) the Theologian: cf. Saturday of Pentecost.
27 Saint Kalistratos: cf. the third Saturday in John.
28 The blessed Chariton: cf. 20 January.
29 Saint Kyriakos (Palestinian anchorite): cf. 21 October.
30 Saint Gregory (the Illuminator) of Greater Armenia: *V + Mt 24:42–47*.

OCTOBER

1 The holy apostle Ananias: cf. 2 September.
2 Saint Cyprian: cf. 3 September.
3 Saint Dionysios (the Areopagite): *IV + Mt 13:44–54a*.
4 Saint Hierotheos: cf. 4 September.
5 The holy martyr Charitine: cf. the tenth Sunday in Luke.
6 The holy apostle Thomas: cf. the first Sunday after Easter.
7 Saints Sergios and Bakchos: cf. 20 September.
8 Saint Pelagia: *I + Jn 8:1–11*.
10 [=9] The holy apostle James: cf. the first Sunday in Luke.
   Note: The scribe incorrectly numbered this reading; he corrects at Saint Nektarios on the eleventh.
11 [=10] Saints Eulampios and Eulampia: *II + Mk 13:9–13*.
11 Saint Nektarios and companions: *II + Mt 5:14–19*.
12 The holy martyrs Probos, Tarachos, and Andronikos: cf. 20 September.
13 Saints Karpos and Papyllos: *V + Mt 7:12–21*.
14 Saint Nazarios and his companions: cf. the third Saturday in John.
    Note: Rubric in gold.
15 Saint Lukianos (bishop of Antioch): cf. 3 September.
16 Saint Longinos: cf. the ninth Passion reading.
17 The holy prophet Hosea: *I + Lk 13:31–35*.
18 The holy apostle Luke: *II + Lk 10:16–21*.
19 The holy prophet Joel: cf. 5 September.
20 Saint Artemios: cf. the third Sunday of Lent.
21 Saint Hilarion (anchorite): *I + Lk 6:17–23*.
22 Saint Averkios: cf. the eleventh Saturday in Luke.
23 The holy apostle James (son of Joseph): cf. 15 September.
24 Saint Arethas: cf. Sunday of All Saints.
    Note: The cross-reference assumes that the user can identify All Saints' Sunday as the first

Sunday in the Matthew readings of the synaxarion, which is designated here only by section and day number.

25 The holy notaries Markianos and Martyrios: *II + Lk 12:2–12*.
26 The great martyr Saint Demetrios: *I + Mt 8:23–27*.
27 Saint Nestor: cf. the third Saturday of Lent.
28 The holy martyr Domna: cf. the seventh Saturday in Luke.
   Note: Not at this point in L(C-R) or L(Greg); Indus and Domna: L(Greg), TypkSS = 3 December. SynaxCP gives, among the saints of this day, Domninos of Thessalonika.
29 Saint Abramios (anchorite): cf. 10 January.
30 Saint Kyriakos (archbishop of Constantinople): cf. 13 November.

NOVEMBER

1 The holy Anargyroi, Kosmas and Damian: *I + Mt 10:1, 5–8*.
   Note: L(C-R) and L(Greg) give a different passage for this day and the saint(s); the scribe identified the reading as from John.
2 Saint Akindynos and companions: *II + Mt 19:23–30*.
   Note: The scribe identified the reading as from Luke.
3 The holy martyrs Akepsimas, Aeithalas, and Joseph: cf. 3 September.
4 The blessed Ioannikios: cf. 20 January.
5 Saints Galaktion and Episteme: cf. 10 October.
6 Saint Paul the Confessor: cf. 25 September.
7 The Thirty-three Holy Martyrs (of Melitene): cf. 15 September.
8 Service for the Archangels: cf. 18 October.
9 Saint Matrona: cf. 11 October.
10 Saint John the Almsgiver: cf. 10 January.
11 Saint Menas and companions: cf. the third Saturday in John.
12 [after the day's number and a gilt initial T, the scribe left a blank space for the name of the saint(s); he then wrote the text:] *III + Jn 10:1–10*.
   Note: L(Greg) and L(C-R) = Saint John the Almsgiver, and Saint Nilos; TypkSS = Martin. The pericope does not accord with those for this day in L(C-R) or L(Greg); the scribe identified it as from Matthew.
13 [After the number the scribe left a blank space, with neither reference nor passage.]
   Note: L(C-R), L(Greg) = John Chrysostom; TypkSS = exile of John Chrysostom.
14 The holy apostle Philip: cf. 25 October.
15 The holy confessors: cf. 10 October.
   Note: L(Greg) = specifically the confessors Gourias, Samonas, and Abibos.
16 The holy apostle Matthew: cf. the fifth Saturday in Matthew.
17 Saint Gregory (the Wonderworker): cf. 1 November.
18 Saint Platon: cf. the third Saturday in John.
19 The holy prophet Abdias: cf. 20 September.

20   Entrance of the All-holy Virgin (into the temple): cf. 8 September.
     Note: This feast is celebrated on 21 November.
21   Saint Kikilia: cf. 4 December.
     Note: Saint Cecilia variously assigned: L(Greg), SynaxCP = 22 November; TypkSS = 24 November.
22   Saint Proklos: cf. 11 October.
     Note: L(C-R) = 22 November; L(Greg) = 23 November; SynaxCP = 20 November.
23   Saint Gregory (of Agrigentum): cf. 30 September.
     Note: L(C-R), L(Greg), TypkSS = 24 November.
24   Saint Clement (of Rome): cf. 20 January.
     Note: L(Greg) = 24 November; L(C-R), TypkSS, SynaxCP = 25 November. Similar variety exists for the next four readings.
25   Saint Alypios: cf. 20 January.
26   Saint James (the Persian): cf. 2 September.
28   Saint Stephen (the Younger): cf. the seventh Saturday in Matthew.
29   Saint Eirenarchos: cf. 10 October.
30   The holy apostle Andrew: cf. Wednesday of Easter week.

DECEMBER

1   The holy prophet Nahum: cf. 5 September.
[2] The holy prophet Habakkuk: cf. 17 October.
     Note: This and the following two numbers have been lost to a binder's knife.
[3] The holy prophet Abdias: cf. 17 October.
     Note: See assignment and reference above at 19 November, which parallels L(C-R), L(Greg); TypkSS = 3 December.
[4] The holy martyr Barbara: *I + Mk 5:24–34.*
5   Our blessed father Sabbas: cf. 2 September.
6   Our blessed father Nikolaos: cf. 20 January.
7   The blessed Ambrose: cf. 3 September.
8   The holy apostle Sosthenos: cf. 22 September.
     Note: Spelling here = L(Greg).
9   Conception of Saint Anne: *V + Mk 11:22–26* (with variant ending: ed. Nestle-Aland, see apparatus at 11:26) + *Mt 7:7–8.*
     Note: The scribe identified the reading as from Luke.
11   [=10]   The holy Martyrs Menas, Hermogenes, and Egraphos: cf. the seventh Saturday in Matthew.
     Note: The scribe has mistakenly numbered this celebration; the day is actually the tenth; the following two are likewise off one day. With Eustratios, the scribe is back in sequence.
12   [=11]   The blessed Daniel (the Stylite): cf. 20 January.
13   [=12]   The blessed Spyridon: *I + Lk 11:1–13* (see Colwell and Riddle, *Prolegomena,* 139, for complete *incipit*).

The New York Cruciform Lectionary

Note: The scribe has identified the reading as from John.

13 Saint Eustratios: cf. 20 September.
14 Saint Thyrsos, and the memory of the terror: *I + Lk 8:22–25.*
    Note: The second part of the day's celebration is unknown to L(Greg) and L(C-R); the TypkSS commemorates an earth tremor, which began on this day in 557.
15 Saint Eleutherios: cf. the eleventh Saturday in Luke.
    Note: Rubric in gold.
16 The holy prophet Haggai: cf. 10 October.
17 The Three Holy Youths of Babylon: *III + Lk 11:43–50a.*
    Note: The scribe has identified the reading as from Matthew.
18 The blessed Phloros: cf. the first Sunday in Matthew.
    Note: Not in L(C-R), L(Greg), but paralleled by TypkSS and SynaxCP.
19 Saint Boniface: cf. the Sunday after the Elevation (of the Holy Cross).
20 Saint Ignatios Theophoros: *I + Mk 9:33–41.*
    Note: The scribe has identified the passage as from Matthew.
21 Saint Juliane: cf. 16 September.
    Note: Rubric in gold.
22 Saint Anastasia: cf. the seventeenth Saturday in Matthew.
23 The Holy Ten Martyrs of Crete: cf. 15 September.
    Saturday before the birth of Christ: cf. the twelfth Saturday in Luke.
    Sunday before the birth of Christ: *Mt 1:1–17* [scribe inserts] Beginning of Morning Service for Christ's birth [then continues:] *25.*
    Evening before Christ's birth: *Lk 2:1–20.*
25 Christ's Nativity: morning lection, cf. Sunday of the Holy Fathers (Abraham, Isaac, Jacob), the Book of Generations. From the middle *+ Mt 2:1–12.*
[26] Service for the Virgin: *Mt 2:13–18* [scribe inserts] End of (Holy) Children (reading) [then continues:] *19–23.*
27 Saint Stephen Protomartyr: cf. the thirteenth Sunday in Matthew.
    Note: Rubric in gold.
28 Saint Theodore, bishop of Constantinople: cf. 3 September.
29 (Holy) Children (killed at Bethlehem by Herod): cf. 26 of this month; go back.
30 The blessed Markellos: cf. the eleventh Saturday in Luke.
    Note: (L(C-R), L(Greg), TypkSS, SynaxCP = 29 December.
31 The blessed Irenaeus: cf. 2 September.
    Note: Not attested on this day in other sources.
    Saturday after Christ's birth: *I + Mt 15b–21.*

JANUARY

1 The circumcision of our Lord Jesus Christ, and Saint Basil: *I + Lk 2:20–21, 40–52.*
2 Our blessed father Silvester (bishop of Rome): cf. 3 September.
   Note: Rubric in gold.

3   The holy prophet Malachi, and Saint Gordos: cf. 5 September.
    Note: Other sources = Gordios.
4   Saints Zosimos, Chrysanthos, and Dareia: cf. 20 September.
    Note: Chrysanthos and Dareia are not known in the lectionaries on this day; TypkSS, BHG = 17 October; but here again below: 19 March = L(Greg).
    Saturday before the (feast of) Lights: *I* + *Mt 3:1–11*.
    Note: The scribe identified the reading as from John.
    Sunday before the Lights: *Mk 1:1–8*.
5   Lesson on the Lights: *Lk 3:1–18*.
6   The holy Theophanies: verses, *Ps 28:3a* [first phrase] + *Ps 28:1a* [first phrase] + *I* + *Mk 1:9–11*.
    Note: The word "verses" appears in the margin.
    [Same feast] for the liturgy: *I* + *Mt 3:13–17*.
7   Service for John the Forerunner: *I* + *Jn 1:29–34*.
    Saturday after the Lights: *I* + *Mt 4:1–11*.
    Sunday after the Lights: *I* + *Mt 4:12–17*.
8   The holy martyrs Julian and Basilissa: cf. on the martyrs.
    Note: Rubric in gold.
9   The holy martyr Polyeuktos: cf. the third Saturday in Easter.
10 Saint Gregory, bishop of Nyssa: cf. 29 September.
11 Our blessed father Theodosios: cf. 21 October.
12 Our blessed father Stephen: cf. 21 October.
    Note: Otherwise unknown on this day.
13 The holy martyrs Hermylos and Stratonikos: cf. the third Saturday in Easter.
14 The Holy Abbots (of Raithou): cf. the eleventh Saturday in Luke.
15 The holy martyrs Babylas and the Youths: cf. the third Saturday in Easter.
16 For the worship of the venerable chains of the holy apostle Peter: cf. Saturday of Pentecost.
17 Our blessed father Anthony (Abbot): cf. 21 October.
18 On the return from exile of Saints Athanasios and Cyril: cf. 2 September.
    Note: Rubric in gold.
19 Our blessed father Theodotos, bishop of Ankyra: cf. 21 October.
    Note: On this day TypkSS, SynaxCP = Theodotos, bishop of Kyrene; the Bishop of Ankyra: SynaxCP = 4 November. No parallel with L(C-R), L(Greg); rubric in gold.
20 Our blessed father Euthymios: *II* + *Mt 11:27–30*.
21 Our blessed confessor Maximos: cf. 6 November.
22 The holy apostle Timothy, and Anastasios (the Persian): cf. Easter Sunday.
23 The blessed martyr Clement (bishop of Ankyra): cf. the first Saturday of Lent.
24 The holy martyr Vikentios (the deacon?): cf. 2 October.
    Note: If Vikentios the deacon, the celebration is unknown to L(C-R), L(Greg), but TypkSS, SynaxCp = 22 January.
25 Saint Gregory the Theologian (of Nazianzus): cf. 21 October.
26 The remembrance of the tremor, at the Exakionion: cf. 26 October.
    Note: The reference is to the earthquake on this day in 450. In the second phrase, the scribe

The New York Cruciform Lectionary

has referred to a quarter of the city located at the end of the Mese outside the Constantinian walls; here there was a column, erected by Constantine, called the Exakionion (R. Guilland, *Etudes de topographie de Constantinople byzantine,* II, Berliner byzantinistische Arbeiten, XXXVII, Berlin, 1969, 62–64). On this day, according to the TypkSS, the Cathedral clergy led a procession commemorating the earthquake, and part of the day's service was observed at the Exakionion. Stational services are common to the TypkSS, but this reference and that on 25 September are the only ones in the lectionary to services possibly held in the city. Perhaps rather than an explicit direction to go to the Exakionion, the phrase simply means that the tremor commemorated was identified by the monument or that part of the city; no parallel in L(C-R) or L(Greg).

27 Saint John Chrysostom: cf. 13 November.
Note: L(C-R), L(Greg) = Translation of Chrysostom's relics; the reference returns to a blank space.

28 Our blessed father Ephrem (the Syrian): cf. 21 October.

29 The translation of the relics of Saint Ignatios (Theophoros): cf. 20 December.

30 The holy hieromartyr Hippolytos, bishop of Rome: cf. Tuesday of the sixth week of Pentecost.
Note: The sixth week is the one before Pentecost; a similar error occurs below at 21 [=23] February.

31 The holy miracle-workers Kyros and John: cf. 1 November.

FEBRUARY

1   Saint Tryphon; cf. the tenth Saturday in Luke.

[2] The Presentation of our Lord Jesus Christ, morning lection: *Lk 1:39* + cf. 8 September + *I* + *Lk 2:22–38* [scribe inserts] End [then continues:] *39–40*.
Note: The scribe has run together the readings for the morning service and liturgy for the day.

3   The holy and just Symeon, and Anna the Prophetess: cf. the feast [i.e., above].
Note: Rubric in gold.

4   Our blessed father Isidore (of Pelusiota): cf. 21 October.

5   The holy martyr Agathe: cf. the seventeenth Saturday in Matthew.

6   The blessed Parthenios, bishop of Lampsakos; cf. 2 September.
Note: L(Greg), L(C-R), TypkSS, BHG = 7 February.

7   Saint Theodore Stratelates: cf. 2 October.
Note: TypkSS = 8 February, but L(Greg), L(C-R) = 7 February.

8   The holy prophet Zachariah: cf. the end of the menologion.

9   [=10] The holy martyr Charalampos: cf. 3 September.
Note: L(Greg), L(C-R), TypkSS = 10 February. Similarly conclusive evidence exists for correcting, within square brackets, the scribe's assignments throughout the rest of February. He perhaps omitted Nikephoros on 10 February.

10 [=11] Saint Blasios (bishop of Sebaste): cf. 4 September.

Saints and Feasts in the Menologion

11 [=12] Our blessed father Meletios, archbishop of Antioch: cf. 2 September.
12 [=13] The blessed Martinianos: cf. 21 October.
13 [=14] Saint Auxentios: cf. the third Sunday in Lent.
14 [=15] The holy apostles Onesimos, Timothy, and Paphnoutios: cf. the seventh Saturday in Luke.
Note: For Timothy, see below at 17 [=19]; Onesimos: SynaxCP = 15 February; Paphnoutios with Euphrosyne: TypkSS, SynaxCP = 15 February L(Greg) gives Paphnoutios on 20 February.
15 [=17] The holy (and) great martyr Theodore Tiron: cf. the first Saturday in Lent.
16 [=18] Our blessed father Leo, pope of Rome: cf. 3 September.
Note: TypkSS shows both Theodore Tiron and Pope Leo together on 17 February; correction here gives weight to other lectionary evidence and to sequence.
17 [=19] The holy martyr Timothy: cf. 21 October.
Note: TypkSS, SynaxCP = 19 February; no lectionary evidence in similar form, but see L(Greg) at 21 February.
18 [=20] Saint Romanos and the youths: cf. 4 September.
Note: TypkSS, BHG = 18 November.
19 [=21?] Our blessed father John the Faster (archbishop of Constantinople): cf. 3 September.
Note: John is also celebrated above on 2 September; TypkSS = 18 February; I propose 21 on the basis of sequence.
20 [=22] Our blessed father Thomas, patriarch: cf. 2 September.
Note: Rubric in gold.
21 [=23] Our blessed father Polycarp (bishop of Smyrna): cf. Tuesday of the sixth week of Pentecost.
Note: The sixth week is the one just before Pentecost; rubric in gold.
24 Discovery of the venerable head of Saint John the Forerunner, for the liturgy: *I* + Mt 11:2–14.
Note: The scribe has identified the reading as from John but has returned to the correct sequence of numbers.
25 Our blessed father Tarasios (archbishop of Constantinople): cf. 3 September.
26 Saint Porphyrios (bishop of Gaza): cf. 2 September.
27 Our blessed father Prokopios the Decapolite: cf. 1 November.
28 Our blessed father Basil (the confessor): cf. 20 January.

MARCH

[For the readings of this month, considerable divergence exists among the sources, and often I have done nothing more than call attention to it.]

1 The holy martyr Eudokia (of Samaria): cf. 4 November.
2 Saint Theodotos, bishop of Kyrenia: cf. 20 September.
3 [=4?] The holy martyrs Paul and Julian: cf. (reading) for the martyrs.

The New York Cruciform Lectionary

Note: L(Greg), SynaxCP = 4 March; TypkSS = 17 August.

4 [=5] The blessed Hsychios, priest, and the holy martyr Konon: cf. 2 September.
Note: L(Greg), SynaxCP = 5 March.

5 [=6] The later Forty-two Holy Martyrs: cf. the ninth of this month.
Note: L(Greg), L(C-R), TypkSS, SynaxCP, BHG = 6 March.

6 [=7?] Our blessed father Markos, and Gerasimos: cf. 2 September.
Note: Markos: TypkSS, SynaxCP, BHG = 5 March. Gerasimos: L(C-R), TypkSS, SynaxCP = 4 March; BHG = 4, 5, 20 March.

7 [=8] Our blessed father Theophylact, bishop of Nicomedia: cf. 6 November.
Note: L(Greg), TypkSS, SynaxCP = 8 March.

[9] The Forty Holy Martyrs of Sebaste: *VI* + *Mt 20:1–16*.
Note: The scribe has identified the reading as from John.

10 Our blessed father Sophronios (archbishop of Jerusalem), and Kodratos: cf. 21 October.
Note: L(Greg), L(C-R), SynaxCP = 11 March; TypkSS = 10 March.

11 The holy hieromartyr Pionios: cf. 2 October.
Note: TypkSS, SynaxCP = 11 March; not in L(C-R), L(Greg) on this day.

12 Our blessed father Theophanes (the Confessor): cf. 21 October.

13 Saint Nikephoros, bishop of Constantinople: cf. 3 September.

14 [=13] The holy martyr Alexander of Pydna: cf. the third Saturday in Easter.
Note: L(Greg), TypkSS = 15 March; SynaxCP = 13 March.

15 [=14] Saint John of Rouphinianais, and our blessed father Benedict, bishop of Rome: cf. 2 September.
Note: L(Greg) = 14 March.

16 Our blessed father Syschemonos, bishop of Lampsakos: cf. 12 November.
Note: Unparalleled in the sources on this day.

17 Alexios, man of God, and the raising of Lazarus, and Saint Marinos: cf. 20 January.

18 Our blessed father Cyril, bishop of Jerusalem: cf. 2 September.

19 The holy martyrs Chrysanthos and Dareia: cf. 4 September.
Note: See above at 4 January.

20 Destruction of our blessed fathers at the monastery of Saint Sabbas, and our blessed father Malachios: cf. 29 September.
Note: Holy Fathers: TypkSS = 16 May; L(Greg) = 20 March as Malchos; Malachios on 2 January = L(Greg).

22 The holy hieromartyr Basil, priest, and Thomas, bishop (of Constantinople): cf. 3 October.

23 Saint Christina: cf. 16 September.

24 The holy martyr Nikon and his two hundred disciples: cf. the seventh Saturday in Luke.
Note: Nikon: L(Greg), BHG = 23 March.

25 Lesson for the All-holy Virgin, morning: Psalm verse, fourth mode, *Ps 71:6* [first five words], verse, *Ps 71:7* [first six words]; lesson: cf. 8 September + *Lk 1:39*.
Note: TypkSS gives these same antiphons for the liturgy.
[Same day and feast] For the liturgy: *Lk 1:24–38*.

26 The Archangel Gabriel: cf. 18 October.
Note: Rubric in gold.

27 The blessed Matrona of Thessalonika: cf. 11 October.
28 Our blessed father and miracle-worker Hilarion (abbot of the monastery of Pelekete): cf. 3 October.
29 Our blessed father John, archbishop of Jerusalem: cf. 3 September.
30 Our blessed father John, author of the Ladder: cf. 28 September.
31 The holy martyrs Menander and Neophytos: cf. the Saturday after Easter.

APRIL

1 The blessed Mary of Egypt: cf. 11 October.
2 The blessed miracle-worker Titus: cf. 1 November.
3 The holy prophets Ezekiel, Zachariah, and Daniel: cf. 5 September.
   Note: Unique on this day.
4 The holy martyrs Theodoulos and Agathapous, and the blessed Joseph the Hymnographer: cf. the Saturday after Easter.
5 The blessed George of Malaios: cf. the third Sunday in Lent.
   Note: L(Greg) = of Maleos.
6 Saint Eutychios, archbishop of Constantinople: cf. 3 September.
7 Saint George, bishop of Mytelene: cf. 13 November.
   Note: Thus in L(C-R), SynaxCP; L(Greg) = of Mitylene; rubric in gold.
8 [=9]   Our blessed fathers Patermouthios and Kopres, and the holy martyr Eupsychios: cf. the tenth Saturday of Luke.
   Note: L(Greg), TypkSS, SynaxCP = 9 April; evidence indicates that the scribe has here skipped a day and thus disturbed the order for the rest of the month.
9 [=10]   The holy martyr Terentios and his companions: cf. the first Sunday in Matthew.
   Note: L(Greg), TypkSS, SynaxCP = 10 April.
10 [=11]   The holy martyr Antipas (bishop of Pergamon): cf. 3 October.
   Note: L(C-R), L(Greg), TypkSS, SynaxCP = 11 April; similar agreement exists for the following corrections.
11 [=12]   Our blessed father and confessor Basil, bishop of Pareios: cf. 6 November.
12 [=13]   The holy martyrs Kriskentios and Theodore: cf. the first Sunday in Matthew.
   Note: SynaxCP as Kriskentinos, spelling here = L(Greg); L(Greg) as Theodosios.
13 [=14]   The holy apostles Aristarchos, Podes, and Trophemos: cf. 18 October.
   Note: Other sources as Poudes.
14 [=15]   The holy martyrs Sabbas the Goth, Leonides, Nikodemos, and their companions: cf. the first Sunday in Matthew.
15 [=16]   Saint Akakios, bishop of Melitene: cf. Tuesday of Pentecost.
16 [=17]   Our blessed fathers Kosmas of Chalcedon, and Agapios, pope of Rome: cf. 2 September.
   Note: TypkSS, SynaxCP as Agapetos; reading here = L(Greg).
17 [=18]   Our blessed father John of Palaiolauritos: cf. 3 October.

The New York Cruciform Lectionary

18 [=19] The holy and great martyr Theodore of Perge, Pamphylia: cf. Friday of the first week of Lent.

19 [=20] The holy hieromartyr Paphnoutios: cf. 5 November.

20 [=21] Our blessed father Theodore of Trichina: cf. the third Sunday of Lent.

21 [=22] Our blessed father Theodore of Sikeon: cf. 13 November.

22 [=23] The holy and great martyr George: cf. the third Saturday of Easter.
Note: Rubric in gold.

23 [=24] The holy martyrs who died at Chalcedon, and the holy martyr Sabbas Stratelates: cf. the seventh Saturday in Luke.

24 [=25] The holy apostle and evangelist Mark: cf. [scribe leaves a blank space for reference].

25 [=26] The holy hieromartyr Basil, bishop of Amaseia: cf. the third Saturday in Easter.

26 [=27] The holy Symeon of Jerusalem, kinsman of the Lord: cf. the third Sunday of Lent.
Note: Rubric in gold.

27 [=28] The holy apostle Iason: cf. the seventh Saturday in Luke.

28 [=29] The holy martyr Memnon, and the Twenty-two Martyrs, and the Twenty-nine Martyrs of Cyzicus: cf. the seventh Saturday in Luke.
Note: BHG, L(Greg) = Nine Martyrs of Cyzicus.

30 The holy apostle James, brother of (John) the Theologian: cf. 9 October.

MAY

1 The holy prophet Jeremiah: cf. 29 June.

2 Our holy father Athanasios, bishop of Alexandria: cf. 2 September.

3 The holy martyr Perouzoe and her children: cf. 29 November.
Note: SynaxCP offers the only parallel.

4 The holy martyr Eirene: cf. 4 November.

5 The holy martyr Pelagia the Virgin: cf. the seventh Saturday in Matthew.

6 [+7] The holy and just Job: cf. [scribe leaves blank]; commemoration of the appearance of the holy cross in the heavens: cf. 3 September.
Note: The sources agree that the Sign of the Cross was celebrated on 7 May; the scribe may have inadvertently combined it with Job.
The same day [=7], the holy martyr Akakios: cf. the third Saturday in Easter.
Note: L(Greg), TypkSS = 7 May.
The same day [=8], Saint John the Theologian: *I + Jn 19:25–27; 21:24, 25.*

7 [=8] Our blessed father Arsenios: cf. 21 October.
Note: L(Greg), SynaxCP = 8 May.

9 The holy prophet Isaiah: cf. Wednesday of the sixth week in Easter.
The same day, The holy and great martyr Christopher: cf. Friday of the first week of Lent.

10 The holy apostle Simon Zelotes: cf. 9 October.

Saints and Feasts in the Menologion

11 The holy hieromartyrs Mokios and Pachomios: cf. the third Saturday of Easter.
12 Our holy fathers Germanos, archbishop of Constantinople, and Epiphanios of Cyprus: cf. 2 September.
13 The holy martyr Alexander: cf. on the Martyrs.
   Note: In some lectionaries, this reading would be found at the end of the manuscript; the scribe did not include the pericope.
14 Our blessed father Pachomios, and Theodore the Sanctified: cf. on the blessed.
   Note: Same as above to 13 May.
15 The holy prophet Zachariah: cf. at end of the menologion.
16 The holy apostle Andronikos: cf. the third Saturday in Easter.
   Note: L(C-R), L(Greg), SynaxCP = 17 May.
17 The holy martyr Thalelaios: cf. Friday of the first week of Lent.
   Note: L(C-R), L(Greg), SynaxCP = 20 May.
21 Our holy rulers Constantine and Helen: cf. 13 November.
22 The holy martyr Basiliskos and his companions: cf. 20 September.
23 Our blessed father Symeon of the Marvelous Mountain: cf. 1 September.
   Note: L(C-R), L(Greg) = 24 May; TypkSS = 23 May.
24 The holy martyr Meletios: II + Jn 14:21–24.
   Note: L(C-R), L(Greg) = 23 May; TypkSS, SynaxCP = 24 May.
28 The holy apostle Karpos, one of the Sixty, and the holy martyr Therapon: cf. 23 February.
   Note: L(C-R) = 26; L(Greg) = 27 May.
29 The holy martyr Theodora: cf. the seventeenth Saturday in Matthew.
   Note: Others all read Theodosia, virgin martyr.
30 The blessed Isaac of the Dalmatos (monastery): cf. 10 November.
   Note: See below at 3 August.
31 The holy martyr Hermeias: cf. the Friday of the first week of Lent.

JUNE

1 The holy martyr Justin: cf. 23 February.
2 Saint Nikephoros, archbishop of Constantinople: cf. 3 September.
3 The holy martyr Loukillianos: cf. the tenth Saturday in Luke.
4 Our father, Saint Metrophanes, archbishop of Constantinople: cf. 3 September.
5 Our father, Saint Eustathios, archbishop of Antioch: cf. 2 September.
6 The holy hieromartyr Dorotheos (bishop of Tyre): cf. the seventh Saturday in Luke.
7 The holy martyr Theodotos of Ankyra: cf. similarly.
8 Saint Theodore Stratelates: cf. the tenth Saturday in Luke.
9 Saint Cyril of Alexandria, and the holy apostle Phourtounatos: cf. 18 October.
10 Saint Timothy, bishop of Prousa: cf. 21 October.
11 The holy apostles Bartholomew and Barnabas: cf. the seventh Saturday in Luke.
12 Our blessed father Onouphrios: cf. 10 November.
13 The holy martyr Akylina: cf. the seventeenth Saturday in Matthew.

14   The holy prophet Elisha: cf. on the Prophets.

15 [=16]   The holy and miracle-working Tychon: cf. 1 November.
Note: L(C-R), L(Greg), TypkSS, SynaxCP = 16 June; similar agreement exists for the following two corrections.

16 [=17]   The holy martyrs Manuel, Sabel, and Ishmael: cf. the third Saturday in Easter.

17 [=18]   The holy martyr Leontios and his companions: cf. similarly.
[There follows a gap of about two lines in which the title to the next reading would have appeared; a pericope follows without author designation:] *I + Lk 6:20–27, 10:23–24, 11:33.*
Note: The reading does not appear in the sources for celebrations between 18 and 22 June.

22   The holy martyr Justin and his companions: cf. 16 September.
Note: Justin unique among sources; TypkSS and SynaxCP read Justos, bishop of Eleutheropolis.

23   Our blessed father Eusebios (bishop of Samosata): cf. 10 November.
Note: L(C-R) = 19; L(Greg), TypkSS, SynaxCP = 22 June.

24   The holy martyr Agrippine: cf. the seventeenth Saturday in Matthew.
Note: L(Greg), TypkSS = 23 June.

25   The birth of Saint John the Forerunner and Baptist, morning service: fourth mode: *Ps 131:17a,* [verse] *Ps 131:1a;* reading: cf. [scribe leaves blank].
Note: L(C-R), L(Greg) = 24 June.
[Same day and feast] For the liturgy: *Lk 1:1–4* [scribe inserts] For the Conception: *incipit* I [then continues:] *5–23* [inserts direction,] Beginning of Conception [then continues:] *24–25, 57–68, 76, 80.*

25   The holy martyr Fevronia: cf. the seventeenth Saturday in Matthew.

26   The blessed David of Thessalonika: cf. 21 October.

27   Our blessed father Sampson Xenodochos: cf. the eleventh Saturday in Luke.

28   The holy martyr Hypatios, bishop of Gangra: cf. the third Saturday in Easter.

29   The holy apostles Peter and Paul: Psalm verse, mode [unspecified], *Ps 18:5;* verse, *Ps 18:1;* reading for morning service: cf. 9 October.
Note: Rubric in gold.
For the liturgy: *I + Mt 16:13–18* [scribe's inserts] End of Consecration [then continues:] *19.*
Note: The reference is to the celebration of the consecration of Saint Sophia on 23 December, but no entry above directs the reader to this passage.

30   The holy Twelve Apostles: *I + Mt 9:36–10:8.*

JULY

1   The holy Anargyroi: cf. 1 November.

2   Deposition of the venerable garment of the All-holy Virgin (in the Blachernae): cf. 8 September, morning.

Saints and Feasts in the Menologion

3   The holy martyrs Hyakinthos and Theodotos: cf. the third Saturday in Easter.

4   Our blessed fathers Andrew of Crete, Theodore of Cyrene and Donatos: cf. 2 September.
Note: L(Greg) = Donatos, but SynaxCP = Doratos.

5   The holy martyr Aetios, Philemon and his companions: cf. 13 October.

6   The blessed Thomas of Malaios: cf. 10 November.

7   The holy martyrs Isauros, Eustathios, Polycarp, and Evangelos: cf. 23 February.
The same day, the blessed Sisoes the Great: cf. 13 October.

8   The holy and great martyr Prokopios: I + *Lk 6:17–19, 9:1–2, 10:16–21*.

9   The holy hieromartyr Pankratios (bishop) of Taormina; cf. 13 October.

10   The Forty-five Holy Martyrs of Nikopolis: cf. the third Saturday in Easter.

11   The holy and great martyr Euphemia of the Mountain: cf. the seventeenth Saturday in Matthew.

12   The holy martyrs Proklos and Hilarion, and Saint Golindouch: cf. on the Martyrs.

13   The holy martyr Sarapion: cf. the third Saturday after Easter.

14   [=13]   Saint Stephen Sabaites: cf. 10 November.
Note: L(Greg) = 13. Until the scribe gets back into sequence on the 24th, the preponderance of evidence indicates that he has mistakenly numbered the following days.

15   [=14]   The holy apostle Akylas: cf. 18 October.

16   [=15]   The holy martyrs Keruakos and Ioulita: cf. the tenth Saturday in Matthew.
Note: SynaxCP = Kerukos and Ioulitta; reading here = L(Greg).

17   [=16]   The holy martyr Anthenogenes and his companions: cf. the third Saturday after Easter.

18   [=17]   The holy and great martyr Marina: cf. the seventeenth Saturday in Matthew.

19   [=18]   The holy martyr Aimelianos: cf. the eighth of this month.

20   [=19]   The holy, blessed martyr Theodosia: cf. the seventeenth Sunday in Matthew.
Note: Rubric in gold.

21   [=20]   The holy prophets Elijah and Elisha: cf. 6 August, liturgy.

22   [=21]   The holy prophet Ezekiel: cf. 9 June.
The same day, our blessed father Symeon, Fool for Christ: cf. 10 November.

23   [=22]   The holy hieromartyr Phokas: cf. the tenth Saturday in Luke.

24   The holy martyr Christina (virgin martyr of Tyre): cf. the seventeenth Saturday in Luke.

25   The death of Saint Anne: cf. the sixth Saturday in Luke.
The same day, the holy women Eupraxia and Olympias: cf. the seventeenth Saturday in Matthew.

26   The blessed Symeon (Stylites, archimandrite) of Mandra, and the holy hieromartyr Ermolaos: cf. the sixth Saturday in Luke.
Note: Others read Hermolaos.

27   The holy and great martyr Panteleimon: cf. the third Saturday in Easter.

28   The holy apostles Prochoros, Nikanor, and Parmenas: cf. the seventh Saturday in Luke.

29   The holy martyr Kalinikos, and Theodotos: cf. 20 September.

30   The holy apostles Silatila and Soulianos, Kriskentios, Epainetos and Andronikos: cf. the seventh Saturday in Luke.

The New York Cruciform Lectionary

Note: The other sources read Silas et al.
31 Saint John Stratiotes: cf. 13 October.
    The same day, The blessed and just Eudokimos: cf. the sixth Saturday in Luke.

AUGUST

1 The holy Macabees: cf. the seventh Sunday in Luke.
2 Discovery of the relics of the protomartyr Saint Stephen: cf. 26 December.
3 Our blessed father Isaac of the Dalmatos (monastery?): cf. the sixth Saturday in Luke.
   Note: Parallel with L(Greg), but SynaxCP = blessed fathers Isaac, Dalmatos, and Phaustos; a change in the case of the article from the entry above at 30 May makes the reading here doubtful, as if the names of Isaac and Dalmatos had been mistakenly joined.
4 The holy, blessed martyr Eudokia: cf. the seventeenth Saturday in Matthew.
5 The holy martyr Eusignios: cf. the third Sunday in Lent.
6 The Transfiguration of our Lord Jesus Christ: morning service: Psalm verse, fourth mode, *Ps 88:13b;* verse: *Ps 88:1b;* morning reading: I + Lk 9:28–34.
   Note: the text breaks at Lk 9:34, where a leaf is now missing; it contained the rest of this reading, to Lk 9:36, and the beginning of the next.
   [Same day and feast: reading for the liturgy; Mt 17:1–8] 9.
   Note: Only the end of the reading for the service survives.
7 [=7+8] Saint Domitios and the blessed Aimilianos (bishop of Cyzicus): cf. the third Sunday of Lent.
   Note: Aimilianos, L(C-R), L(Greg), SynaxCP = 8 August.
8 [=9?] The holy apostle and evangelist Matthew: cf. 1 November.
   Note: L(C-R), L(Greg) = 7; TypkSS, SynaxCP = 9 August.
9 [=10] The holy martyr Lawrence: cf. the third Saturday in Easter.
   Note: L(C-R), L(Greg), TypkSS, SynaxCP = 10 August; similar evidence exists for those corrected below.
10 [=11] The holy martyr Euplos: cf. the tenth Saturday in Luke.
11 [=12] The holy martyrs Photios and Aniketos: cf. 20 September.
12 [=13] Our blessed father Maximos (the Confessor): cf. 6 November.
13 [=14] Our blessed father Markelos and his sixty disciples: cf. the eleventh Saturday in Luke.
15 The death of the Virgin: cf. 8 September readings.
16 Saint Diomedes: cf. 2 October.
17 The holy martyr Myron: cf. 15 September.
18 The holy martyrs Phloros and Hilarion: cf. 15 October.
    Note: All other sources read Phloros and Lauros.
19 Saint Andrew Stratelates: cf. 2 October.
20 The holy apostle Thaddeus: cf. 1 November.
21 The holy martyr Bassa, and her companions: cf. the tenth Saturday in Matthew.
22 The holy martyr Agathonikos: cf. the third Saturday in Easter.

23 The holy martyrs Eirenaios and Oros and Horopsa: cf. 20 September.
    Note: Others give Oropsa.
24 The holy martyr Euphrosyne: cf. 20 January.
    Note: Not in any of the sources at this point.
25 The holy apostle Titus (of Gortyna): cf. 2 September.
26. The holy martyrs Adrianos and Natalia: cf. 25 October.
27 The blessed Sabbas: cf. 3 September.
28 The blessed Poimenos, and Moses (the Ethiopian): cf. 20 January.
29 The beheading of the Forerunner: *I + Mk 6:14–30.*
[30] The holy apostle Thaddeus: cf. 18 October.
    Note: The sources all agree on celebrating Thaddeus on 20 August, as here above.
31 Deposition of the venerable girdle of the Virgin in the (church) of the Chalke: cf. the fifteenth Sunday in Luke.
    The same day, our holy patriarchs Alexander, John, and Paul the Younger: cf. 2 September.
    Lection for the holy prophet Zachariah: read 5 September; *III + Mt 23:27–39.*

END OF MENOLOGION

[Eleven morning readings of Resurrection follow before the end of the manuscript.]

SAINTS AND FEASTS

The following abbreviations are used: a = apostle; ab = archbishop; b = bishop; cfs = confessor; comps = and companions; Cple = Constantinople; hm = hieromartyr; m = martyr; pr = prophet; pt = patriarch; ww = wonderworker. An asterisk (★) means that I have made a choice between possible readings.

Abbots (of Raithou), 14 January (Lk 12:32–40)
Abdias, 19 November, [3] December (Lk 21:12–19/ Lk 13:31–35)
Abramios (anchorite), 29 October (Lk 6:17–23)
Adrianos and Natalia, 26 August (Lk 12:2–12)
Aetios, 5 July (Mt 7:12–21)
Agapios [Agapitos], pope of Rome, 16 [=17] April (Mt 5:14–19★)
Agathe, 5 February (Mt 25:1–13)
Agathonikos, 22 August (Jn 15:17–16:2)
Agrippine, 24 June (Mt 25:1–13)
Aimelianos, m, 19 [=18] July (Lk 6:17–19, 9:1–2, 10:16–21)
Aimilianos (b Cyzicus), 7 [=8] August (Mk 8:34–9:1)

Akakios, m, 6 [=7] May (Jn 15:17–16:2)
Akakios, b Melitene, 15 [=16] April (Mt 4:25–5:13)
Akepsimas, Aeithalas, and Joseph, 3 November (Jn 10:9–16)
Akindynos comps, 2 November (Mt 19:23–30)
Akylas, 15 [=14] July (Lk 10:16–21)
Akylina, 13 June (Mt 25:1–13)
Alexander, m, 13 May (no reading)
Alexander of Pydna, 14 March (Mk 15:43–16:8)
Alexander, John, and Paul the Younger, pp Cple, 31 August (Mt 5:14–19)
Alexios, man of God, 17 March (Mt 11:27–30)
Alypios, 25 November (Mt 11:27–30)
Ambrose, 7 December (Jn 10:9–16)
Ananias, 1 October (Mt 5:14–19)

Anargyroi, 1 July; cf. also Kosmas and Damian (Mt 10:1, 5–8)
Anastasia, 22 December (Mt 25:1–13)
Anastasios (the Persian), 22 January (Jn 1:1–17)
Andrew, a, 30 November (Jn 1:35–52)
Andrew of Crete, Theodore of Cyrene, and Donatos, 4 July (Mt 5:14–19*)
Andrew Stratelates, 19 August (Jn 10:9–16)
Andronikos, 16 May (Jn 15:17–16:2)
Anna, pr, 3 February (Lk 1:39–49, 56 / Lk 2:22–38)
Anne, conception (of Virgin), 9 December; death, 25 July; cf. Joachim (Mk 11:22–26 / Lk 8:16–21)
Anthemios, b Nicomedia, 3 September (Jn 10:9–16)
Anthenogenes comps, 17 [=16] July (Jn 15:17–16:2)
Anthony (Abbot), 17 January (Lk 6:17–23)
Antipas (b Pergamon), 10 [=11] April (Mt 13:44–54a)
Aquilas: cf. Akylas
Aquilina: cf. Akylina
Archangel Gabriel, 26 March (Lk 10:16–21)
Archangel Michael at Chonae, 6 September (Lk 10:16–21)
Archangels, 8 November (Lk 10:16–21)
Arethas, 24 October (Mt 10:32, 33, 37, 38, 19:27–30)
Aristarchos, Podes [Poudes], and Trophemos, 13 [=14] April (Lk 10:16–21)
Arsenios, 7 May (Lk 6:17–23)
Artemios, 20 October (Mk 8:34–9:1)
Athanasios, b Alexandria, 2 May (Mt 5:14–19*)
Athanasios and Cyril, return from exile, 17 January (Lk 6:17–23)
Auxentios, 13 [=14] February (Mk 8:34–9:1)
Averkios, 22 October (Lk 12:32–40)
Babylas and the (Eighty-four Holy) Children, 4 September (Lk 10:19–21)
Babylas and the Youths, 15 January (Jn 15:17–16:2)
Barbara, [4] December (Mk 5:24–34)
Bartholomew and Barnabas, 11 June (Lk 9:1–6)
Basil, b Amaseia, 25 [=26] April (Jn 15:17–16:2)
Basil, b Pareios, 11 [=12] April (Lk 8:22–25)
Basil (cfs), 28 February (Mt 11:27–30)
Basil, priest, 22 March (Mt 13:44–54a)
Basiliskos comps, 22 May (Lk 21:12–19)
Bassa comps, 21 August (Mt 17:24–18:4)
Benedict, b Rome, 15 March (Mt 5:14–19*)
[Blank space], 12, 13 November; 24 [=25] April
Blasios (b Sebaste), 10 [11] February (Lk 10:19–21)
Boniface, 19 December (Mk 8:34–9:1)
Cecilia: cf. Kikilia

Chains of Saint Peter, 16 January (Jn 21:14–25)
Charalampos, 9 [=10] February (Jn 10:9–16)
Charitine, 5 October (Lk 13:10–17)
Chariton, 28 September (Mt 11:27–30)
Christ, circumcision, 1 January; birth, 25 December; presentation in the temple, [2] February; transfiguration, 6 August (Lk 2:20–21, 40–52 / Mt 1:1–25, 2:1–12 / Lk 1:39–49, 56, 2:22–40 / Lk 9:28–34[–36] / [Mt 17:1–8] 9)
Christina, 23 March (Lk 7:36–50)
Christina (virgin martyr of Tyre), 24 July (Lk 20:46–21:4)
Christopher, 9 May (Jn 15:9–16)
Chrysanthos and Dareia, 4 January, 19 March (Lk 21:12–19 / Lk 10:19–21)
Clement (b Ankyra), 23 January (Mk 2:23–3:5)
Clement (of Rome), 24 November (Mt 11:27–30)
Constantine and Helen, 21 May (no reading)
Cyprian, 2 October (Jn 10:9–16)
Cyril of Alexandria, 9 June (Lk 10:16–21)
Cyril, b Jerusalem, 18 March (Mt 5:14–19*)
Daniel (pr), 3 April (Mt 23:27–39)
Daniel (the Stylite), 12 [=11] December (Mt 11:27–30)
David of Thessalonika, 26 June (Lk 6:17–23)
Demetrios, 26 October (Mt 8:23–27)
Diomedes, 16 August (Jn 10:9–16)
Dionysios (the Areopagite), 3 October (Mt 13:44–54a)
Domitios, 7 August (Mt 8:34–9:1)
Domna, 28 October (Lk 9:1–6)
Donatos, 4 July (Mt 5:14–19*)
Dorotheos (b Tyre), 6 June (Lk 9:1–6)
Earthquake, 14 December; (of 450) 26 January; 25 September (Lk 8:22–25 / Mt 8:23–27 / Lk 8:22–25)
Eirenaios and Oros and Horopsa [Oropsa], 23 August (Lk 21:12–19)
Eirenarchos, 29 November (Lk 5:1–11)
Eirene, 4 May (Mt 11:27–30)
Eleutherios, 15 December (Lk 12:32–40)
Elijah and Elisha, 21 [=20] July ([Mt 17:1–8]9)
Elisha, 14 June, 21 [=20] July (Mt 23:27–39)
Ephrem (the Syrian), 28 January (Lk 6:17–23)
Epiphanios of Cyprus, 12 May (Mt 5:14–19*)
Ermolaos [Hermolaos], 26 July (Lk 8:16–21)
Eudokia, 4 August (Mt 25:1–13)
Eudokia (of Samaria), 1 March (Mt 11:27–30)
Eudokimos, 31 July (Lk 8:16–21)
Eudoxios comps, 6 September (Mk 12:28–38a)

Eulampios and Eulampia, 11 [=10] October (Mk 13:9–13)

Eumenios (b Gortyna), 18 September (Mt 5:42–48)

Euphemia [as daughter ?] of Paneuphemos, 16 September; and of the mountain, 11 July (Lk 7:36–50 / Mt 25:1–13)

Euphrosyne, 24 August (Mt 11:27–30)

Euplos, 10 [=11] August (Lk 10:19–21)

Eupraxia and Olympias, 25 July (Mt 25:1–13)

Eupsychios, 8 [=9] April (Lk 10:19–21)

Eusebios (b Samosata), 23 June (Lk 6:17–23)

Eusignios, 5 August (Mk 8:34–9:1)

Eustathios, ab Antioch, 5 June (Mt 5:14–19*)

Eustathios, comps, 20 September (Lk 21:12–19)

Eustratios, 13 December (Lk 21:12–19)

Euthymios, 20 January (Mt 11:27–30)

Eutychios, ab Cple, 6 April (Jn 10:9–16)

Ezekiel, 3 April, 22 [=21] July (Mt 23:27–39 / Lk 10:16–21)

Ezekiel, Zachariah, and Daniel, 3 April (Mt 23:27–39)

Fathers of Raithou: cf. Abbots . . .

Fathers of Saint Sabbas, 20 March (Lk 6:17–23)

Feast of Lights, 5 January (Lk 3:1–18)

Fevronia, 25 June (Mt 25:1–13)

Fire (of 461), 1 September (Lk 4:16–22a)

Forerunner: cf. John the Baptist

Galaktion and Episteme, 5 November (Lk 5:1–11)

George, 22 [=23] April (Jn 15:17–16:2)

George of Malaios, 5 April (Mk 8:34–9:1)

George, b Mytelene, 7 April (no reading)

Gerasimos, 6 [=7] March (Mt 5:14–19*)

Germanos, ab Cple, 12 May (Mt 5:14–19*)

Golindouch, 12 July (Mt 23:27–39)

Gordos [Gordios], 3 January (Mt 23:27–39)

Gregory (of Agrigentum), 23 November (Mt 24:42–47)

Gregory (the Illuminator), 30 September (Mt 24:42–47)

Gregory the Theologian (of Nazianzus), 25 January (Lk 6:17–23)

Gregory of Nyssa, 10 January (Lk 6:17–23)

Gregory (the Wonderworker), 17 November (Mt 10:1, 5–8)

Habakkuk, [2] December (Lk 13:31–35)

Haggai, 16 December (Lk 5:1–11)

Hermeias, 31 May (Jn 15:9–16)

Hermione, 4 September (Mt 25:1–13)

Hermolaos: cf. Ermolaos

Hermylos and Stratonikos, 13 January (Jn 15:17–16:2)

Hierotheos, 4 October (Mt 25:1–13*)

Hilarion, 21 October (Lk 6:17–23)

Hilarion: cf. Proklos

Hilarion (abbot of Pelekete), 28 March (Mt 13:44–54a)

Hippolytos, b Rome, 30 January (Jn 12:19–36)

Holy Children (killed at Bethlehem by Herod), 29 December (Mt 2:13–18)

Holy Confessors, 15 November (reference ambiguous)

Holy Cross, adoration of the wood of, [10], 11, 12, 13 September; elevation, 14 September; sign of in the heavens, 6 [=7] May (Jn 11:47–54 / Jn 8:21–30 / Jn 8:31–42a / Jn 12:25–36 / Jn 19:6, 9b–11a, 13–20, 25b–26a, 30b–35a / Jn 10:9–6)

Holy Fathers of Saint Sabbas, 20 March (Lk 6:17–23)

Hosea, 17 October (Lk 13:31–35)

Hsychios, priest, 4 [=5] March (Mt 5:14–19*)

Hyakinthos and Theodotos, 3 July (Jn 15:17–16:2)

Hypatios, b Gangra, 28 June (Jn 15:17–16:2)

Iason, 27 [=28] April (Lk 9:1–6)

Ignatios (Theophoros), 20 December; translation of relics, 29 January (Mk 9:33–41 / ibid.)

Innocents: cf. Holy Children . . .

Ioannikios, 4 November (Mt 11:27–30)

Irenaeus, 31 December (Mt 15:14–19)

Irene: cf. Eirene

Isaac, of the Dalmatos (monastery), 30 May, 3 August (Lk 6:17–23 / Lk 8:16–21)

Isaiah, 9 May (Jn 12:36–47)

Isauros, Eustathios, Polycarp, and Evangelos, 7 July (Jn 12:19–36)

Isidore (of Pelusiota), 4 February (Lk 6:17–23)

James (anchorite), 10 [=9] October (Lk 5:1–11)

James (a, son of Joseph), 23 October (Mt 10:16–22)

James, a, brother of (John) the Theologian, 30 April (Lk 5:1–11)

James (the Persian), 26 November (Jn 15:9–16)

Jeremiah, 1 May (Mt 16:13–19*)

Joachim and Anne, 9 September (Lk 8:16–21)

Job, 6 May (no reading)

Joel, 19 October (Mt 23:27–39)

John the Almsgiver, 10 November (Lk 6:17–23)

John the Baptist, 7 January; beheading, 29 August; birth, 25 June; conception, 23 September; discovery of head, 24 February (Jn 1:29–34 / Mk 6:14–30 / Mt 25:1–13 / ibid. / Mt 11:2–14)

John Chrysostom, 27 January (no reading)
John Climacus, 30 March (Mt 11:27–30)
John the Evangelist, 6 [=8] May; death, 26 September (Jn 19:25–27, 21:24, 25 / Jn 21:14–25)
John the Faster, 19 [=21?] February (Jn 10:9–16)
John (the Faster) and Paul the Younger, 31 August, 2 September (Jn 15:9–16 / ibid.)
John, ab Jerusalem, 29 March (Jn 10:9–16)
John of Palaiolauritos, 17 [=18] April (Mt 13:44–54a)
John of Rouphinianais, 15 March (Mt 5:14–19*)
John Stratiotes, 31 July (Mt 7:12–21)
Jonah, 21 September (Lk 11:29–33)
Joseph the Hymnographer, 4 April (Jn 3:22–33*)
Julian and Basilissa, 8 January (no reading)
Julian of Ankyra, 12 September (Jn 15:17–16:2)
Juliane, 21 December (Lk 7:36–50)
Justin, 1 June (Jn 12:19–36)
Justin comps, 22 June (Lk 7:36–50)
Kalinikos, 29 July (Lk 21:12–19)
Kalistratos, 27 September (Jn 15:17–16:2)
Karpos, one of the Sixty, 28 May (Jn 12:19–36)
Karpos and Papyllos, 13 October (Mt 7:12–21)
Keruakos and Ioulita, 16 [=15] July (Mt 17:24–18:4)
Kikilia, 21 November (Mt 5:24–34)
Kodratos, 10 March (Lk 6:17–23)
Konon, 4 [=5] March (Jn 15:9–16)
Kosmas and Damian, 1 November; cf. also Anargyroi (Mt 10:1, 5–8)
Kosmas of Chalcedon, 16 [=17] April (Mt 5:14–19*)
Kriskentios and Theodore [Theodosios], 12 [=13] April (Mt 10:32, 33, 37, 38, 19:27–30)
Kyriakos (ab Cple), 30 October (no reading)
Kyriakos (Palestinian anchorite), 29 September (Lk 6:17–23)
Kyros and John, 31 January (Mt 10:1, 5–8)
Lawrence, 9 [=10] August (Jn 15:17–16:2)
Lazarus, his resurrection, 17 March (Mt 11:27–30)
Leo, pope of Rome, 16 [=18] February (Jn 10:9–16)
Leonides, Nikodemos comps, 14 [=15] April (Mt 10:32, 33, 37, 38, 19:27–30)
Leontios comps, 17 [=18] June (Jn 15:17–16:2)
Longinos, 16 October (Jn 19:25–37)
Loukillianos, 3 June (Lk 10:19–21)
Luke, 18 October (Lk 10:16–21)
Lukianos (b Antioch), 15 October (Jn 10:9–16)
Macabees, 1 August (Lk 8:41–56)
Malachi, 3 January (Mt 23:27–39)
Malachios, 20 March (Lk 6:17–23)

Mamas, 2 September (Jn 15:9–16)
Manuel, Sabel, and Ishmael, 16 [=17] June (Jn 15:17–16:2)
Marina, 18 [=17] July (Mt 25:1–13)
Marinos, 17 March (Mt 11:27–30)
Mark, 24 [=25] April (no reading)
Markellos, 30 December (Lk 12:32–40)
Markelos and his Sixty Disciples, 13 [=14] August (Lk 12:32–40)
Markianos and Martyrios, 25 October (Lk 12:2–12)
Markos, 6 [=7] March (Jn 15:9–16*)
Martinianos, 12 [=13] February (Lk 6:17–23)
Martyrs of Chalcedon, 23 [=24] April (Lk 9:1–6)
Martyrs, Ten of Crete, 23 December (Mt 10:16–22)
Martyrs, Twenty-two, 28 [=29] April (Lk 9:1–6)
Martyrs, Twenty-nine of Cyzicus, 28 [=29] April (Lk 9:1–6)
Martyrs, Thirty-three (of Melitene), 7 November (Mt 10:16–22)
Martyrs, Forty of Sebaste, [9] March (Mt 20:1–16)
Martyrs, Forty-two, 5 [=6] March (Mt 20:1–16)
Martyrs, Forty-five of Nikopolis, 10 July (Jn 15:17–16:2)
Mary of Egypt, 1 April (Mt 5:14–19)
Matrona, 9 November (Mk 13:9–13*)
Matrona of Thessalonika, 27 March (Mt 5:14–19*)
Matthew, a, 16 November (Mt 9:9–13)
Matthew, a, and Evangelist, 8 [=9?] August (Mt 10:1, 5–8)
Maximos the Confessor, 21 January; 12 [=13] August (Lk 8:22–25 / ibid.)
Meletios, 24 May (Jn 14:21–24)
Meletios, ab Antioch, 11 [=12] February (Mt 5:14–19*)
Memnon, 28 [=29] April (Lk 9:1–6)
Menander and Neophytos, 31 March (Jn 3:22–33*)
Menas, Hermogenes, and Egraphos, 11 [=10] December (Mt 10:37–11:1)
Menas and companions, 11 November (Jn 15:17–16:2)
Menodora, Metrodora, and Nymphodora, [10] September (Mt 25:1–13)
Metrophanes, ab Cple, 4 June (Jn 10:9–16)
Mokios and Pachomios, 11 May (Jn 15:17–16:2)
Moses (the Ethiopian), 28 August (Mt 11:27–30)
Myron, 17 August (Mt 10:16–22)
Nahum, 1 December (Mt 23:27–39)
Nazarios comps, 14 October (Jn 15:17–16:2)
Nektarios comps, 11 October (Mt 5:14–19)

Neophytos, 31 March (Jn 3:22–33)
Nestor, 27 October (Mk 2:14–17)
Nikephoros, ab Cple, 2 June; 13 March (Jn 10:9–16 / ibid.)
Niketas, 15 September (Mt 10:16–22)
Nikolaos, 6 December (Mt 11:27–30)
Nikon and his two hundred disciples, 24 March (Lk 9:1–6)
Onesimos, Timothy, and Paphnoutios, 14 [=15] February (Lk 9:1–6)
Onouphrios, 12 June (Lk 6:17–23)
Pachomios, 11, 14 May (Jn 15:17–16:2 / no reading)
Pankratios, (b) of Taormina, 9 July (Mt 7:12–21)
Panteleimon, 27 July (Jn 15:17–16:2)
Paphnoutios, 19 [=20] April (Lk 5:1–11)
Parthenios, b Lampsakos, 6 February (Mt 5:14–19*)
Patermouthios and Kopres, 8 [=9] April (Lk 10:19–21)
Paul the Confessor, 6 November (Lk 8:22–25)
Paul the Younger: cf. Alexander, and John the Faster
Paul and Julian, 3 [=4?] March (no reading)
Pelagia, 8 October (Jn 8:1–11)
Pelagia the Virgin, 5 May (Mt 10:37–11:1)
Peter: cf. Chains of Peter
Peter and Paul, 29 June (Mt 16:13–19)
Perouzoe and her children, 3 May (Mk 13:9–13)
Philemon comps, 5 July (Mt 7:12–21)
Philip, 14 November (Lk 12:2–12)
Phloros, 18 December (Mt 10:32, 33, 37, 38, 19:27–30)
Phloros and Hilarion, 18 August (Jn 10:9–16)
Phokas, 22 September, 23 [=22] July (Mt 25:1–13 / Lk 10:19–21)
Photios and Aniketos, 11 [=12] August (Lk 21:12–19)A
Phourtounatos, 9 June (Lk 10:16–21)
Pionios, 11 March (Jn 10:9–16)
Platon, 18 November (Jn 15:17–16:2)
Poimenos, 28 August (Mt 11:27–30)
Polycarp (b Smyrna), 21 [=23] February (Jn 12:19–36)
Polyeuktos, 9 January (Jn 15:17–16:2)
Porphyrios (b Gaza), 26 February (Mt 5:14–19*)
Probos, Tarachos, and Andronikos, 12 October (Lk 21:12–19)
Procession to the Campus, 25 September (Lk 8:22–25)
Procession to the Exakionion, 26 January (Mt 8:23–27)

Prochoros, Nikanor, and Parmenas, 28 July (Lk 9:1–6)
Prodrome /-os: cf. John the Baptist
Proklos, 22 November (Mt 5:14–19)
Proklos and Hilarion, 12 July (no reading)
Prokopios, 8 July (Lk 6:17–19)
Prokopios the Decapolite, 27 February (Mt 10:1. 5–8)
Raising of Lazarus: cf. Lazarus
Romanos and the youths, 18 [=20] February (Lk 10:19–21*)
Sabbas, 5 December, 27 August (Jn 15:9–16* / ibid.)
Sabbas the Goth, 14 [=15] April (Mt 10:32, 33, 37, 38, 19:27–30)
Sabbas Stratelates, 23 [=24] April (Lk 9:1–6)
Saint Sabbas: cf. Fathers of . . .
Sampson Xenodochos, 27 June (Lk 12:32–40)
Sarapion, 13 July (Jn 15:17–16:2)
Sergios and Bakchos, 7 October (Lk 21:12–19)
Sign of the Cross in the heavens: cf. Holy Cross
Silatila and Soulianos, Kriskentios, Epainetos, and Andronikos, 30 July (Lk 9:1–6)
Silvester (bishop of Rome), 2 January (Jn 10:9–16)
Simon Zelotes, 10 May (Lk 5:1–11*)
Sisoes the Great, 7 July (Mt 7:12–21)
Sophia, Pistes, Elpes, and Agape, 17 September (Mt 25:1–13)
Sophronios (ab Jerusalem), 10 March (Lk 6:17–23)
Sosthenos, 8 December (Mt 25:1–13)
Sozon, 7 September (Jn 15:17–16:2)
Spyridon, 13 [=12] December (Lk 11:1–13)
Stephen, 12 January (Lk 6:17–23)
Stephen Protomartyr, 27 December; discovery of relics, 2 August (Mt 21:33–42 / Mt 2:13–23)
Stephen (the Younger), 28 November (Mt 10:37–11:1)
Stephen Sabaites, 14 [=13] July (Lk 6:17–23)
Symeon, 3 February (Lk 2:22–38)
Symeon the Fool, 22 [=21] July (Lk 6:17–23)
Symeon of Jerusalem, 26 [=27] April (Mk 8:34–9:1)
Symeon of the Marvelous Mountain, 23 May (Lk 4:16–22a)
Symeon Stylites, 1 September; (archimandrite) of Mandra, 26 July (Lk 4:16–22a / Lk 8:16–21)
Syschemonos, b Lampsakos, 16 March (Jn 10:1–10)
Tarasios (ab Cple), 25 February (Jn 10:9–16)
Terentios comps, 9 [=10] April (Mt 10:32, 33, 37, 38, 19:27–30)
Thaddeus, 20 August, [30] August (Mt 10:1, 5–8 / Lk 10:16–21)

The New York Cruciform Lectionary

Thalelaios, 17 May (Jn 15:9–16)

Thekla, 24 September (Mt 25:1–13)

Theodora, 11 September (Jn 8:1–11)

Theodora, 29 May (Mt 25:1–13)

Theodore, b Cple, 28 December (Jn 10:9–16)

Theodore of Cyrene and Donatos, 4 July (Mt 5:14–19*)

Theodore of Perge, Pamphylia, 18 [=19] April (Jn 15:9–16)

Theodore the Sanctified, 14 May (no reading)

Theodore of Sikeon, 21 [=22] April (no reading)

Theodore Stratelates, 7 February; 8 June (Lk 10:19–21)

Theodore Tiron, 15 [=17] February (Jn 1:44–52)

Theodore of Trichina, 20 [=21] April (Mk 8:34–9:1)

Theodosia, 20 [=19] July (Mt 15:21–28)

Theodosios, 11 January (Lk 6:17–23)

Theodotos, 29 July (Lk 21:12–19)

Theodotos, b Ankyra, 19 January; 7 June (Lk 6:17–23 / Lk 9:1–6)

Theodotos, b Kyrenia, 2 March (Lk 21:12–19)

Theodoulos and Agathapous, 4 April (Jn 3:22–33)

Theophanes (the Confessor), 12 March (Lk 6:17–23)

Theophanies, 6 January (Mk 1:9–11 / Mt 3:13–17)

Theophylact, b Nicomedia, 7 [=8] March (Lk 8:22–25)

Theotokos: cf. Virgin

Therapon, 28 May

Thomas, a, 6 October (Jn 20:19–31)

Thomas, p, b Cple, 20 [=22] February, 22 March (Mt 5:14–19* / Mt 13:44–54a)

Thomas of Malaios, 6 July (Lk 6:17–23)

Three Holy Youths of Babylon, 17 December (Lk 11:43–50a)

Thyrsos, 14 December (Lk 8:22–25)

Timothy, a, 22 January (Jn 1:1–17)

Timothy, m, 17 [=19] February (Lk 6:17–23)

Timothy, b Prouse, 10 June (Lk 6:17–23)

Titus (the Wonderworker), 2 April (Mt 10:1, 5–8)

Titus (of Gortyna), 25 August (Mt 5:14–19*)

Trophimos, 19 September (Mt 10:16–22)

Tryphon, 1 February (Lk 10:19–21)

Twelve Apostles, 30 June (Mt 9:36–10:8)

Tychon, 15 June (Mt 23:27–39)

Vikentios (deacon?), 24 January (Jn 10:9–16)

Virgin (Mary), [26] December; birth, 8 September; presentation in temple, 20 November; annunciation to, 25 March; relic in the Blachernae, 2 July; relic in the Chalke, 31 August; death, 15 August (Mt 2:13–23 / Lk 1:39–49, 56; Lk 10:38–42, 11:27–28 / ibid. / Lk 1:24–38 / Lk 1:39–49, 56; Lk 10:38–42, 11:27–28 / ibid.)

Zachariah (pr), 5 September, 8 February, 3 April, 15 May (all Mt 23:27–39)

Zosimos, Chrysanthios, and Dareia, 4 January (Lk 21:12–19)

Biblical Passages Reproduced or Cited (S/ denotes a reading found in the synaxarion.)

Psalms

18:1a, 5a: Peter and Paul, morning.

28:1a, 3a: Holy Theophanies (morning).

44:11a, 18a: Birth of the Virgin, morning.

71:6a, 7a: Virgin, morning.

88:1b, 13b: Transfiguration of Christ, morning.

131:1a, 17a: Birth of John the Baptist, morning.

Matthew

1:1–25: Sunday before Christ's birth.

1:18–25; 2:1–2:[11] Christ's birth, morning service.

---

11. I use the reading in L(Greg) to fix the first part of the reading.

2:13–18: (Holy) Children (killed at Bethlehem by Herod).

2:13–23: Discovery of the relics of Stephen Protomartyr; Virgin.

3:1–11: Saturday before Feast of Lights.

3:13–17: Holy Theophanies, liturgy.

4:1–11: Saturday after Feast of Lights.

4:12–17: Sunday after Feast of Lights.

4:25–5:13: Akakios, b Melitene.

5:14–19: Agapios pope of Rome; pts (of Cple) Alexander, John and Paul the Younger; a Ananias; Andrew of Crete; Athanasios, b Alexandria; Benedict, b Rome; Cyril b Jerusalem; Epiphanios of Cyprus; Eustathios, ab Antioch; Gerasimos; Germanos, ab Cple; Hsychios, priest; Irenaeus; pts John the Faster and Paul the Younger; John of Rouphinianais; Kosmas of Chalcedon; Nektarios comps; Markos; Mary of Egypt; Matrona of Thessalonika; Meletios, ab of Antioch; Parthenios, b Lampsakos; Porphyrios (b Gaza); Proklos; Theodore of Cyrene and Donatos; Thomas, pt (Cple); a Titus of Gortyna.

5:42–48: Eumenos (b Gortyna).

7:12–21: m Aetios; John Stratiotes; Karpos and Papyllos; hm Pankratios (b) of Taormina; Philemon comps; Sisoes the Great.

8:23–27: Demetrios; earthquake; procession to Exakionion.

S/9:9–13: a Matthew.

9:36–10:8: Twelve Apostles.

10:1, 5–8: Anargyroi; m Eirene; Gregory (the Wonderworker); Kosmas and Damian; Kyros and John, ww; a Matthew; Prokopios the Decapolite; a Thaddeus; Titus, ww; Tychon, ww.

10:16–22: a James (son of Joseph); m Myron; m Niketas; Ten Martyrs of Crete; Thirty-three Martyrs (of Melitene); Trophimos.

S/10:32, 33, 37, 38, 19:27–30 (= Sunday of All Saints): Arethas; mm Kriskentios and Theodore; Phloros; Sabbas the Goth; Leonides, Nikodemos comps; m Terentios comps.

S/10:37–11:1: mm Menas, Hermogenes, and Egraphos; Pelagia the Virgin; Saturday before Adoration of Venerable Wood; Stephen (the Younger).

11:2–14: Discovery of the Head of John the Baptist, liturgy.

11:27–30: Alexios, man of God; Alypios; Basil the Confessor; Chariton; Clement (of Rome); Daniel (the Stylite); Eirene; Eudokia (of Samaria); m Euphrosyne; Euthymios; Ioannikios; John Climacus; Marinos; Moses (the Ethiopian); Nikolaos; Poimenos; Raising of Lazarus.

12:15b–21: Saturday after Christ's Nativity.

13:44–54a: m Antipas (b Pergamon); hm Basil, priest; Dionysios (the Areopagite); Hilarion (abbot of Pelekete); John of Palaiolauritos; Thomas b (Cple).

S/15:21–28: m Theodosia.

16:13–18: [Consecration of Saint Sophia.]

16:13–19: pr Jeremiah; aa Peter and Paul, liturgy.

17:[1–]9: Elijah and Elisha; Transfiguration of Christ, liturgy.

S/17:24–18:1: m Bassa comps; mm Keruakos and Ioulita.

19:23–30: Akindynos comps.

20:1–16: Forty Martyrs of Sebaste; Forty-two Martyrs.

S/21:33–42: Stephen Protomartyr.

23:27–39: pr Daniel; pr Elisha; pr Ezekiel; prr Ezekiel, Zachariah and Daniel; Gordos; pr Joel; pr Malachi; pr Nahum; Tychon; pr Zachariah.

24:42–47: Gregory (of Agrigentum); Gregory (the Illuminator) of Greater Armenia.

S/25:1–13: m Agathe; m Agrippine; Akylina; Anastasia; conception and birth of John the Baptist; m Eudokia; m Euphemia; Eupraxia and Olympias; m Fevronia; m Hermione; Hierotheos; m Marina; mm Menodora, Metrodora, Nymphodora; Phokas; Sophia, Pistes, Elpes, and Agape; a Sosthenos; Thekla; m Theodora.

MARK

1:1–8: Sunday before Feast of Lights.

1:9–11: Holy Theophanies.

S/2:14–17: Nestor.

S/2:23–3:5: Clement (b Ankyra); death of John the Baptist.

5:24–34: m Barbara; Kikilia.

6:14–30: Beheading of John the Baptist.

S/8:34–9:1: Aimilianos (b Cyzicus); Artemios; Auxentios; Boniface; Domitios; m Eusignios; George of Malaios; Sunday following Elevation (of the Holy Cross); Symeon of Jerusalem, kinsman of the Lord; Theodore of Trichina.

9:33–41: Ignatios Theophoros; Ignatios, translation of relics.

11:22–26, Mt 7:7–8: Conception of Saint Anne.

12:28–38a: m Eudoxios comps.

13:9–13: Eulampios and Eulampia; Matrona; Perouzoe and her children.

S/15:43–16:8: Alexander of Pydna.

LUKE

1:1–25, 57–68, 76, 80: Birth, and Conception of John the Baptist.

1:39–49, 56: Birth of the Virgin, morning; relic of Virgin at Blachernae.

1:39–49, 56, 2:22–38: Presentation of Christ, morning.

1:39–49, 56, 2:22–40: Presentation of Christ, liturgy.

2:1–20: Evening before Christ's birth.

2:20–21, 40–52: Circumcision of Christ.

3:1–18: Feast of Lights.

4:16–22a: Beginning of the indiction; Fire (of 461); Symeon of the Marvelous Mountain; Symeon Stylites.

S/5:1–11: Eirenarchos; Galaktion and Episteme; pr Haggai; James (anchorite); a James, brother of (John) the Theologian; hm Paphnoutios; aa Peter and Paul; a Simon Zelotes.

6:17–23: Abramios (anchorite); Anthony (Abbot); Arsenios; Athanasios and Cyril, return from exile; David of Thessalonika; Destruction of fathers at Saint Sabbas; Ephrem (the Syrian); Eusebios (b Samosata); Gregory the Theologian (of Nazianzus); Gregory b Nyssa; Hilarion; Isaac of the Dalmatos (monastery); Isidore (of Pelusiota); John the Almsgiver; Kodratos; Kyriakos (anchorite); Malachios; Martinianos; Onouphrios; Sophronios (ab Jerusalem); Stephen; Stephen

Sabaites; Symeon the Fool; Theodosios; Theophanes (the Confessor); Thomas of Malaios; m Timothy; Timothy, b Prousa.

6:17–19, 9:1–2, 10:16–21: Aimelianos; m Prokopios.

6:20–27, 10:23–24, 11:33: Blank in June.

7:36–50: Christina; Euphemia; Juliane; m Justin comps.

S/8:16–21: Death of Saint Anne; hm Ermolaos; Eudokimos; Isaac of the Dalmatos (monastery?); Joachim and Anne; Symeon (Stylites, archimandrite) of Mandra.

8:22–25: cfs Basil, b Pareios; earthquake, 25 September, 14 December; cfs Maximos; Maximos the Confessor; Paul the Confessor; Procession to Campus; Theophylact, b Nicomedia; Thyrsos.

8:41–56: Macabees.

S/9:1–6: aa Bartholomew and Barnabas; Domna [28 October]; hm Dorotheos (b Tyre); a Iason; Martyrs of Chalcedon; m Memnon; Nikon and his two hundred Disciples; aa Onesimos, Timothy, and Paphnoutios; aa Prochoros, Nikanor and Parmenas; m Sabbas Stratelates; aa Silatila and Soulianos, Kriskentios, Epainetos, and Andronikos; m Theodotos, b Ankyra; Twenty-two Martyrs; Twenty-nine Martyrs of Cyzicus.

9:28–[36]: Transfiguration of Christ, morning.

10:16–21: a Akylas; Archangel Gabriel; Archangel Michael at Chonae; Archangels; Aristarchos, Podes and Trophemos; Cyril of Alexandria; Ezekiel; a Luke; a Phourtounatos; a Thaddeus.

S/10:19–21: Babylas and children; Blaise (b Sebaste); Chrysanthos and Dareia; m Euplos; m Eupsychios; m Loukillianos; Patermouthios and Kopres; hm Phokas; Romanos and youths; Theodore Stratelates; Tryphon.

10:38–42, 11:27–28: Birth of the Virgin, liturgy; Death of the Virgin; Entrance of the Virgin in the Temple; Virgin.

11:1–13: Spyridon.

11:29–33: pr Jonah.

11:43–50a: Three Youths of Babylon.

12:2–12: mm Adrianos and Natalia; Markianos and Martyrios; a Philip.

S/12:32–40: Abbots (of Raithou); Averkios; Eleutherios; Markellos; Markelos and his Sixty Disciples; Sampson Xenodochos.

S/13:10–17: m Charitine.

S/13:19–29: Saturday before Christ's birth.

13:31–35: pr Abdias; pr Habakkuk; pr Hosea.

S/19:1–10: Deposition of the relic of the Virgin in Chalke.

S/20:46–21:4: m Christina.

21:12–19: pr Abdias; m Basiliskos comps; Chrysanthos and Dareia; mm Eirenaios and Oros and Horopsa; Eustathios comps; Eustratios; m Kalinikos; mm Photios and Aniketos; Probos, Tarachios, and Andronikos; Sergios and Bakchos; Theodotos; Theodotos, b Kyrenia; Zosimos.

John

S/1:1–17: Anastasios (the Persian); a Timothy.

1:29–34: John the Baptist.

S/1:35–52: a Andrew.

S/1:44–52: Theodore Tiron.

3:13–17: Sunday before Adoration (of the Venerable Wood).

S/3:22–33: Joseph the Hymnographer; Menander and Neophytos; Neophytos; Theodoulos and Agathapous.

8:1–11: Pelagia; Theodora (of Alexandria).

S/8:21–30: Adoration of the Venerable Wood; Saturday following the Elevation of (the Holy Cross).

S/8:31–42: Adoration of the Venerable Wood.

10:1–10: 12 November, blank; Syschemonos, b Lampsakos.

10:9–16: Akepsimas, Aeithalas, and Joseph; Ambrose; Andrew Stratelates; hm Anthemios, b Nikomedia; Appearance of the Cross in the heavens; m Charlampos; Cyprian; Diomedes; Eutychios, ab Cple; John, ab Jerusalem; John the Faster; Leo, pope of Rome; Lukianos (b Antioch); Metrophanes, ab Cple; Nikephoros b, ab Cple; mm Phloros and Hilarion; hm Pionios; Sabbas; Silvester (bishop of Rome); Tarasios (ab Cple); Theodore b Cple; m Vikentios (deacon?).

S/11:47–54: Adoration of Holy Wood.

S/12:19–36: Hippolytos, b Rome; mm Isauros, Eustathios, Polycarp and Evangelos; m Justin; a Karpos, one of the Sixty; Polycarp (b Smyrna); m Therapon.

12:25–36b: Adoration of the Venerable Wood, liturgy.

12:28b–36: Adoration of the Venerable Wood, morning.

S/12:28b–50(?):[12] Elevation of the Holy Cross, morning.

S/12:36–47: p Isaiah.

14:21–24: m Meletios.

S/15:9–16: m Christopher; m Hermeias; James (the Persian); Konon; Mamas; Markos; Sabbas; m Thalelaios; m Theodore of Perge.

S/15:17–16:2: m Agathonikos; m Akakios; a Andronikos; m Anthenogenes comps; mm Babylas and youths; hm Basil, b Amaseia; Forty-five Martyrs of Nikopolis; m George; Hermylos and Stratonikos; mm Hyakinthos and Theodotos; m Hypatios, b Gangra; m Julian of Ankyra; Kalistratos; m Lawrence; m Leontios comps; mm Manuel, Sabel and Ishmael; Menas comps; hmm Mokios and Pachomios; Nazarios comps; Pachomios; m Panteleimon; Platon; m Poleuktos; m Sarapion; m Sozon.

19:6, 9b–11a, 13–20, 25b–26a, 30b–35a: Elevation of the Holy Cross, liturgy.

19:25–27; 21:24, 25: John the Evangelist.

S/19:25–37: Longinos.

S/20:19–31: a Thomas.

S/21:14–25: Chains of Saint Peter; death of John the Evangelist.

Although I reproduce and index the menologion to make it available for comparative study, several comments on the calendar can be offered. I begin with the specific. The scribe wrote out a total of sixty-two Gospel passages, and of them he incorrectly identified the author a full ten times, nearly one out of every six instances. The script does not suggest amateur or low-quality workmanship. The scribe was a man whom we might characterize as a professional, although we must recognize that this category has limited validity; priests and readers who used manuscripts in church were

---

12. I use tables in L(Greg) to fix the reading.

often the ones who copied them.¹³ Perhaps the errors were in the source. Even if they were already present, a moment's reflection would have revealed some of the mistakes, but the scribe rarely seems to have paused for reflection. The errors in numbering are also troublesome. Some, like those on 9 and 10 October, look like simple lapses of attention and do not greatly mar the calendar. Far more serious are the entire runs of days out of sequence in February, April, and August. A saint was skipped, or two were erroneously combined in a single service, and the rest of the month's readings were thrown out of order. On the face of it, the scribe appears to have been careless.

The saints' names may provide further insight into the scribe's attitudes and assumptions. In transcribing names he almost never deviated from contemporary usage. Double consonants (Kallinikos-Kalinikos, Kallistratos-Kalistratos, Markellos-Markelos, Palyllos-Papylos, Sabbas-Sabas) and occasionally errant breathing marks (Horopsa-Oropsa, Hermolaos-Ermolaos) may be discounted as significant. His inclusion of the martyr Domna on 28 October is unique and so is open to question. For this same day the synaxarion gives Domninos of Thessalonika. Perhaps Domna is the result of a moment of distraction, after looking away from the source; it is, however, a mistake that required shifting gender in three words in addition to the name. His assignment of Phloros and Hilarion on 18 August goes against tradition, which gives Phloros and Lauros on this day; the scribe possibly thought of the pair Proklos and Hilarion that he had just written for 12 July. The list of Paul's disciples at Corinth proves to be more difficult; Silas, Silouanos, Kriskentios, Epainetos, and Andronikos became Silatila and Soulianos, Kriskentios, and so on. The Silouanos (from the Latin Silvanus) to Soulianos transformation is simple, but how Silas became the otherwise totally unknown Silatila defies logic, for it presents more than a simple question of doubt arising from the tendency to abbreviate the ends of words (Charalampos, Charalampios, Charalampes). Although the utility of such lists may be founded upon complete accuracy, the questionable spellings do not seem particularly troublesome. Occasionally saints with similar names were celebrated on the same day. Thus 8 December finds the Church recognizing Sophonios, bishop of Jerusalem; Sophronios, bishop of Constantia; and Sositheos. The lists of variant readings and spellings in the Saint Sophia Typikon and the Constantinopolitan Synaxarion occasionally show what look like the results of confusion arising from this tendency to form groups. The New York scribe's version, Sosthenos, cannot be found in BHG but is paralleled by the reading for the day in the lectionary table assembled by Colwell and Riddle. It may turn out that other manuscripts read Domnina on 28 October.

If there is a remarkable trait revealed by the calendar of the New York Lectionary, it is found in the simplification of lists and identifying tags. Some saints are members of recognized groups: Paul's disciples at Corinth or others like Akepsimas, Aeithalas, and Joseph (3 November). The scribe often wrote only the first name of such groups followed by "and companions." This phrase is perfectly acceptable in itself, but it is used frequently when other sources list all the names (for example, at 31 January, 24 May, 17 June, 26 July, 2 and 14 October, and others). In addition, the scribe often omits information, such as ecclesiastical rank or city of birth or death, that would conclusively identify the saint of the day; names of all the members of a group fall into the category of identifying information. The calendar is stripped down to its essentials. Perhaps the scribe assumed that his audience had sufficient knowledge to require little more than a few simple clues. Apart from assuming a body of common knowledge, the scribe may have counted on information

---

13. For examples of such activity, see chapter II, notes 19–21.

The New York Cruciform Lectionary

being available from other sources. In the eleventh and twelfth centuries, calendar icons became popular; one located in a church would have provided information to those about to hear the day's lesson. A reading taken from a synaxarion or menologion (by which terms I refer to separate liturgical manuals) also would have given valuable information. We are, nevertheless, presented with a problem by the calendar in all its aspects.

The following is quite conceivable. The deacon got up and identified the reading for the day as from Matthew and the saint's name; he then proceeded to sing a passage from John that was assigned as the lesson for a different day. If we change places, moving from a place in the congregation to the role of deacon, some further difficulties in the use of the manuscript arise. The menologion relies heavily on references to Gospel passages already written in full; occasionally the passage cited had not yet been copied when the reference was made. The cross-references are not as innocent as they appear. Some, which are references to references, lead the reader on a chase throughout the manuscript. The month of December, for instance, contains twenty-four cross-references, of which fourteen are to other days in the menologion. Nine are direct; the reader finds the pericope on the first try. In three cases he is led to another reference; one has him hunting through two more references before finding the passage. Finally, one reference is incorrect because it refers to a misnumbered passage. The references for the anchorite Abramios, remembered on 29 October, are particularly frustrating. The first one takes the reader to 10 January, where he is led back to 29 September and then on to 21 October, just a page above the original citation, where the reading is given in full. Partway through the reading for the service held on 29 June is a note, End of Consecration (reading), that allowed the passage to be used on two different occasions requiring pericopes of slightly varying length. The commemoration to which the note refers, the consecration of Saint Sophia, was celebrated on 23 December, but no reference on the twenty-third directs the user to turn back to 29 June. There are also references to the lessons for the martyrs (8 January, 3 March, 13 May) and for the blessed (14 May), lessons that were sometimes written at the end of the menologion. Of these catchall readings, the scribe reproduced only the pericope for the prophets; the other two are dead-ends as written. Again, some degree of knowledge is required to sort out what the scribe has written in order to use the manuscript correctly. On the face of it, the lectionary exists to reduce a complex set of procedures to a matter of turning successive pages. But time and again the execution of the manuscript denies the ideal of utility. What might give us even greater pause is the absence of corrections or additions—which could have been simply and discreetly added. Can there be some significance to this, especially since the Gospel text shows signs of correction?

Kurt Weitzmann has written that the Gospel lectionary was used in procession and then placed on the altar as a book so holy that "in many instances" it was never opened, even to provide the day's reading.[14] For those times in Byzantine history when the Incarnation was of deepest concern, the Gospel lectionary (or Gospel book) might have provided an objective analogy for the understanding of Christ's physical reality; under such circumstances the concern for utility could have been transcended by an acutely felt theological issue. These times are hundreds of years before the period of the New York Lectionary; moreover, by the ninth century images like the Virgin holding

---

14. "The Narrative and Liturgical Gospel Illustrations," *Studies*, 248.

the Child had already begun to provide a more direct analogy for the concept of the Incarnation as it related to the liturgy. It is true that a mid-twelfth-century lectionary in Jerusalem[15] contains a full-page miniature of the Virgin holding Christ, but the subject also appears in contemporary psalters,[16] probably as a result of growing veneration of the Virgin in Byzantine society.[17] Although the eighth-century commentator Germanos linked the Gospels to the Incarnation,[18] the actual characterization of the lectionary pronounced at every service proclaimed it to be holy wisdom.[19] The direct evidence required to sustain the assertion that lectionaries were often not opened must be sufficiently strong to overcome the sharpest sensation such books create, and I do not refer to their look, feel, or heft. When opened, they tend to reek of incense; occasionally they are marked with the drippings of candles. The unambiguous literary statements from throughout the Middle Ages required to take the lectionary as a symbol do not, to my knowledge, exist. We have, though, the indirect but powerful testimony of the difficulty a reader would encounter in using the New York Lectionary. Perhaps it was never really intended for use. Ultimately I do not think that the state of the calendar of the New York Lectionary serves as evidence for the idea that often lectionaries did not actually serve their apparent function. The best explanation for the manuscript's uncorrected defects may prove to be far more mundane. The Lectionary betrays a peculiarly Byzantine attitude toward craftsmanship. This attitude is demonstrated in the frequently disconcerting juxtaposition of the finest materials and workmanship in some areas with a blind indifference to quality and execution in others. Anyone who has handled Byzantine manuscripts has at some time been struck by the extreme care taken in painting miniatures or writing text on parchment of appalling quality (especially when judged by the standards of Western medieval bookmaking). The construction of Byzantine ivory caskets or the building and decoration of churches often reveal the same attitude as the New York Lectionary. The deacon who used the manuscript would have had to verify, either alone or with the help of the *skevophylax* or *ekklesiarch,* the day's reading in the *typikon*.

The patterns of references and errors in transcribing the menologion contribute to the study of liturgical calendars and the lectionary. The manuscript may contain clues as to how such lists were compiled. The embedded references at first appear to be evidence for the growth of the menologion over the course of time. Without a concerted effort at weeding, references simply grew a few at a time, until by the twelfth century the system had grown quite cumbersome. The different kinds of

---

15. Greek Ecumenical Patriarchate, Mar Ibrahim, cod. 9: Lake, *Dated Greek MSS,* I, pls. 19, 20.

16. For example, Berlin, Universitätssammlung, cod. 3807; Vienna, Nationalbibliothek, theol. gr. 336; Washington, D.C., Dumbarton Oaks, cod. 3: A. Cutler, *The Aristocratic Psalters in Byzantium,* Bibliothèque des Cahiers archéologiques, XIII, Paris, 1984, figs. 100, 314, 319.

17. As suggested by the instances in which a donor figure venerates the Virgin holding the Christ child: for instance, Mount Athos, Dionysiou monastery, cod. 65: ibid., fig. 364.

18. References above, Introduction, note 6.

19. If there is one image of Christ associated with the early and some later lectionaries, it is not the child on his mother's lap but the adult Christ; cf. Lavra cod. A.92 (Weitzmann, *Byz. Buchmalerei,* fig. 179) and Sinai, gr. 204 (ibid., 28); see also Athens cod. 2645 (Marava-Chatzinicolaou and Toufexi-Paschou, *Manuscripts of the National Library of Greece,* fig. 318), a late eleventh-century lectionary that bears traces of an earlier style, in which the image of Christ has been shifted to before the *synaxarion* section, and perhaps also the portrait of Christ now bound in Princeton Garrett 6 (Weitzmann, *Byz. Buchmalerei,* fig. 374) and the twelfth-century cover of the lectionary of the Treasury of the Great Lavra, Mount Athos (*Treasures of Athos,* III, ill. p. 24). The combination of Evangelists and standing Christ in Vat. gr. 756 (G. Galavaris, *The Illustrations of the Prefaces in Byzantine Gospels,* Byzantina Vindobonensia, XI, Vienna, 1979, figs. 83, 84) looks like lectionary influence on a Gospel book. The popularity of the image in other media, most interestingly the coinage (P. Grierson, *Catalogue of the Byzantine Coins in the Dumbarton Oaks Collection and the Whittemore Collection,* III/1, *Leo III to Nicephorus III,* Washington, D.C., 1973, 160–64 discusses), suggests that unraveling the significance of the standing Christ figure will prove to be difficult.

titles given episcopal saints—bishop, archbishop, and patriarch of Constantinople (Thomas I appears twice under different titles)—might further endorse this view. There may be some appeal to this analysis, but it eventually fails to account for all the evidence. By and large, the calendar of saints appears to be a unified creation.

The errors in identifying the authors of the pericopes in the menologion (ten wrong out of sixty-two) contrast with the mere three mistakes in identifying the Evangelists in the more than one hundred and forty readings of the synaxarion. These numbers do of course require substantial qualification. The menologion readings follow no order, whereas those of the synaxarion tend to be grouped: mostly John lessons, followed by ones from Matthew, then a set entirely from Luke, concluded by a short section from Mark. The scribe must still remain alert, since a reading from Matthew, for example, may appear in the midst of the John section. Although not as dramatic as it might first seem, the differences in accuracy between the two sections could be accounted for by the way the two parts were made, if not in this exact case, then at least in some instances. The section of daily and weekly readings varies little, if at all, in content; the synaxarion is either daily throughout or contains select readings from Matthew onward (the case here). The New York calendar in comparison with others reveals a degree of choice in selecting saints; in addition, the Gospel readings assigned the saints are not unvarying. Some scribes making lectionaries may have compiled calendars from lists. The way in which cross-references tend to cluster and become impacted within others suggest as much. The use of lists is only partly hypothetical, since they were routinely added to medieval Gospel books to allow their use in church. The impacted references in the New York Lectionary follow patterns, but ones interlocked in so confusing a way that it would be difficult to work backwards and recompile the scribe's source, assuming that in this case it was a list.

Underlying the system of cross-references are a number of basic texts to which saints can be assigned by name or characteristic feature. That for Gregory the Illuminator and Gregory of Agrigentum (Mt 24:42–47) begins on the word "watch" (*gregoreite*), a play on the name. Matthew 25:1–3, to which is assigned a large number of women, relates the parable of the wise and foolish virgins. Groups composed largely of men of episcopal rank are associated with Matthew 5:14–19 (". . . but he who does them and teaches them [the Law and Commandments] shall be called great in the kingdom of heaven") and John 10:9–16 ("So there shall be one flock, one shepherd"). Saints known for their healing powers and the sainted physicians, Kosmas and Damian, are associated with Matthew 10:1, 5–8 ("Heal the sick, raise the dead, cleanse lepers, cast out demons. You received without pay, give without pay"). Not all the assignments are clear, but few may turn out to require knowledge of theological literature or an exegetical tradition. A patron or scribe could have added names to the list quite easily; the existence of readings under general rubrics (prophets, martyrs, the blessed) demonstrates the need for some flexibility. The readings assigned are those typical of the lectionaries and are generally, but not invariably, those found in the Typikon of the Cathedral. The Typikon gives many more saints but fewer readings. Sometimes the variations can be difficult to evaluate. For 25 September and the commemoration of the earthquake, the Saint Sophia Typikon gives Matthew 7:7–11 as the reading, whereas the lectionary(ies) give Luke 8:22–25. The reading from Luke recounts Christ's calming the storm and ends on the words: "Who then is this, that he commands even wind and water?" The Matthew reading does not accord with the celebration in nearly as clear a fashion.

Saints and Feasts in the Menologion

The last point pertains to the matter of flexibility. I should stress at the outset that when the calendar of the lectionary is compared with the list compiled by Gregory, and with the Typikon of the Great Church and the synaxarion, the most important impression is of uniformity in liturgical practice, despite each document's having its individual character and purpose. The elaborate services and rich litanies of the cathedral church were, judging by the lectionaries, not followed in all places. The calendar of the New York manuscript is more selective than that of the Typikon. Generally, when divergence exists, our manuscript sides with the lectionaries, especially the calendar given by Gregory.[20] Sometimes, though, the only parallel is with the Typikon. If one were to take the investigation a step further into the variant readings in the apparatus of the Typikon and Synaxarion, it might prove to be the case that separately drafted texts in time influenced one another. Sometimes a reading in the lectionary(ies) has it parallel not in the established text of J. Mateos but in readings found in the later manuscripts. Generally, though, the menologion of the Lectionary contains few surprises, but this of course is its very essence.[21]

The calendar of the Lectionary expresses above all else the concept of the universal Church as a living reality. Much of it has been devoted to the founders of the Church, the Apostles and early martyrs, and to the bishops of Rome, Constantinople, Antioch, and other cities; it celebrates monks and nuns, hermits and stylites. Yet it also embraces those in secular life: the emperor Constantine and his mother, Helen, holy physicians and notaries, and the sainted innkeeper Sampson. It commemorates disasters that threatened to destroy the city. Through fixed celebrations in its calendar the Church led the community in remembering the great fires and earthquakes of the past; in this way the congregation was prepared to face the uncertainties of the future. How puny and mundane must the state alternatives to a stable structure for daily life have seemed: regulation of weights and measures, criminal and small claims courts, the bureaucratic apparatus for tax collection.

The success of the calendar depended upon its homogenous character. Room for some flexibility did exist in both design and execution. In the menologion of the New York Lectionary, two means in particular call attention to specific saints generally found in lectionaries. One is illustration. In addition to the portraits of Symeon Stylites and Theodore Tiron, there are preparatory drawings for portraits of Niketas, Luke, and Demetrios (Figs. 21, 29, 35–37). The second way in which the makers of the manuscript called attention to a select number of saints was through gold titles. The scribe wrote in gold the first entry of each month and every rubric above a pericope written in full. Outside of this systematic use, a number of other rubrics are in gold: the Archangel Gabriel; the return from exile of Saints Athanasios and Cyril; Eleutherios; the great martyr Saint George and George, bishop of Mytelene; Joachim and Anne; Julian and Basilissa; Juliane; Nazarios and his companions; Peter and Paul; Polycarp of Smyrna; Silvester, bishop of Rome; Sozon; Stephen Protomartyr; Symeon and Anna the Prophetess; Symeon of Jerusalem; Theodosia; Theodotos of Ankyra; and the patriarch Thomas. Not one of these happens also to be portrayed; the groups do not overlap. Are we to think of these saints and the Archangel as somehow special to the church for which the manuscript was made,

---

20. That of Colwell and Riddle, *Prolegomena,* is much less similar.

21. The list could be contrasted with the saints illustrated in the Theodore Psalter of 1066: S. Der Nersessian, *L'illustration des Psautiers grecs du Moyen âge,* II, Londres, Add. 19,352, Bibliothèque des Cahiers archéologiques, V, Paris, 1970, 116–17. Virtually every saint portrayed by Theodore can be found in the calendar of the New York Lectionary, but the Studite monk is highly selective in his choices.

or are their names often picked out in gold? Only after much more such information has been made available will students of manuscripts and the liturgy be able to begin sorting out the places of production and the use of medieval lectionaries. As it now stands, though, the contribution of the calendar to our appreciation of the New York Lectionary is considerable.

IV

The Cruciform Lectionary in the Twelfth Century

There is a kind of poetry in which the length of line changes so that the verses form an image on the page. Such poetry has had many names—*carmina figurata, Figurengedichte, Augenpoesie,* concrete poetry, *poésie visuelle*—but perhaps none more appropriate than an ancient Greek compound used in modern criticism to describe shaped verse. The term is *technopaignion,* in which are joined the contrasting ideas of refined technique and childish playfulness. The small number of ancient examples of shaped verse known to us today was of course preserved by the Byzantines. The Paris fragment of the *Palatine Anthology* shows a good tenth-century scribe at work copying *carmina figurata,* Simias's "Axe," Dosiades' "Altar," and the "Pipes," attributed to Theocritus.[1] Although the Byzantines did not measurably contribute to this genre, they did delight in shaped text. Marginal commentary especially can be found written in various forms, including recognizable ones like crosses and columns,[2] in one case a bird.[3] The cruciform pages of Gospels in the New York Lectionary belong to the tradition of shaped text.

The cumulative effect created by page after page of cruciform text is a kind of wonder at the scribe's single-minded pursuit, and the sense of astonishment and admiration his work inspires may be well worth noting as we try to place the book in the history of Byzantine art. Doing so requires recognizing the long heritage of cruciform text. Writing in the shape of a cross is not an innovation for which we can credit the scribe of the New York Lectionary. Throughout the Middle Ages others took the opportunity to write various parts of manuscripts in the shape of a cross. Most often, though, these parts are prefatory materials of strictly limited length: tables of contents,[4] prologues,[5] the Eusebian *Letter.*[6] An example of opening Gospel

---

1. Paris. suppl. gr. 384: *Anthologia palatina: Codex palatinus et codex parisinus phototypica editi,* Codices graeci et latini photographice depicti duce Scatone De Vries, xv/2, ed. C. Preisendanz, Leiden, 1911, pls. 669–74. The last two compositions are well known to art historians because they occur in illustrated, or elaborated, versions in the thirteenth-century Paris. gr. 2832: Omont, *Miniatures,* pl. cxxx. W. Hörandner, "Visuelle Poesie in Byzanz. Versuch einer Bestandsaufnahme," *Jahrbuch der Österreichischen Byzantinistik,* XL, 1990, 1–42.

2. See the commentary of the Florence Prophets, Cod. Laur. Plut. 5.9: H. Belting and G. Cavallo, *Die Bibel des Niketas,* Wiesbaden, 1979, pl. 12. See also J. Lowden, *Illuminated Prophet Books,* University Park, Pa., and London, 1988, fig. 29.

3. Copenhagen, Kongelige Bibliotek, Cod. GKS 9: Belting and Cavallo (as in note 2), pl. 17; H. Hunger, "Minuskel und Auszeichnungsschriften im 10.–12. Jahrhundert," *La paléographie grecque et byzantine,* Paris, 1977, fig. 13.

4. For example, Paris. gr. 580, fol. iv, and Vat. Reg. gr. 1, fol. 1.

5. For example, Ambros. B.80.sup.; Marc. gr. 1.18 (= 1276).

6. Athen. cod. 74, Lond. Add. 11,300, and Paris, Coisl. 20 are written in pure cruciform; the Codex Mavrocordatianus, Bratislava; Laur. conv. soppr. 159, Marc. gr. 1.18 (= 1276), Princeton. Garrett 2 and Scheide 1, Vat. urb. gr. 2 are written in a large quatrefoil reminiscent of the cross (and probably related to the quatrefoil and rectangle design of Athen. gr. 57, Oxon. Cromwell 15, Paris. gr. 64 and gr. 70, Vat. gr. 364 and Urb. gr. 2).

The New York Cruciform Lectionary

leaves is also known.[7] When the end of a text would not fill an entire page, scribes occasionally wrote the final lines in the shape of a cross;[8] in addition, at least one cruciform subscription survives.[9] Few if any of the rather large number of individual leaves written in a cruciform pattern required much planning or a separate ruling system, and for this reason nearly all the earlier examples differ significantly from the New York Lectionary.

It is important to emphasize the rarity of books written throughout in the shape of a cross. Before the twelfth century only one Greek manuscript copied entirely cruciform survives, the ninth-century Gospel book in Princeton, Garrett 1.[10] Yet datable to about the same time as the New York Lectionary are two more books written in cruciform and another partly transcribed in the shape of the cross. All three manuscripts also happen to be lectionaries. In making them the scribes left large amounts of expensive parchment empty; doubtless they did so at the order of patrons whose motives went beyond simple piety. One might successfully contend that an interest in the material richness of donations is especially marked in twelfth-century Byzantium. This we would infer from book ornament of the time. For explicit, written proof of interest in the materials of the book, one can turn to a contemporary manuscript dedication in which the donor, writing in verse, directs the reader's attention to the quality of the parchment and gold ornament.[11] Given the Byzantine interest in calligraphy, the ubiquity of the cross, and the twelfth-century predilection for grand display, finding three other cruciform lectionaries may be sheer coincidence. On the other hand, some connection may run from the New York Lectionary to one or more of the others.

Since part of the appreciation of a work of art is its relationship to other, similar objects of the time, I will describe briefly the cruciform lectionaries in London, Washington, D.C., and on Mount Athos. For those in the Dumbarton Oaks Collection and the British Library, I can offer firsthand observations.[12] I have not seen the example in the Iviron Monastery; in fact, it is relatively little known on account of its having long been the lectionary used in the services. In the course of summary discussion I will mention some of the problems I think one faces in trying to circumscribe the manuscripts as part of a distinct movement.

London, British Library, Add. MS 39,603

We can reclaim some of the colorful history of the cruciform lectionary in the British Library.[13] The earliest evidence of its movements outside its probable place of origin, Constantinople, is the note written on fol. 1 (Fig. 43), which reads:[14]

---

7. Paris. gr. 64, with illustrations, like the few leaves in Jerusalem, cod. Taphou 14.

8. As four of many examples, I cite: Lond. Harley 5785, fol. 143, Princeton. Garrett 3, fol. 260, Vat. gr. 463, fol. 183v, and Vat. Pal. gr. 189, fol. 314v.

9. Mount Athos, Iviron monastery, cod. 16: Lake, *Dated Greek MSS*, III, pl. 177.

10. K. Clark, *A Descriptive Catalogue of Greek New Testament Manuscripts in America*, Chicago, 1937, 61–63, pl. VII; W. Hatch, *The Principal Uncial Manuscripts of the New Testament*, Chicago, 1939, pl. LX; *Manuscripts from American Collections*, 56–57, fig. 2.

11. Cod. Sinai. gr. 339: J. Anderson, "The Illustration of Cod. Sinai. Gr. 339," *Art Bulletin*, LXI, 1979, 167–68.

12. For the opportunity to examine the manuscripts, I wish to thank Susan Boyd, Curator of the Byzantine Collection, Dumbarton Oaks, and Derek Turner, former Keeper of Manuscripts, the British Museum.

13. Aland, *Liste*, 218 (l:233); British Museum (Department of Manuscripts), *Catalogue of Additions to the Manuscripts, 1916–1920*, London, 1933, 84–85; see also XVIII, correcting the date to "perhaps rather XII" than the eleventh-century attribution given on p. 84.

14. I wish to thank Professor N. Oikonomides for his help in reading the signature.

The Cruciform Lectionary in the Twelfth Century

ἀφιερώται παρὰ τοῦ σεβασμιου γέρον(τος) ἁγίου Ἡρακλει(ας) κυρίου Μεθοδίου ὡς δ[. . .] ἱστορι(ας) ἔχομεν βασιλικῶν χειρῶν ἔργον ἐστι Ἀλεξίου ἢ Ἐμμανοήλου τῶν Κομνηνῶν.

Ὁ Ἡρακλείας Μεθόδιας

The inscription is faint and the words are difficult to read, but the following can be said. At some time the book came under the control of a bishop of Heraklia named Methodios; he gives no date in the inscription, but quite likely he is the Methodios who held office between 1760 and 1794. He wrote the inscription when he donated to some church or monastery a lectionary that he believed to be the work of a Byzantine emperor, Alexios or possibly Manuel Komnenos. We next hear of the manuscript in the Xenophon monastery on Mount Athos. It was there that Robert Curzon discovered and purchased the book in 1837. Curzon's story of the discovery, handwritten on paper sheets bound into the lectionary, makes for lively reading; I reproduce the text as an appendix to this chapter. The account reads like an archetypal confrontation between the city slicker and the rustics; the Englishman goes looking for precious books, discovers one whose inscription supports some expectation and its owners, rather than disabuse him, simply feign ignorance. According to the Athos monks, the lectionary came from the Pantokrator monastery, an otherwise undocumented owner. Finally, in 1917 Darea Curzon donated the manuscript to the British Museum (the end paper bears a sticker with the shelfmark, 84.19, that it bore in Curzon's library at Parham Park, Sussex).

The contents of the unillustrated manuscript are as follows: fols. i–ix are a miscellany of writings pertinent to the manuscript: a letter dated 26 November 1855 from Frederick H. Scrivener to Robert Curzon, as well as handwritten and printed copies of Scrivener's notice on the Greek manuscripts at Parham Park.[15] The content of the lectionary (fols. 1–196) consists of daily readings from Easter to the Lenten vigils, that is, those from John (1–41v), Matthew (42–111v), and Luke (112–96); the final readings, beginning on fol. 196, are in fact references for Monday through Thursday of the vigils, which end with the complete text sung on Friday. A block of ornament at the end of the last reading signifies the end of the volume; because of its makeup, only three headpieces were required.

The London Lectionary has 196 folios, measuring 37½ by 29¼ cm; the ruling pattern is given to scale in Figure C (fol. 144, typical); the vertical text measures 9.7 by 23.6 cm and the horizontal is 17.4 by 8.8 cm. There are 25 lines per leaf: 7 above, 10 in crossbar, and 8 below. The leaves are ruled on the flesh side on good heavy sheets of parchment. Gatherings are numbered at front and back in the lower margin toward the gutter by a hand perhaps not contemporary with that of the text; I–IV are quaternions (although IV comprises two bifolia and four individual sheets), V is a quaternion plus single sheet (with it ends one section of the manuscript, VI–XIII quaternions, XIV a ternion (with it ends another section of manuscript), XV–XX quarternions, XXI a ternion with single sheet, XXII–XXIV quaternions, XXV a ternion. The hand occasionally varies from the highly controlled style with which the manuscript opens, but the book is probably the work of one scribe. The text is in brown ink and the ekphonetic notation is in carmine.

---

15. F. Scrivener, *An Exact Transcript of the Codex Augiensis, A Graeco-Latin Manuscript of S. Paul's Epistles, Deposited in the Library of Trinity College, Cambridge,* London, 1859, xlvii, cited the lectionary in passing and stated that it once "belonged to the Emperor Alexius Comnenus."

The New York Cruciform Lectionary

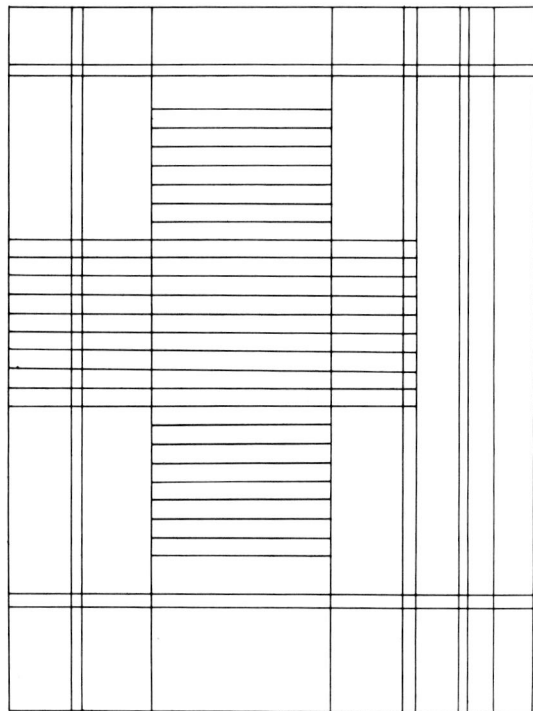

Fig. C. Ruling pattern, Lond. Add. 39,603

The manuscript contains no portraits, and there are no offprints to suggest that it ever had any. Polychrome finials were painted around the text on each leaf and all the initials were executed in polychrome flower-petal style; only two of them have figural decoration, fols. iv (*epsilon* with gesturing hand at the first reading from John; Fig. 44) and 195v (deer grazing on foliage hanging from an *epsilon;* Fig. 47). There are three cruciform headpieces and a block of polychrome ornament painted at the end of the last lection. The cruciform headpieces signal the major divisions: at fol. 1 (cross-shaped headpiece with title marking the beginning of the manuscript: The Holy and Great Sunday of Easter; the Gospel according to John, Fig. 43), fol. 42 (cross-shaped headpiece to mark beginning of Matthew readings; inscribed: Monday of Pentecost Week, of the Holy Spirit; Beginning of the Text of Daily Readings from Matthew's Gospel, Fig. 45), and fol. 112 (cross-shaped headpiece to mark the beginning of the Luke readings; the inscription, written in half-uncial, announces the start of readings from Luke's Gospels and continues giving directions for the period of time covered by the lections, Fig. 46).[16]

In both text type and size, the London manuscript differs from the others. It is somewhat larger and contains daily lessons to the Lenten vigils. Although the manuscript is not illustrated and the scribe occasionally allows his manner of writing to relax, this is an extremely handsome book. It does not appear to have been written by the same hand as the New York Lectionary. The script of the London manuscript has a slightly higher proportion of minuscule forms on the pages illustrated. It would be difficult if not impossible to base attributions on the manner of script. Bold, highly

---

16. Gregory, *Textkritik,* 353, transcribes.

legible forms of minuscule appear early in the eleventh century for texts used in the service.[17] Over the course of the century a significant number of manuscripts were written in this way: menologia, psalters, sermon collections, and others in addition to the lectionary. Many scribes gained experience as the need for service manuals of all kinds remained strong. The demands on the scribe writing service minuscule were simplicity and legibility at a distance, requirements that effectively eliminated the individual flourish or expressive idiosyncracy upon which precise attributions depend. In fact, the scripts are difficult even to date with any degree of confidence. In comparison with lectionaries like London, British Library, Add. MS 5153, made in 1033, or Mount Athos, Panteleimon monastery, cod. 27, dated 1072,[18] the cruciform manuscripts all share elements perhaps more often found in twelfth-century service hands. The letters tend to be perpendicular to the rulings and, although often softly rounded, they are easily inscribed within a square. The scribes pack the letters more tightly than in earlier books and limit the number of ligatures to create a freestanding look that happens to balance the full (for example, Fig. 43) and half-uncial titles (Fig. 46). One dated book written in a thoroughly comparable style can be found in the Vatican Library, cod. Pal. gr. 24, written in 1144.[19]

Format presents one important difference between the writing of the London and New York manuscripts. When copying the text of the New York Lectionary, the scribe indented lines with the various initials in mind. A few of the opening leaves of the London manuscript contain readings with slight indentations; but after the first gathering the text was written flush with the rulings. The two systems could reflect the commissions: one manuscript to be illustrated, the other not. If one examines eleventh- and twelfth-century Byzantine manuscripts with initial ornament, no particular pattern emerges to sustain the hypothesis; the presence or absence of indentation seems to be a matter of scribal habit. In the case of the London Lectionary, a scribe's own tendency may have been encouraged by unusually wide margins.

Like the New York Lectionary, the London manuscript contains cruciform headpieces at the main divisions of the text. The final two (Figs. 45, 46) consist of narrow bands of ornament drawn and painted so precisely and with such relatively small, tight detail they might easily pass as ornament of the early second half of the eleventh century. The opening headpiece (Fig. 43), though, is a markedly wide band filled more freely. Its style, which sets the tone of the manuscript, belongs to the twelfth century, though it too appears quite simple and restrained. When the opening headpieces in the New York and London manuscripts are compared (Figs. 2, 43), we can better grasp the nature of their differences. Birds perch on the horizontals of the New York Lectionary and hide within the rinceau of its filler ornament. From the baseline rise fantastic plants growing out of overgrown acanthus calyxes. The decoration in the London manuscript begins simply and becomes ever more restrained. The same holds true of the New York manuscript. In actual style the filler ornament of the framing bands is executed with equivalent precision and detail, but throughout the cruciform headpieces the illuminator of the New York Lectionary paints animals and lush and complicated foliage. The manuscripts are separated not so much by style as by tone—by what appears to be a conscious decision regarding how ornament will be used. The choice may be an all-

17. See London, British Library, Add. MS 5153, a lectionary written in 1033: Lake, *Dated Greek MSS*, II, pl. 124.

18. For the former, see note 17; for the latter, see Lake, *Dated Greek MSS*, III, pl. 185.

19. Ibid., VIII, pls. 576–78.

The New York Cruciform Lectionary

encompassing one that relates to the absence of Evangelist portraits and narrative images. In one respect the decoration of the London manuscript is unusually extensive. When lectionaries were illuminated, it was customary to execute the initials to the Saturday and Sunday readings in polychrome but those for the weekdays in gold. In the London Lectionary every reading begins with a polychrome letter, though nearly all are relatively simple in design. The opening *epsilon* is one of only two initials with figural ornament, and for this manuscript it is extensively decorated (Fig. 44). The initial design may be common, but its rich execution betrays more than any other ornament in the book twelfth-century elements of style. Tendrils sprout from the top and grow luxuriantly out of the base. The letter extends and flattens along the page following the manner of the ornament of the title pages in the New York Lectionary. The second initial is a deer biting on a piece of foliage pendant from the *epsilon* that opens the Sunday reading of the first week of Lent (Fig. 47); it is an animal comparable in kind and style to those found in the Lenten headpiece of the New York Lectionary (Fig. 21, top corners).

The few points of contact between the two manuscripts alert us to the degree to which what at first appear to be differences in date in fact result principally from differences of intention in the execution of the two commissions. Restraint was exercised throughout the London Lectionary. The two more simple headpieces are crosses formed of narrow bands of tight decoration placed with elegant understatement against a wide expanse of perfectly empty parchment. The decorative style of the Iviron manuscript presents yet another approach.

Mount Athos, Iviron Monastery, unnumbered lectionary

The third cruciform lectionary is at the Iviron monastery on Mount Athos (Figs. 48–51). The Iviron Lectionary has no library or inventory number and went unnoticed until the publication of the illuminated manuscripts of Mount Athos,[20] on which I rely for the following brief description. Presumably, the manuscript was used in the monastery church and therefore was unavailable for study. Neither C. Gregory nor K. Aland listed it among the manuscripts of the New Testament. The Iviron Lectionary contains 333 folios (defective at end) measuring 25 by 32 cm. It is cruciform throughout and decorated, like the New York and London lectionaries, with finials on each leaf. No Evangelist portraits have been cited, and the illustration does not seem to go beyond the historiated initial on fol. 1, a badly flaked portrait of John writing in the initial *epsilon,* his outstretched arm forming the cross-stroke of the letter (Fig. 48).

The nonfigural ornament of the Iviron Lectionary is as rich as that of the London manuscript is restrained. The frames of the title pages (Figs. 48–51) are the traditional *pi*-shape (found in innumerable Byzantine manuscripts, as well as on fol. 230 of the New York Lectionary). Filling the lower quadrants and occasionally rising from the headpieces are fanciful growths, some comparable in form to ones in the New York manuscript (Figs. 16, 48). The use of plants rising from curving calyxes may be traced back to the middle of the eleventh century. Examples appear on the canon tables of the famous Vienna Gospels, theol. gr. 154.[21] By the last quarter of the eleventh century

---

20. *Treasures of Athos,* II, 344–45.

21. P. Buberl and H. Gerstinger, *Die byzantinischen Handschriften,* II, *Die Handschriften des X.–XVIII. Jahrhunderts,* Die illuminierten Handschriften und Inkunabeln der Nationalbibliothek in Wien, VIII/4, Leipzig, 1938, pl. VI, 1, 2.

they have started to appear on miniature frames, as in the Evangelists of Vat. gr. 1156,[22] and on headpieces: one in a copy of sermons by Gregory of Nazianzus at Vienna[23] and in another copy of the sermons, made at the monastery of Saint George Manganes in Constantinople.[24] Though the decorative pattern had been used for some time, its use in title-page ornament is not especially common, though neither is it sufficiently rare to indicate that the lectionaries were made by the same craftsmen.

Washington, Dumbarton Oaks Collection, cod. 1 (acc. no. 39.12)

The Dumbarton Oaks Lectionary is the one other lectionary with narrative images; in its case, though, illustration and cruciform format are nearly exclusive. The scribe of the manuscript began copying the text in the usual two-column format, and only at gathering seven did he change to the shape of the cross. All but three of the illustrations, which are mainly historiated initials, occur in the first six gatherings.

The lectionary was bought at Sotheby's in 1939 by Mr. and Mrs. Robert Woods Bliss, who subsequently (1940) presented it to the Dumbarton Oaks Research Library. A prior owner signed his initials at the top of nearly every leaf (Fig. 53). A nonscribal entry on fol. 65 (Fig. 53) gives information on the readings and calendar and thus attests to nothing more than use of the manuscript at the time it was written, perhaps in the thirteenth or fourteenth century. Folios 1 through 140v contain the synaxarion; the menologion began on a now-lost leaf; preserved is the portion beginning with the end of the reading for 1 September to the reading for 10 October on the manuscript's last page, fol. 149v.

The lectionary text was written on 149 folios, measuring 32½ by 25 cm, arranged as follows in twenty-two gatherings, each numbered by the scribe (Fig. 53: an *iota,* for X, in the bottom right corner). Quite a few leaves have been removed from the manuscript; in the following quire description the losses are noted within parentheses at the appropriate places: I (leaf cut from between fols. 6 and 7)—II quaternions; III ternion with single leaf, fol. 18; IV (two leaves excised between fols. 27 and 28)—V quaternions; VI ternion; VII (two leaves excised between fols. 44 and 45, one replaced with paper glued to stub)—X (the entire bifolio has been removed between fols. 65 and 66 and the conjugate half of 65 cut) quaternions; XI–XIV (two leaves cut between fols. 94 and 95)—XV (leaves cut between fols. 104 and 105 and after 105) quaternions; XVI probably quaternion that has the leaf before 106 excised; XVII ternion; XVIII quaternion; XIX one bifolio (fols. 127 and 129) and four single leaves (fols. 127, 130, 131, 132); XX three bifolia and one single leaf (fol. 139); XXI quaternion; XXII now consists of two single leaves, fols. 148, 149. The scribe ruled gatherings I–VI in a two-column format of twenty-four lines per column as reproduced in Figure D. The remainder of the leaves he ruled in a cruciform pattern reproduced in Figure E; the cross consists of eight lines in each of its three parts. Ruling is on the hair side and pricking is occasionally visible. The scribe wrote fols. 1–8v in carmine ink that he dusted with gold powder; fols. 9–41v are in carmine only and the

---

22. O. Demus, *Byzantine Art and the West,* New York, 1970, fig. 60.

23. Vind. theol. gr. 126; Buberl and Gerstinger (as in note 21), pl. XLIV, 1.

24. G. Galavaris, *The Illustrations of the Liturgical Homilies of Gregory Nazianzenus,* Studies in Manuscript Illumination, VI, Princeton, 1969, 214–15, fig. 431.

The New York Cruciform Lectionary

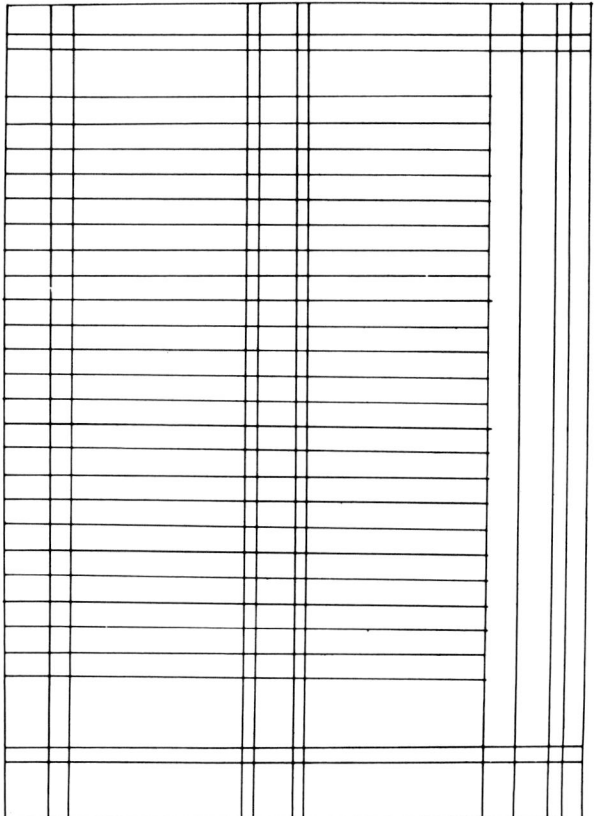

Fig. D. Ruling pattern, Dumbarton Oaks, MS 1 (double-column text)

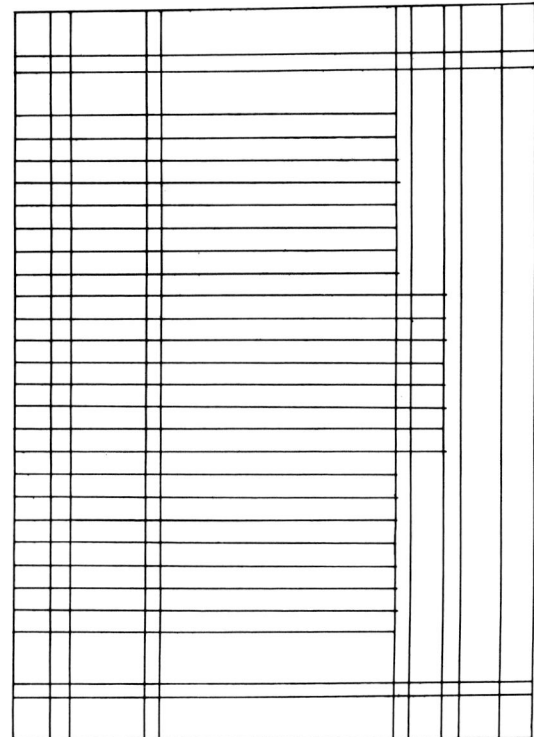

Fig. E. Ruling pattern, Dumbarton Oaks, MS 1 (cruciform text)

remainder of the manuscript is in brown ink. Despite the changes in format and ink, the text was probably written by only one scribe.

The lectionary was illustrated and headpieces placed at the major text divisions; no doubt a number of images and headpieces have been lost to vandalism. Those remaining are:

Fol. 1: John the Evangelist enthroned holding a book has been posed to form the initial *epsilon:* Easter Sunday reading. This first illustration to the first reading is framed by a large headpiece.
Fol. 2: Initial *theta* with illustration of Christ enthroned with a book; reading for Monday of Easter week (Jn 1:18–28).
Fol. 2v: Initial *tau* with portrait of Peter running toward Christ's tomb, which is depicted in the opposite margin; reading for Tuesday of Easter Week (Lk 24:12–35).
Fol. 4v: Initial *tau* with portrait of John the Baptist, his right hand upraised to gesture; reading for Wednesday of Easter week (Jn 1:35–52).
Fol. 5v: Initial *tau* with portrait of Nicodemus, bearded and in a short tunic; reading for Thursday of Easter week (Jn 3:1–15).
Fol. 6v: Initial *tau* with Christ in an energetic pose, walking holding a length of rope (the "whip of cords"); reading for Friday of Easter week (Jn 2:12–22).

Fol. 7: Initial *omicron* framing Thomas's trying the wound in Christ's side: reading for the Sunday after Easter, or second Sunday (Jn 20:19–31).

Fol. 8: Christ in the initial *tau* gestures across text to a servant filling tall jars in the opposite margin: reading for Monday of the second week after Easter (Jn 2:1–11).

Fol. 8v: Initial *epsilon* formed of Christ enthroned gesturing in speech: reading for Tuesday of the second week after Easter (Jn 3:16–21).

Fol. 9 Christ enthroned within the initial *epsilon*; reading for Wednesday of the second week (Jn 5:17–24).

Fol. 11v: Initial *tau* formed of standing figure of Christ; reading for Saturday of the second week (Jn 6:14–27).

Fol. 12v: Initial *tau* formed of Joseph of Arimathea, with white beard and short tunic, raising both hands upward; reading for the third Sunday (Mk 15:43–16:8).

Fol. 15v: Initial *epsilon* with Christ enthroned speaking; reading for the Saturday of the third week (Jn 15:17–16:2).

Fol. 16v: Christ stands to form part of the initial *tau*; he gestures across the column to the youthful paralytic, who has his bed on his back; Sunday of the Paralytic (Jn 5:1–15).

Fol. 19: Christ stands, holding a book and gesturing, to form part of the initial *tau*; reading for the Wednesday of the fourth week (Jn 7:14–30).

Fol. 22 (Fig. 52): Christ seated forms the initial *tau*; he gestures across the margin to the woman drawing water from the well with an amphora; behind her is the city of Samaria; reading for the fifth Sunday (Jn 4:5–42).

Fol. 26: Christ standing forms the initial *tau*; he holds a loaf and across the column of text are the Disciples filling cylindrical containers; reading for the Wednesday of the fifth week (Jn 6:5–14).

Fol. 31: Christ enthroned forms part of the initial *epsilon*; reading for Wednesday of the sixth week (Jn 12:36–47).

Fol. 32: The Ascension of Christ has been depicted in an unusual fashion: its parts are scattered over the entire leaf; a tree and three disciples (Peter and Andrew among them) form the initial *alpha*; reading for the morning service on Ascension Thursday (Mk 16:9–20). The leaf has been reproduced.[25]

Fol. 32v: Christ standing forms the initial *tau*; reading for the liturgy on Ascension Thursday (Lk 24:36–53).

Fol. 35: Initial *tau* formed of Christ, his hands upraised in a gesture of prayer to a segment of heaven depicted just above the initial; reading for the Sunday of the Holy Fathers of Nicaea (Jn 17:1–3).

Fol. 39v: Initial *tau* formed of Christ gesturing across the column to Saint Peter; reading for Pentecost Saturday (Jn 21:14–25).

Fol. 40v: Initial *tau* formed of Christ standing holding a book; reading is for Pentecost Sunday liturgy (Jn 7:37–52, 8:12).

Fol. 65 (Fig. 53): Cruciform headpiece to mark the start of the reading from Luke and the New Year.

Fol. 88: Cruciform headpiece at the beginning of the Mark readings and commemoration of Saint Theodore Tiron.

Fol. 111v: Initial *epsilon* formed by Christ enthroned; initial begins the first of the Passion readings (Jn 13:31–18:2).

---

25. *Greek Manuscripts from American Collections*, fig. 44.

The New York Cruciform Lectionary

Fol. 122v (Fig. 54): In the left quadrant Saint Peter kneels, his hands upraised; across the leaf is a rooster; illustrates the end of the third Passion reading (Mt 26:57–75).

Fol. 145: An image of Christ, dead on the cross, appears within the block of text; the reading illustrated is that for 14 September, the feast of the Elevation of the Holy Cross. This unusual representation of a figure within the text of a lectionary reading has been published.[26]

Saints of the Menologion

What little survives of the contents of the menologion is listed here. The abbreviations used are those of chapter III. An asterisk (★) denotes a saint not found in the New York Lectionary.

SEPTEMBER: [first leaf of text lost, now begins at Lk 1:42–56]. 2, Saint Mamas; cf. Monday of Pentecost week. 3, Saint Anthemios; cf. 13 November. 4, Saint mm Babylas and Children: *Inc. II + Lk 10:19f.* 5, Saint pr Zachariah: *Inc. V + Mt 23:29f.* 6, Archangel Michael; cf. 8 November. 7, Saint Sozon; cf. 7 October. 8, Birth of All-Holy Virgin, morning; cf. morning reading for first of the month; liturgy: *Inc. I + Lk 8:16f.* 9, Joachim and Anna: *Inc V + Lk 8:16f.* 10, Saint mm Nymphodora, Menodora, and Metrodora; cf. eleventh of the month [?]. 11, Blessed Theodora; cf. fourth morning lection. 12, Saint hm Autonomos★; cf. 6 December Saturday before the Adoration (of the Holy Cross); cf. seventh Saturday in Matthew, Sunday before the Adoration: *Inc. V + Jn 3:13f.* 14, Elevation of the Holy Cross: *Inc + Jn 19:6f.* 15, Saint Great m Niketas; cf. third Saturday after Easter. 16, Saint m Euphemia; cf. eleventh of the month. 17, Saints mm Sophia, Pistes, Elpes, and Agape; cf. seventeenth Saturday in Matthew. 18, Blessed Sosanna★; cf. eighteenth Sunday in Matthew. 19, Saint m Trophimos; cf. All-Saints Sunday. 20, Saint m Eustathios and comps: *Inc. II + Lk 21:12f.* 21, Saint a Kodratos: *Inc. II + Lk 10:16f.* 22, Saint m Phokas; cf. third Sunday after Easter. 23, Conception of John the Prophet; cf. 24 June. 24, Saint m Thekla; cf. seventeenth Saturday in Matthew. 25, Blessed Euphrosyne: *Inc. V + Mt 11:27f.* 26, Death of Saint John the Theologian; cf. Pentecost Saturday. 27, Saint m Kallistratos: *Inc. II + Lk 12:2f.* 28, Blessed Chariton; cf. [?]. 29, Blessed Kyriakos; cf. third Sunday in Lent. 30, Saint Gregory of Greater Armenia: *Inc. V + Mt 24:42f.* OCTOBER: 1, a Annios [= Ananias]; cf. 21 September. 2, Saint m Cyprian; cf. 2 September. 3, Saint Dionysios the Areopagite; cf. Tuesday of Pentecost week. 4, Saint m Hierotheos, and Peter★; cf. 4 September. 5, Saint Charitine and Mamelchtha★; cf. seventeenth Saturday in Matthew. 6, Saint a Thomas; cf. Sunday of week after Easter. 8, Blessed Pelagia; cf. fourth morning lection. 9, Saint James: *Inc. I + Mt 10:1f.* 10, Saints Eulampios and Eulampia: *Inc. II + Mt 10:16f.* End of text and manuscript.

Despite the changes in ink and in ruling, the manuscript appears to have been written by one scribe and to have been planned from the start for illustration. The ruling patterns for the two parts are actually quite similar. In both, twenty-four lines of text cover just over twenty-three centimeters, title guides are exactly the same width and about the same distance from the text. That the manuscript was written with illustration in mind is proven by the way the text was written around the

---

26. Ibid., fig. 43.

figure of Christ crucified, on fol. 145. The illustration is uniform throughout the manuscript and is the work of a single hand, perhaps that of the scribe. Text and image dovetail on fol. 145 in such a way as to suggest that the Crucifixion was sketched before the page was written.

Nothing in the style of either script, ornament, or illustration expressly calls to mind the New York Lectionary or either of the other two cruciform manuscripts. As a point of specific comparison one might begin with the miniature cycle. Most of the miniatures fall in the section written in two columns, fols. 1 to 40v. Some of their subjects happen to be found in the New York Lectionary but not in remarkably similar form. The two versions of the Woman at the Well, for instance (Figs. 11, 22), resemble one another because their respective painters drew from a well-established tradition of composition: Christ sits and addresses the woman who stands facing him but separated from him by the well. Some differences might be attributed to format. The illuminator of the Dumbarton Oaks Lectionary consistently used the initials as part of his compositions. The illustration for the Sunday following Easter consists of Christ and a small figure of Thomas, both enclosed in the initial *omicron* (fol. 7). In the New York Lectionary the same subject grandly unfolds over four entire quadrants (Figs. 6, 7); but had illuminator A been confined to just an initial, his solution might have been similar to that of the painter of the Dumbarton Oaks manuscript. The illuminator of the eleventh-century Morgan Lectionary, cod. 639, was able to get Thomas, Christ, and other disciples into the space of the *omicron* owing to his unusually delicate touch.[27] Of possibly greater importance in evaluating the relationship between the works are the number of subjects in the Dumbarton Oaks manuscript that are not in the New York Lectionary. The Cleansing of the Temple (shown as Christ striding vigorously with the whip), the Marriage Feast at Cana (he orders the servant to fill jars), or the Miracle of Loaves and Fishes (he commands the Disciples to gather up what remains) are succinct narratives that do not occur in the New York Lectionary. The illustration for Monday of the first week of the synaxarion (Christ depicted in the *theta* in illustration of the opening words, "No one has ever seen God; the only Son, who is in the bosom of the Father, he has made him known") can be paralleled not by the New York Lectionary but by at least one other, Dionysiou cod. 587, which shows Christ on the lap of the Ancient of Days.[28] The illuminator of the Dumbarton Oaks manuscript knew lectionary illustration. Perhaps he copied some other manuscript. If the latter proves to be the case, the work he copied was not the New York manuscript, nor was it one close to it in subject matter, at least for the bulk of the miniature cycle. The opening part of the manuscript, either directly or indirectly, is in no way similar to the New York Lectionary.

What is remarkable about the Dumbarton Oaks Lectionary is that only the illustrations in the cruciform section even begin to recall ones in the New York manuscript. The first of the Passion readings opens with an image of Christ (though an enthroned figure in the Dumbarton Oaks manuscript), and both show Peter and the Cock in the margin of the third Passion reading (Figs. 27, 28, 54). Both manuscripts contain an image of the Crucifixion in illustration of the 14 September reading. In trying to gauge the importance of these parallels (over the greater number of differences), one might turn to the headpiece ornament in the cruciform part of the book. The First Saturday in Luke (Beginning of the New Year) is marked by a headpiece at fol. 65 (Fig. 53). The proportions of the design are unlike those of the New York manuscript, whose cruciform headpieces are narrower and taller. In both cases, the headpieces were drawn within the guides used in

27. Weitzmann, "Morgan 639," fig. 298.

28. *Treasures of Athos*, I, fig. 191.

The New York Cruciform Lectionary

writing the text, so their proportions simply mirror differences created at an earlier stage and carried throughout both manuscripts. The text columns of the Dumbarton Oaks manuscript are closer to those of the London Lectionary (Figs. 44, 54), but the headpieces in the latter manuscript are handsomely simple, much closer to those in the New York Lectionary. In the Dumbarton Oaks manuscript, the headpiece design is a complicated one; a quatrefoil frames an uncial title inelegantly inscribed above the initial and seven lines of Gospel text. Arcs and flowers in circles appear around the quatrefoil, and all are finally framed by the cross and its simple teardrop finials. The filler to the outside frame recalls that used in the Evangelist portraits of the New York Lectionary (for example, Fig. 1), but it is treated in a different manner.

As a last basis for comparison one might turn to the testimony of the menologion, unfortunately preserved in fragmentary condition. When the menologia in the Dumbarton Oaks and New York manuscripts are compared as calendars of approximately contemporary manuscripts of the same type, it is their differences that are most striking. Four saints in the Dumbarton Oaks Lectionary (Autonomos, Sosanna, Peter with Hierotheos, and Mamelchthas) do not appear in the New York menologion. Some (Hermione, Sergios, and Bakchos) in the New York menologion are not found in the Dumbarton Oaks fragment or are reported in a different fashion (Archangel Michael—Michael at Chonae); still others are celebrated in the New York Lectionary in entirely different months (Kodratos, Euphrosyne). Where texts are given by reference or a passage written in full, and in some cases with the associations of text and saint, these vary also. Finally, the way titles are used tends to differ. The menologion texts of these two manuscripts were not copied one from the other, nor can they be derived from a common model or list. Indeed they represent quite different strands within the common medieval tradition.

Some conclusions can be offered. The early part of the Dumbarton Oaks manuscript, written in double columns and illustrated, bears no relationship to the New York Lectionary or to the tradition it seems to represent. The one part that does recall the New York manuscript, that written in cruciform with just a handful of miniatures, contains in part a text distinctly different within the tradition. All that really connects the manuscripts is an idea. The patron of the Dumbarton Oaks Lectionary saw or heard of a cruciform manuscript like that in New York and commissioned one similar to it from a scribe who did not have the benefit of seeing his source.

Together, the four cruciform lectionaries comprise an unlikely family. Standing farthest from the group in terms or style is the Dumbarton Oaks Lectionary; the composition of its illustrations and their distribution by subject matter and lection distance it from the only other one with miniatures, the New York manuscript. The miniatures, script, and ornament of the Dumbarton Oaks Lectionary strengthen the parallel between the New York and London manuscripts. The one contrast also serves to draw the Iviron Lectionary (to the extent that we know it) closer to the New York and London lectionaries. In all three the ornamental plants tend to be thick and the movement of their stems controlled in a way oddly antithetical to the otherwise expansive lushness; the flowers that fill the frames are delicate and carefully drawn. Such care runs conspicuously through the ornament of the London manuscript, though its maker indulged in few of the flourishes that might help us relate him to the makers of the New York or Iviron manuscripts. Although attributions are at present impossible, the cruciform lectionaries enhance our knowledge of twelfth-century Byzantine art. From all indications, they were made at Constantinople.

The Cruciform Lectionary in the Twelfth Century

The provenance of the New York and London lectionaries leads to Constantinople. According to the inscription on fol. 2, the New York Lectionary was given to the Constantinopolitan church of Saint George in the Cypresses by the Patriarch Konstantios II (1834–35). Although late, and involving a rededication, the note puts the manuscript unequivocally in the capital. The London Lectionary's tradition of provenance proves to be more elusive. Robert Curzon's account of the book's movements pertains to nineteenth-century Greece. What he writes was told to him by the lectionary's owners, whose interest would have been served by a colorful provenance that led back to the hands of Alexios and Manuel Komnenos, who are believed to be the actual scribes. But how much faith can be invested in this tale?

In examining the tradition related by Robert Curzon, we might begin with what speaks against it. The source of the important information is a note of dedication written by Methodios, bishop of Heraklia, on fol. 1; in it he remarks that the manuscript was of imperial hands, those of *either* Alexios *or* Manuel Komnenos. One manuscript written by a high government official does survive, but it was made under unusual circumstances.[29] No evidence allows us, much less encourages us, to suppose that members of the aristocracy often copied books for donation or that emperors ever did. The use of chrysography does not entail an imperial autograph, as Curzon avers; in fact, gold writing was common in the Middle Ages. (A great deal of the Dumbarton Oaks Lectionary was transcribed in gold, although no one has claimed it for an imperial autograph.) The note on fol. 1 of the London manuscript was clearly written centuries after the time the book was made. The names Alexios and Manuel Komnenos were common and need not denote, especially from the late vantage of the inscription, the twelfth-century emperors. The unusually expensive format of the manuscript could conceivably lead to a tradition claiming it to be an imperial dedication. A great deal speaks against the inscription and the account the monks of the Xenophon monastery gave to Curzon. Yet one fact survives: the manuscript was probably made sometime during the reigns of those emperors named Alexios and Manuel (Alexios I, 1081–1118; Manuel I, 1143–77, Alexios II, 1180–83). Is the late inscription the result of a guess or is it an informed attribution? Perhaps it was made on the basis of evidence no longer available to us. One medieval book cover made in metal and inscribed with the name of the donor survives.[30] Names of imperial donors generally appear on opening leaves of the manuscript, the very place where damage most frequently occurs.[31] Also, if the full lectionary included a second volume, then we lack it and possibly further information regarding the original dedication, information customarily written at the end of a work. At one time the manuscript might have contained evidence upon which the tradition was based. Attributing it to the cupidity of some monks eager to dupe a foreign collector seems not only cynical but also inaccurate in light of the inscription. Members of the Komnenos family were active donors who especially prized manu-

29. Paris. gr. 479: Lake, *Dated Greek MSS,* IV, pl. 240.

30. Venice, Bibl. Marc., lat. cl. 1: V. Laurent, "Monogrammes byzantins," *Epeteris Hetaireias Byzantinon Spoudon,* XXXIX–XL, 1972–73, 325–29. Other examples appear in T. Velmans, "La couverture de l'Evangile dit de Morozov et l'évolution de la reliure byzantine," *Cahiers archéologiques,* XXVIII, 1979, 121–23; and in G. Galavaris, "A Constantinopolitan Lectionary in the Great Lavra on Mount Athos 'Embellished' by the Wallachian Voevods," *Festschrift für Klaus Wessel zum 70. Geburtstag,* ed. M. Restle, Munich, 1988, 117–23.

31. Dedicatory poems and miniatures, alone or together, occur in such works as: the Paris Gregory (Paris. gr. 510: Omont, *Miniatures,* pls. XVI–XIX), the Menologium (Vat. gr. 1162) and Psalter (Marc. gr. 479) of Basil II (for both: I. Ševčenko, "The Illuminators of the Menologium of Basil II," *DOP,* XVI, 1962, 272 and n. 92), the Barberini Psalter (Vat. Barb. gr. 372: J. Anderson, "The Date and Purpose of the Barberini Psalter," *Cahiers archéologiques,* XXXI, 1983, 35–36, 62, figs. 1, 2), Paris. Coisl. 79 (Omont, *Miniatures,* pls. LXI–LXIV), and others.

The New York Cruciform Lectionary

scripts. That one member of the family commissioned the lectionary is plausible; the date and circumstances at the core of the tradition are altogether reasonable.

For two of the manuscripts the provenance leads to Constantinople. I see no reason to doubt that all four were made in the capital during the twelfth century. The attempt to date the manuscript more accurately requires comparisons that also point to Constantinople as the place where the lectionaries were made, perhaps by a loose consortium of scribes and illuminators. The intriguing similarities and differences might also resolve in a temporal sequence—work produced over more than one generation.

APPENDIX:

Robert Curzon's Account of the Purchase of the London Lectionary (Add. MS 39,603)

The text on fol. ix has been abridged, but without emendation:

This venerable manuscript was formerly preserved in the apsis behind the Altar of the monastery of Pantocratoras at Mount Athos, from whence it was brought out on great occasions only, and shown on feast days to the populace with the relics of the saints and benefactors of the Christian church among whom the Emperor Alexius Comnenus held a chief place for he was the founder of many a Monastery in Greece. . . . So much was the memory of the great king respected in the monasteries of his foundation, that so long as the golden binding gleaming with many a ruby and many a fair pearl and many a rich diamond remained on the book which he had written for the use of the sacred community remained, it was preserved with care in the most holy place, and brought forth with veneration for above 700 years to be displayed before the eyes of a grateful and admiring congregation on the most sacred festivals of the Church. Now it came to pass in these latter days that the patriotic feelings of the Greeks rebelled against the rule of the Mahomedan Sultan of Constantinople the haralch or capitulation tax was an abomination unto them. . . . Machmond was overthrown and Otho of Bavaria reigned in his stead. During 8 years of war the ceremonies of Religion were neglected reliquaries were melted down, and the sacred[iv] relics were scattered to the wind the books which had so long been preserved with pride and care were despoiled of the jewels with which the piety of former days had covered them and this book with many others was thrown aside to be neglected for a while, and then by accident to fall into the hands of a descendent from one of those barbarians whom he had feared and betrayed when they passed through his dominions on their way to the conquest of the Holy Land.

Some time during the Greek revolution this book found its way across the peninsula of Mount Athos to the monastery of Xenophou where I found it lying on the ground under a 3 legged stool with a fine MS of the 4 Gospels with a commentary bound in a faded red velvet lying on it. Looking at the note on the first leaf I suspected it might be the book mentioned by Dr. Carlysle and enquired its history of the monks. They said they knew that the 2 MSS above mentioned were precious books and that they were set aside under the stool that they might be preserved more carefully as they had something to do with some king or other but who or what he was they did not seem to understand.

[He then describes negotiations for purchase; at the end of five hours Curzon bought the manuscripts for twenty pounds.][32]

The note on the opposite page is written out below, in a more modern hand; by which, it seems, that this book is said to be an autograph of the Emperors Alexius and Emanuel Comnenus, the two first pages are written in purple ink, dried with gold dust, according to the usage of the Byzantine Emperors, the signature below the note is written in the form of a cypher, such as is used by the Patriarchs of the Greek Church, in imitation of the toura of the Sultan.

ἀφιορῶθη πάρα τού σεβασμιοτάτου γερουτος
ἀγίου Χιρίλου κυρίου μεθόδου ὡς δια της
ιστοριας ἔχομεν βασιλικῶν χειρῶν ἔργον ἐστιν
αλεξιου καὶ ἐμμανοήλου τῶν Χομνηνῶν

R. Curzon
Constantinople
August 22. 1837.

---

32. The story of the negotiations, only lightly reworked from the notes in the manuscript, was told by Curzon in his *Visits to Monasteries in the Levant,* reprinted: Ithaca, N.Y., 1955, 320–22; latest edition of the work first published in 1849.

V

Conclusion and Remarks on Style and Date

THE BYZANTINE CRUCIFORM LECTIONARIES form a loose collection of unusually handsome and expensive books. Their value is aptly expressed in the story of the imperial donation of the London Lectionary. Centering on Alexios or Manuel Komnenos bent over writing, the tale of the manuscript's creation reveals an assumption borne out by the study of the manuscripts. Although the content of the lectionary helped direct the worship of Christ and the saints, the Patriarchal church did not control the actual making of the manuscripts through a central office of book production. This was left to individuals, to the many scribes and donors, and from the available evidence these makers and users followed the lead of the patriarch. The provenance of the New York Lectionary, like that of the London manuscript, leads to the seat of the patriarch, Constantinople. The style of these two cruciform lectionaries likewise suggests Constantinople as the place where they were copied and illuminated. The New York Lectionary, in particular, contributes to our knowledge of painting in twelfth-century Byzantium.

The painting styles of the New York Lectionary's two principal illuminators are quite distinct. Of the two, Illuminator A was more responsive to innovations begun in the early decades of the twelfth century. Artists at work then had inherited methods of depicting the figure that had evolved early in the eleventh century as ones based on a conception of the figure that we read as flat; the methods of articulation tend to rely on systems of lines that lie comfortably on the picture plane. Early twelfth-century artists seemed to realize that such lines of drapery articulation could be curved to make the representation seem three-dimensional; moreover, when handled correctly, the lines imbued the figure with energy. One of the earliest dated works to combine energetic line and sculptural form is the portrait of Moses teaching in the Mount Athos psalter, Gregoriou cod. 157 (Fig. 62). A. Cutler has dated the manuscript to around 1108 on the basis of paschal tables (that had gone unnoticed).[1] The painter of the seated Moses created a complex three-dimensional pose. The overgarment ripples along its edges and breaks in tight undulating folds as it falls over the left arm. Here is the beginning of the "Dynamic Style," which E. Kitzinger has outlined for the second half of the twelfth century.[2] Illuminator A of the New York Lectionary is a virtuoso at interlocking small

---

1. First published by A. Cutler, *The Aristocratic Psalters in Byzantium*, Bibliothèque des Cahiers archéologiques, XIII, Paris, 1984, 21, figs. 33–36; *Treasures of Athos*, I, 465–69.

2. "Byzantium and the West in the Second Half of the Twelfth Century: Problems of Stylistic Relationships," *Gesta*, IX, 1970, 49–56; his claim that the style emerges in the 1160s may place too much emphasis on invention rather than on a period of gestation before the signal monument, Saint Panteleimon at Nerezi. On this manner, see also K. Weitzmann, "Eine spätkomnenische Verkündigungsikone des Sinai und die zweite

forms in complex spatial patterns. Four fine examples of his approach survive in the portrait of Christ on fol. 56, the two of Peter reacting to the denial, and the image of the council seated in judgment (Figs. 13, 25, 28, 14). All are highly expressive but show one of the liabilities of taking this approach. Passages that appear to be strongly three-dimensional—a convincing arm, portrait, or part of a leg—fail to cohere into a satisfying whole. The figure of Christ standing against the initial *tau* seems to have been divided into shell-like segments, each quite sculptural but none more than vaguely coordinated with an overall conception of a man standing and speaking.

Illuminator A's treatment of the early Dynamic Style may be contrasted with that of the illuminator responsible for the figure of Moses in the Gregoriou Psalter (Fig. 62). The early twelfth-century illuminator employed an overlay of lines to create the impression of a gauzy fabric waving with every movement. Illuminator A drew wider lines (as did his colleague, B) that curve and bend in concentric patterns, so that the material seems thicker. Despite the small scale on which he worked, Illuminator A created complex bunches of heavy material, as in those in the portrait of Saint Peter on fol. 167v (Fig. 25); one he pulls to his eyes and the other he tugs at nervously. This thick fabric, bent and twisted, is featured in other work of the period. An especially close counterpart can be found in the scene in the Seraglio Octateuch of the Israelites harvesting the quail and manna (Fig. 63). In the rippling of the garments at the hemline and over the arms, the facile highlights, and the treatment of the shadow along the face are parallels that point to a powerful style developing at Constantinople around the middle of the eleventh century. The drapery of the man seated second from the left in the council picture (Fig. 14) breaks around the feet in a series of deep folds that recall somewhat the use of drapery in the frescoes of Saint Panteleimon at Nerezi, commissioned by Alexios Komnenos Angelos and dated 1164.[3] The strong highlighting by itself, or in the way thin short lines emerge from islands of bright color, can be found in the Martorana at Palermo, executed in the 1140s.[4] Such highlighting likewise occurs throughout the miniatures of the Vatican edition of the monk James's Sermons on the Life of the Virgin, illustrated by one of the artists who worked on the Seraglio Octateuch.[5]

Illuminator A's methods of portraiture also contribute to dating his work. As a starting point for an appreciation of his conception of the face, one might return to the early twelfth-century Gregoriou Psalter. When painting the face of Moses (Fig. 62), the Psalter illuminator drew a hook under the eye and a prominent patch of red on the cheek, in themselves common Byzantine conventions. But this artist has strongly shaded the faces; and in emphasizing the fold under the eye and the rouging of the cheek, both of which he nearly ran together, he again proves to be a noteworthy figure in the early phase of the Dynamic Style. Both Illuminator A and the illuminator of the Octateuch miniature paint a solid zone of shadow running from beneath the eye down the

---

byzantinische Welle des 12. Jahrhunderts," *Festschrift für Herbert Von Einem zum 16. Februar 1965*, Berlin, 1963, 299–312, and L. Hadermann-Misguich, *Kurbinovo: les fresques de Saint-Georges et la peinture byzantine du XIIe siècle*, Bibliothèque de Byzantion, VI, Brussels, 1975, who painstakingly dissects the elements of the manner.

3. V. Lazarev, *Storia della pittura bizantina*, Turin, 1967, 199–200, figs. 301–4; P. Miljković-Pepek, *Nerezi*, Belgrade, 1966. For the patron and date, see G. Zacos and A. Veglery, *Byzantine Lead Seals*, I/3, Basel, 1972, 1527.

4. See especially the figure of Symeon: O. Demus, *The Mosaics of Norman Sicily*, London, 1949, fig. 50b. They also appear prominently in Berlin, Staatsbibl., gr. qo. 66, though at a later date: H. Buchthal, "Studies in Byzantine Illumination of the Thirteenth Century," *Jahrbuch der Berliner Museen*, XXV, 1983, figs. 30–32.

5. See his related method of treatment throughout Vat. gr. 1162: C. Stornajolo, *Miniature delle omilie di Giacomo Monaco (Cod. Vat. gr. 1162) e dell'Evangeliario greco Urbinate (Cod. Vat. Urbin. gr. 2)*, Rome, 1910, pls. 1–82.

Conclusion and Remarks on Style and Date

face. In the scene of the council (Fig. 14) the shadow takes the form of a sharp triangle, as it does in the frescoes at Nerezi.[6] Without question, this element of facial articulation gives the portraits in the manuscripts an appearance of emotional stress, although not necessarily one of sorrow. Sorrow is read in context, as, for example, when Peter weeps at the sound of the cock (Fig. 25). Primarily, at least at its beginning in early twelfth-century painting, the shadow appears to have been a way of adding greater plasticity to faces.

Illuminator A, it seems clear, takes part in the development of a manner of expression that begins at Constantinople and becomes increasingly strong over the course of the twelfth century; it is found in monuments of different media for various patrons, some foreign. The Gregoriou Psalter of 1108 is a related, yet earlier, treatment of what was more explicitly evoked in the Lectionary miniatures and the Octateuch. Documentary evidence places the execution of the Octateuch between the years 1138 and c. 1152.[7] What we can surmise about the career of its most prominent contributor makes a date within the range of the 1140s or early 1150s a likely choice. The similarities Illuminator A's style bears with that of this other illuminator, the Kokkinobaphos Master, lead me to propose that the Octateuch and Lectionary are roughly contemporary works of art, both made around the middle of the century. The differences between the manuscripts and the frescoes of Saint Panteleimon at Nerezi tend to support this assertion. In all, the stylistic parallels accord with the other documentation: the manuscripts were made at Constantinople during the height of the Komnene period: the final decade of John II's reign and the early part of Manuel's.[8]

The comparisons that put the execution of the New York Lectionary around the middle of the twelfth century are general ones; they relate the work of the first illustrator to a movement that can be tracked through a number of dated works of art. More precise parallels do exist but in undated manuscripts; their contribution to understanding Illuminator A's art speaks to the issue of the circumstances under which he and Illuminator B came to work together on the Lectionary. Evangelist portraits closely resembling those of the Lectionary survive in two other manuscripts: Mount Athos, Panteleimon, cod. 2 (Fig. 57),[9] and Paris, Bibliothèque Nationale, gr. 189 (Fig. 55).[10] The Athos manuscript is a Gospel lectionary with narrative illustrations; these were cited in chapter I and sometimes found to parallel ones in the New York manuscript. (The Panteleimon Lectionary also contains full-page scenes and some portraits whose style is unrelated to that of the initials and Evangelist portraits.[11]) The manuscript at Paris is a Gospel book with commentary, though the Gospels are arranged in lectionary order: John, Matthew, Luke, and Mark. Long ago, Albert M. Friend undertook the study of such portraits and discovered that Byzantine illuminators tended to use only a handful of compositions.[12] Actual portrait features were of course also fixed. One must therefore treat similarities with deliberate care. The Mark portraits in the two lectionaries follow a composition used variously for either Matthew or Mark in any number of medieval manuscripts;

---

6. Miljković-Pepek (as in note 3), figs. 14, 36–38.

7. Anderson, "Seraglio Octateuch," 86.

8. In general, this dating agrees with that attributed to the London manuscript when it is said to have been the work of Alexios or Manuel Komnenos; Manuel reigned from 1143 to 1180, and his successor, Alexios II, from 1180 to 1183. The source of the tradition is of course unknown.

9. Huber, *Athos*, figs. 89–91; *Treasures of Athos*, II, figs. 274–76.

10. Omont, *Miniatures*, pls. LXXXVIII–LXXXIX.

11. These miniatures have received greater attention than have those of the parent manuscript; see *Treasures of Athos*, II, figs. 277–81, 284–95, and Huber, *Athos*, figs. 92–110.

12. "The Portraits of the Evangelists in Greek and Latin Manuscripts," *Art Studies*, V, 1927, 113–47, and (part II) VII, 1929, 1–29; an outline of his final types is given by R. Bergman in *Greek Manuscripts from American Collections*, 44–47.

The New York Cruciform Lectionary

the portraits of John and Luke follow types very common in Byzantine art. As for the framing ornament, the step pattern is not exceptionally rare. It can be found, for instance, around the portraits of a Gospel book whose text was written in 948: Mount Athos, Vatopedi monastery, cod. 949.[13] The portraits in this tenth-century manuscript prove to be helpful in showing what is distinctive about the other sets. The Vatopedi portraits seem at first to be related.

When the portraits of the four manuscripts are compared author by author, similarities and differences appear. The composition for the portrait of John in the Vatopedi Gospels is not the same as that in the New York Lectionary and Paris Gospels. Furthermore, the relationship between figure and furniture differs throughout, as do the fundamental elements of style: proportions, drapery articulation, and the sense of movement and mood. The portraits in Vatopedi cod. 949 simply reveal how close the other three are to one another: compositions and drapery folds follow essentially the same patterns. The portrait of Mark, which appears in all three manuscripts, may serve as the basis of comparison. In each of the miniatures (Figs. 20, 55, 57), the Evangelist dominates the field of gold. His footrest juts into the foreground and the left leg slightly overlaps the writing desk; the illuminators thus specify the spatial relationships among the major elements of the composition. Illuminator A of the New York Lectionary brings the stool and desk nearly to the edge of the frame, and the footrest he paints actually touches it. The illuminators of the other two portraits leave a more ample strip of space (set by guides incised into the parchment) between the furniture and the frame. Slight differences in the designs of the stools and desks, as well as in precisely how folds were drawn, show that illuminators probably did such portraits from memory, improvising minor details as they went along. If we carefully examine just some of these details, the three sets divide into groups by style. Those of the New York and Panteleimon lectionaries are closer in execution to each other than either is to that of the Paris Gospels. The shading of Mark's eyes, for example, creates an illusion of relatively deep sockets in the Paris portrait, whereas the surfaces are flatter in the other two. The Paris Gospels may have been done before either the New York or Panteleimon Lectionary.

Aspects of how the Paris Gospels was made can supplement what we learn from style. The portraits in the Gospel book were each painted on a single leaf of parchment ruled specifically for them, without the mass of lines required by the text, especially text with commentary. The gatherings at the start of each Gospel are also regular quaternions, in two cases preceded by short gatherings (ends of John and Luke) with which the portrait leaves were bound. The approach to quire makeup is thus the same in the Paris Gospels and the New York and London lectionaries. Ornament in the Paris Gospels (Fig. 56) recalls that of the London Lectionary (Figs. 43–46). In both cases the work is precise and restrained; patterns tend to be small and the ornament relatively tight. The headpieces in the Gospel book are all rectangles; that of the opening to John's Gospel (Fig. 56: on which the first verse rather than the title is framed) is typical in the use of delicately drawn and modeled ornament of the traditional flower-petal type. The headpieces can be related to the portraits in the use of the same crenelated frame and the round finials at the upper corners. From the base rise smaller plants growing from delicate stems; they too recall the decoration of the London Lectionary,

---

13. Friend (as in note 12, part I), figs. 132–35; Lake, *Dated Greek Manuscripts*, III, pl. 152, publish at full scale the Luke and John portraits. The text of the manuscript was written by the celebrated scribe Ephrem: J. Irigoin, "Pour une étude des centres de copie byzantins, II, Quelques groupes de manuscrits," *Scriptorium*, XIII, 1959, 177–83.

specifically the *epsilon* that begins the first reading (Fig. 44).[14] The portraits in the Gospel book cannot be attributed to either Illuminator A or B, yet they belong to the same group of work, one coherent not because of copying but owing to a tradition of illustration shared by craftsmen over time. The Gospel book serves as a link, albeit attenuated, between two of the cruciform lectionaries.

The portraits in the Panteleimon Lectionary have traits that suggest a date later than the Paris Gospels or New York Lectionary. In all three sets (Figs. 20, 55, 57) a nearly continuous fold runs around the figures' shoulders, down their backs, and under the right leg, in most cases diminishing only at the right knee. In the New York and Paris manuscripts this fold is variously treated as a streamlined arc, broken into two parts in the New York manuscript, or, in the Paris manuscript, in a series of stately folds. The illuminator of the portrait of Matthew in the Panteleimon Lectionary (Fig. 57) gave the fold a slightly nervous quality by means of an uneven outline. This fold line can be found, strongly exaggerated, in the mosaics of Monreale[15] and in the frescoes of the church of the Holy Anargyroi, Kastoria,[16] both from the last quarter of the century. I would not suggest that the Panteleimon Lectionary was made that late, but the motif, as one exploited in monumental painting, allows us to date it after the other two sets of portraits.

The connection between Illuminator A's Evangelists in the New York Lectionary and the portraits in Panteleimon cod. 2 can be enhanced by considering the painting style of Illuminator B. Unlike his colleague, Illuminator B remained far more rooted in a flat style distinctly eleventh century in flavor. Yet related work can be found in two other lectionaries, including the narrative illustrations of Panteleimon cod. 2. The format of the Athos manuscript follows the customary two columns of bold script, which posed a constraint for twelfth-century illuminators. Most of the narrative illustration involves the initials, for example, Christ standing against the *tau* as he heals the possessed or the blind youth (Figs. 58, 59). Both subjects were painted in a bold, simple style; the initials first appear to be portraits to which only a crossbar has been added for the sake of the letter. To a certain degree, the same observation could be made of eleventh-century historiated initials, such as those found in Dionysiou cod. 587[17] or Morgan MS 639 (Fig. 64).[18] But since the time of these two lectionaries, the nature of initial ornament has changed markedly. Figures in the two earlier manuscripts are tall and thin and their drawing remarkably delicate and lively. The illuminators comfortably scatter large groups of figures in the thin margins between the text: Christ addresses his Disciples in Dionysiou cod. 587, or he ascends to heaven in the narrow space between the columns of Morgan MS 639.[19] In the scene of the miracle at Bethesda in Morgan MS 639, the small-scale figures tumble down the page and into the lower margin. Figure scale prevents such elaboration by Illuminator B and the painter of the initials in the Panteleimon Lectionary. The scene of Christ healing the youth is a compact, two-figure group that slightly invades the margin (Fig. 58); in the healing at Gadara the opposite margin comes into play (Fig. 59). In method of composition, these images easily compare with their counterparts in the New York Lectionary (Figs. 12, 15).

---

14. Often the script of the Paris Gospels resembles quite closely hands as early as the mid-eleventh century, but Omont, *Miniatures*, 47, presumably basing his remark on handwriting, attributes the manuscript to the twelfth century.

15. Demus (as in note 4), pls. 67a, 69, 72, 73, 75a; E. Kitzinger, *The Mosaics of Monreale*, Palermo, 1960, figs. 9, 17, 18 and pls. 6, 7, 44, 49, 54.

16. S. Pelekanides, *Kastoria*, I, Thessalonika, 1953, pls. 6, 7.

17. *Treasures of Athos*, I, figs. 191, 200.

18. Weitzmann, "Morgan 639," figs. 296–99, 301–6, for some further examples.

19. *Treasures of Athos*, I, fig. 226 (which reproduces a substantial amount of the leaf, from which one can judge the overall scale of initials, writing and pictures); Weitzmann, "Morgan 639," fig. 305.

They are also similar in style. Figures are broad, with occasional emphasis on the size of the head. Much of the drapery articulation was done through a simple pattern of wide shadow lines gently curving over the surface. The illustrations in the Panteleimon Lectionary appear to have been more heavily polychromed and the drawing of the faces seems cruder (possibly the result of the technique). This brings us to the second manuscript whose illustration recalls the work of Illuminator B.

In the National Library at Athens is another comparable lectionary (cod. 190)[20] written in double columns. Its illustration is even more strictly confined to the initials, as, for instance, in the healing of the blind youth. The illuminator simply depicted the youth.[21] Only in representing the miracle at Gadara did the illuminator make use of both the initial and the opposite margin: Christ stands against the *tau* gesturing to the two figures across the column of writing (Fig. 61). The similarities to the work of Illuminator B, considering both style and technique, can be striking. The illuminator of the Athens Lectionary tends to rely on his drawings, which he covers with successive washes; the figures' faces appear to have been more lightly colored than the drapery. The portraits of Saint Peter (both for Tuesday of Easter week: Figs. 4, 60) bear close comparison in the drawing of the hairline, the filling of the faces, and the emphasis on the simple sweep of the drapery. The hemlines of many of the figures in the Athens manuscript are asymmetrical; a small knob of fabric projects from the body.[22] Illuminator B occasionally draws the bottom of the tunic in the same way (Figs. 12, 15, 23, 30a, 32, 33), whereas Illuminator A uses other, more effective means to enliven figures. Some differences between the styles of Illuminator B and the painter responsible for the Athens Lectionary must also be pointed out. Faces in the Athens manuscript are drawn with an emphasis on the lower jaw; they are wider at the bottom than those done by Illuminator B in the New York Lectionary. In addition, the heads tend to be proportionately larger throughout the Athens manuscript. Similarities nonetheless remain, and they are strong enough to suggest the possibility of Illuminator B's having had experience with lectionary illustration before beginning work on the New York manuscript; style, in other words, reinforces the results of the analysis of subject matter and composition. Although he had the quadrants of the page in which to expand while still retaining an overall scale throughout his compositions, with few exceptions he failed to exploit the opportunity. His scenes, some of which depict the same subjects as those in the Athens and Panteleimon manuscripts, rarely go beyond minimal requirements: Saint Peter and the sepulcher; John, his disciples, and Christ; Christ and the woman at the well (Figs. 4, 5, 11).

The books most closely related in style of illustration to the New York Lectionary are the Gospel book Paris. gr. 189 and the lectionaries Panteleimon cod. 2 and Athens cod. 190. All were probably made over a period that covers, at the outside, the years from about 1120 to 1170. The three share elements of style and technique, as well as compositional patterns that involve both illuminators. It is noteworthy that the closest comparisons are with such books. In the study of how the New York Lectionary was made (chapter II), I suggested that it seemed to be a coordinated project executed by a scribe and illuminators who regularly worked together and not an informal collaboration of independent craftsmen. The relatively broad span of time that the books encompass makes exact attributions difficult, yet in these three we may have further indication that the New York Lectionary

20. Marava-Chatzinicolaou and Toufexi-Paschou, *Manuscripts of the National Library of Greece*, 154–61, figs. 349–81. I wish to express my thanks to Christopher Walter for his help in obtaining photographs of the manuscript.
21. Ibid., fig. 359.
22. Ibid., figs, 351, 354–56, 361, 370.

was made by a group. The group was successful over much of the twelfth century and prominent in the making of one kind of text. This hypothesis advances the claim that the other two cruciform lectionaries are likewise related as part of its production. The tightly controlled decoration of the London Lectionary (Figs. 43–47) reflects the nature of its commission as well as the date of execution; it can be compared in style to the headpieces in the Paris Gospels. The ornament of the Iviron Lectionary is much closer to that of the New York manuscript, and it should probably be considered as a roughly contemporary book. Not only does it have the luxuriant finials, it also has the step-frame motif in the border of the headpiece at the beginning of the menologion (Fig. 51), the same device that appears around the frames of the Evangelist portraits in the Paris Gospels and the New York and Panteleimon lectionaries and the headpieces of the Paris Gospels (Fig. 56).

The ornament in the cruciform lectionaries and the three related manuscripts appears to be competent, though not inspired; by and large the patterns are routine, and their execution moves in a range from exacting through desultory. Many of the patterns can be called traditional, since they have been in use since the mid-tenth century. The illuminators worked variations on the enclosed iris motif: small and delicately articulated blossoms alone (Figs. 45, 46) or combined with birds and animals (Figs. 2, 16, 21), large flowers with less illusionistic highlighting (Figs. 29, 43), and intricate patterns of geometrically interlocked flowers and stems (Figs. 48–51). In the headpieces of the New York and Iviron lectionaries the addition of the lush foliage that fills the quadrants creates slightly jarring juxtapositions: sometimes delicate patterns in the headpieces confront the thick and slightly unnatural plant designs of more recent popularity. The way in which these plants were boldly drawn in large scale (for example, Figs. 2, 16, 49) accords with the figural style of Illuminator B, as well as with the styles of those responsible for the Athens and Panteleimon lectionaries; the coherence becomes especially apparent when the figures and ornament are contrasted with the earlier, finer work in Morgan MS 639 (Fig. 64) or Dionysiou cod. 587. What further betrays the date is the relentless accumulation of decorative motifs: overgrown plants, birds flanking fountains, other birds standing on crossbars. The illuminators used the crenelated frame around headpieces and painstakingly added finials to each leaf of text. The emphasis on ornamental luxury increasingly looms as a feature of Byzantine illumination from the second quarter of the twelfth century. The agglomeration of patterns can be found in contemporary manuscripts like the Sinai. gr. 339 and Paris, gr. 550.[23] It is against this background that the Kokkinobaphos Master, in the decades before the middle of the century, invented new forms of ornament that quickly became popular in Byzantine illumination.[24] Those responsible for the cruciform lectionaries were either unaware of these inventions or chose the traditional paths of enrichment. We should of course be wary of putting a premium on innovation until it has been shown that twelfth-century Byzantines both recognized novelty and considered it important; certainly the spread of decorative innovations tended to follow a course that skirted the Gospel lectionary.[25]

Alone, the cross format of these manuscripts attests to the interest in decorative richness and becomes a hallmark of twelfth-century Byzantine art. Page after page of text written in the shape of the cross does give the lectionaries a particular place in contemporary art. The format is an unmistak-

---

23. Both illustrated in G. Galavaris, *The Illustrations of the Liturgical Homilies of Gregory Nazianzenus*, Studies in Manuscript Illuminations, VI, Princeton, 1969, figs. 377–97 and 398–427.

24. Specifically for the Vat. gr. 1162: Stornajolo (as in note 5), pls. 2, 8, 22, 33, 47, 59.

25. See the works discussed and illustrated in Buchthal (as in note 4), 45–46, figs. 19, 21, 23.

ably conspicuous mark of luxury. The amount of text on the leaves of the manuscripts varies. The scribe of the Dumbarton Oaks Lectionary was able to create the cross shape but squeeze a great deal of text into it by adopting a wide vertical segment (Fig. 54). In other regards the production of this manuscript seems to have been at a lower level than of others. One must wonder if this was apparent to the patron, or if the sums paid for luxury manuscripts reflected a knowledge of quality parallel to ours in modern times. The combined use of double columns and a cross format that allows for each page to hold a relatively large amount of text must be considered in conjunction with the pedestrian quality of miniatures and ornament. The headpiece ornament in the Dumbarton Oaks manuscript (Fig. 53) is not as commanding as that in the New York and London lectionaries (for example, Figs. 2, 43). One reason for this lack of presence is the Washington scribe's reluctance to use an entire side of parchment to write only the few words of a title. Although their subjects in no way suggest poor, untutored, or amateur work, the miniatures are executed without a strong sense of the expressive values of the artist's time. In the figures' proportions emphasis falls on the size of the heads and hands at the expense of the bodies; the articulation of faces or drapery tends to be weak and unfocused. Such work is not uncommon, though it is not often published and consequently is difficult to date precisely.[26] In general, nothing in the script or illumination contradicts a twelfth-century attribution for the manuscript. It is, I suspect, a book produced to emulate one of the other cruciform lectionaries.

Perhaps no object better transmits the ideals of the Orthodox Church and its conception of history and salvation than does the medieval lectionary. The lectionary's dramatic rise in popularity from the start of the eleventh century attests to a widespread need. Strong traditions of decoration and illustration seem to predate the medieval text. The result of so many factors—ancient roots, the response to deeply felt needs, and the prestige of the Church—was a book of more than average devotion and beauty. The illustration of some lectionaries was designed to express devotion to a particular saint[27] or to stress a distinctive set of feasts,[28] but even in such cases the specific finds its expression within the accepted framework of tradition. Each of the twelfth-century cruciform lectionaries was made with a particular church in mind; one or more lectionaries may have been tailored to the recipient, but we remain insufficiently informed to identify, on the basis of internal testimony, even one of those churches. The cumulative effect of page after page of crosses and finials is that of an imperial project carried forward without regard for cost. The patronage may well not have been imperial, but an impression of unusual luxury is an intended consequence of the format. Fittingly, the object of such attention was the Gospel lectionary. In time, our knowledge of the text, illustration, and decoration of such manuscripts may allow more accurate identification of their makers, patrons, and users.

26. The miniatures might be compared in style with those of London, British Library, Harley 5785, or Oxford, Christ Church College, gr. 14.

27. Peter of Monabata in Sinai. gr. 204 (K. Weitzmann, *Illustrated Manuscripts at St. Catherine's Monastery on Mount Sinai,* Collegeville, Minn., 1973, fig. 14) or John the Baptist in Dionysiou cod. 587; K. Weitzmann, "An imperial Lectionary in the Monastery of Dionysiou on Mount Athos: Its Origin and Its Wanderings," *Liturgical Gospels and Psalters,* XII, 244–47, who notes the unusually large number of subjects dedicated to John the Baptist and surmises a connection with the Studios monastery; I would debate the nature of the connection, as he construes it from possibly too early a date.

28. The Skevophylakion Lectionary of the Great Lavra: K. Weitzmann, "Das Evangelion im Skevophylakion zu Lavra," *Liturgical Gospels and Psalters,* XI, argues that the manuscript was the gift of Nikephoros Phokas to the Lavra; although I believe that the manuscript was probably made closer to the second quarter of the twelfth century, the arguments regarding the intended recipient nevertheless hold.

Index

Agony in the Garden, 11
Aland, Kurt, 80
Alexios I Komnenos, Emperor, 77(?), 77 n. 15(?), 87, 88–89(?), 91(?), 93 n. 8
Alexios II Komnenos, 77(?), 77 n. 15(?), 87, 88–89(?), 91(?), 93 n. 8
Alexios Komnenos Angelos, 92
Anastasis, 27
Ancient of Days, 85
Ann Arbor, University of Michigan, MS 171, 11 n. 69
Annunciation, 7, 27
anonymous scholar and schoolmaster, 37
antipascha, 29
arche/telos, 2
Ascension, 7, 27, 83
Athens, Ethnike Bibliotheke (National Library):
   cod. 57, 75 n. 6
   cod. 74, 75 n. 6
   cod. 93, 39 n. 33
   cod. 190, 9, 16, 17, 18, 19, 20, 21, 22, 26, 27, 96–97, Figs. 60, 61
   cod. 2645, 11 n. 69, 71 n. 19

Bačkovo, Theotokos Petritziotissa monastery, 9
   inventory, 3 n. 13
   typikon, 41 n. 3
Barlaam and Joasaph, 11
Basel, Universitätsbibliothek, cod. AN.3.12, 2, 7
Basil, priest and calligrapher, 37
Basil I, Emperor, 7
Basil Menologium. *See* Vat. gr. 1613
Berlin, Deutsche Staatsbibliothek, gr. qo. 66, 92 n. 4
Berlin, Universitätsammlung, Abteilung für christliche Archäologie und kirchliche Kunst, cod. 3807, 71 n. 16
Bliss, Mr. and Mrs. Robert Woods, 81
book cover(s), 6, 9 n. 53, 31, 31 n. 1, 71 n. 19, 87
Bratislava, Lycaeum Augustanum, Codex Mavrocordatianus, 75 n. 6

calendar, 2, 3, 4, 5, 7, 8, 11, 69, 71, 72, 86
Calvary, 23, Fig. 31a
Cambridge, University Library, cod. Nn.2.41 (Codex Bezae), 5
carmine, 3, 14 n. 5, 16, 18, 20, 22, 32–33, 77, 81
Chalcedon, Galakrenai monastery, 37
chanting, 3, 4
Christ:
   and Ancient of Days, 85
   arrest, 22
   Baptism, 7, 24, 27, Fig. 38
   cleansing the Temple, 82, 85
   Crucifixion, 23, 27, 84, 85, Fig. 34
   enthroned, 82, 83
   in Gethsemane, 22, 23
   heals blind, 11, 18–19, 27, 28, 35, 95, 96, Figs. 12, 58
   heals demoniac, 20, 35, 36, 40, 95, Fig. 17
   heals demoniac at Gadara, 19–20, 27, 95, 96, Figs. 15, 59
   heals daughter of Syrophoenician woman, 20
   heals paralytic at Bethesda, 18, 27, 28, 36, 83, 95, Figs. 8, 9, 64
   heals woman with issue of blood, 20
   images, 11
   and lawyer, 32
   miracle at wedding at Cana, 83, 85
   miracle of loaves and fishes, 83, 85
   on Mount of Olives, 21, Fig. 22
   Nativity, 7, 27
   and Peter, 83
   portrait, 19, 22, 71 n. 19
   prays, 83, Fig. 30a
   presentation in Temple, 24, 27, Fig. 39
   and priests and pharisees, 19, 36, 92, Fig. 14
   raises son of widow of Nain, 20, 27, 33–34, 36, Fig. 18
   raising Lazarus, 27
   sends Disciples into Jerusalem, 23
   story of rich man and Lazarus, 20–21, Fig. 19
   teaching, 22, 23, 27, Figs. 10, 13, 17, 30b
   teaching at Capernaum, 18, 20, 35, 36, 40, Fig. 10
   and Thomas, 11, 17, 28, 36, 83, 85, Fig. 7
   Transfiguration, 24, 27, 33, Fig. 40
   washes Disciples' feet, 11
   and women of Samaria, 18, 28, 35, 83, 84, 96, Figs. 11, 52
Christodoulos, 36
Cirta Constantina, 1
Codex Bezae. *See* Cambridge, University Library
Codex Ephraemi Rescriptus. *See* Paris. gr. 9
Colwell, Ernest Cadman, 42, 69
concrete poetry, 75
Constantine, priest, 10 n. 67, 37
Constantine I, Emperor, 1, 50
Constantinople/Istanbul, 5, 8, 12, 87
   Chalkoprateia School, 10 n. 67, 37
   Exakionion, 50
   Hebdomon, 44
   Library of the Greek Ecumenical Patriarchate, cod. 8, 9
   Mese, 50
   monastery of the Prodromos-Petra, 36
   monastery of Saint George Manganes, 37, 81
   monastery of Saint John Studios, 36, 98 n. 27
   monastery of the Theotokos Evergetis, 41, 42
   Saint George in the Cypresses, 14, 87
   Saint Sophia, 5, 6, 8, 41
      Patriarchal Oratory, 37
      Typikon, 3, 8–9, 22, 69, 72, 73
   Topkapı Sarayı Müzesi, cod. 8 (Seraglio Octateuch), 35, 36, 38, 39 n. 33, 92, 93, Fig. 63
Copenhagen, Kongelige Bibliotek, cod. GKS 9, 75 n. 3
Council of Constantinople (381), 6 n. 32
Council of Ephesus (431), 6
Council of Nicaea (787), 6
cruciform text, 11, 13, 25, 27, 75–76, 79, 81, 91, 97
Curzon, Darea, 77
Curzon, Robert, 77, 88–89

Index

Cutler, Anthony, 91
Cyril of Alexandria, 6

Darrouzès, Jean, 9
deacon, 1, 2, 6, 8, 25, 70, 71
diakainesimos, 28
Doisiades, "Altar," 75
Dura Europos, 1
Dynamic Style, 91, 92

Easter, 2, 7, 16, 78, 82
ekklesiarch, 25, 41, 42, 71
ekphonetic notation, 3, 5, 14, 18, 33, 77
Elijah, 24
Eusebius, 1
  Letter to Carpianus, 75
Eustathios Boilas, 9
evangelion, 3
Evangelist(s), 2, 7, 72
  John, 10, 15, 16, 82, 94, Figs. 1, 3
  Luke, 15, 24, 27, 94, Fig. 36
  Mark, 15, 21, 93–94, Figs. 20, 55, 57
  Matthew, 10, 15, 93, 95
  portraiture, 10, 11, 24, 31, 71 n. 19, 93

Feast(s). For New York Lectionary, see 59–64
Feast of Lights, 24
First Entrance, 1, 8
Florence, Biblioteca Laurenziana
  conv. soppr. 159, 75 n. 6
  Plut. 5.9, 75 n. 2
  Plut. 6.23, 16, 17, 18, 19, 20, 23
Friend, Albert M., Jr., 93

gatherings, 15, 32, 77, 94
Germanos I, Patriarch, 1–2, 6, 6 n. 33, 71
Godescalc Gospels. *See* Paris, nouv. acq. lat. 1203
Golgotha, 23
Gospel book, 2, 3, 4, 5, 6, 7, 8, 9, 10, 11, 25, 26, 70, 71 n. 19, 72
Gregory, Caspar René, 42, 73, 80
Gregory of Nazianzus (sermons), 8, 11, 37, 38 n. 27, 81
Gregory Pakourianos, 9

Holy Cross, Feast of Exaltation, 2, 7, 23, 27, 84
Holy Fathers of Nicaea, 42 n. 7, 83
Holy Thursday, 21, 27

Iconoclasm, 7
illuminator(s), 7, 10, 26, 27, 29, 39
Incarnation, 2, 6, 7, 8, 10, 11, 70, 71
incipit(s), 2, 7, 16, 23, 42, 42 n. 10
initial(s), 7, 16 n. 7, 11, 25, 32, 38, 39, 80
inscriptions, 38
Isaiah, 42 n. 7
Italy, 5

Jerusalem, 18
  Orthodox Patriarchate, library
    cod. Mar Ibrahim 9, 71 n. 15
    cod. Taphou 14, 76 n. 7
John, monk and scribe of the Great Lavra, 37
John II Komnenos, Emperor, 93
John Chrysostom, Patriarch, 11
John Climacus, *Heavenly Ladder*, 11
John Kaloploïmos, priest, 37
Joseph of Arimathea, 83
Justin Martyr, 1, 5
Justinian, Emperor, 1, 3

Kastoria, church of the Holy Anargyroi, 95
kathemerinon, 3 n. 13
Kennerley, Mitchell, 14
Kitzinger, Ernst, 91
Kokkinobaphos Master, 92, 93, 97
Konstantios II, Patriarch (1834–35), 14, 87

Lake, Kirsop and Silva, 37
lectionary:
  incipits, 42 n. 10
  names, 3
  narrative illustration, 11
  origin, 3–7
  structure, 2
Leningrad, Gosudarstvennaja Publičnaja Biblioteka im. M.E. Saltykova-Ščedrina (M.E. Saltykov-Ščedrin State Public Library), cod. 21, 11
Lent, 2, 21, 78, 80
liturgy, 1, 3, 4, 6, 7, 11 n. 70, 71
London, British Library:
  Add. MS 5153, 79, 79 n. 17
  Add. MS 11,300, 75 n. 6
  Add. MS 19,352, 22 n. 15, 36
  Add. MS 39,603, 32, 40, 42 n. 6, 76–80, 86, 87, 91, 94, 97, Figs. 43–47
  Harley 5598, 25 n. 20
  Harley 5785, 76 n. 8, 98 n. 26
Louis the Pious, Emperor, 6 n. 37

Madrid, Biblioteca Nacional, cod. vitr, 26–2 (Madrid Skylitzes), 38
Manuel I Komnenos, Emperor, 77(?), 87, 88–89(?), 91(?), 93 n. 8
Mateos, Juan, 9, 73
Maximos the Confessor, 6
menologion, 2, 12, 22, 25, 27, 70, 72, 81
Menologion of Metaphrastes, 11
Methodios, bishop of Heraklia (1760–94), 77
Michael II, Emperor, 6 n. 37
Michael Attaliates, 9
Milan, Biblioteca Ambrosiana, B.80.sup, 75 n. 5
Miracle of Quail and Manna, 92, Fig. 63
Monreale, cathedral, mosaics, 95
Moscow, Gosudarstvennij Istoričeskij Muzej (State Historical Museum), gr. 129, 22 n. 15
Moses, 23, 24, 91, 92, Figs. 31, 40, 62
  and brazen serpent, 23, Fig. 31b
Mount Athos:
  Dionysiou monastery:
    cod. 65, 71 n. 17
    cod. 587, 9, 16, 17, 18, 19, 21, 22, 23, 24, 26, 27, 28, 39 n. 34, 85, 95, 97, 98 n. 27
  Great Lavra, 37, 98 n. 28
    cod. A.86, 7, 11, 16 n. 7
    cod. A.92, 10, 71 n. 19
    cod. B.52, 5
    skevophylakion, unnumbered lectionary, 9–10, 98 n. 28
  Gregoriou monastery, cod. 157, 91, 93, Fig. 62
  Iviron monastery:
    cod. 16, 76 n. 9
    unnumbered lectionary (cruciform), 40, 80–81, Figs. 48–51
  Panteleimon monastery:
    cod. 2, 10, 16, 17, 19, 20, 21, 22, 27, 93–96, 97, Figs. 57–59
    cod. 27, 79
  Pantokrator monastery, 77, 88
    cod. 61, 22 n. 15
  Stauronikita monastery, cod. 15, 37 n. 18, 81
  Vatopedi monastery, cod. 949, 93
  Xenophon monastery, 77, 87, 88
Mount Sinai, monastery of Saint Catherine:
  gr. 48, 33 n. 5, 36
  gr. 204, 5, 10, 71 n. 19
  gr. 208, 11 n. 69, 98 n. 27
  gr. 210, 5 n. 19, 8 n. 46
  gr. 339, 38 n. 27, 76 n. 11, 97
  gr. NE Meg. Perg. 12. *See* gr. 210

Nerezi, St. Panteleimon, frescoes, 91 n. 2, 92, 93
New Testament, 1, 4, 5, 80
New Year, 7, 20, 22, 83, 85
New York, Metropolitan Museum of Art, Egyptian Dept., Inv. no. X455, 5 n. 23
New York, Pierpont Morgan Library:
 cod. M 639, 9, 10, 16, 17, 18, 19, 21, 22, 24, 27
 cod. 647, 10 n. 65
Nicodemus, 82
Nikephoros Phokas, Emperor, 98 n. 28
Niketas, Admiral of the Fleet, 37, 38
Niphon, reader and scribe, 37

Odessa, Gosudarstvennij Istoriko-Kraevedčeskij Muzej (State Historical and Regional Museum), PI-2251 (Aland l 1554), 9 n. 56
Old Testament, 1, 5
ornament, 5, 7, 13, 25–26, 33, 76, 78, 79, 80, 86, 94, 97
Oxford, Bodleian Library:
 Canon. gr. 92, 5 n. 27
 Cromwell 15, 75 n. 6
Oxford, Christ Church College, gr. 14, 98 n. 26

Palatine Anthology, 75
Palermo, Martorana, mosaics, 92
Palestine, 5
Palm Sunday, 7, 21
Paris, Bibliothèque Nationale:
 Coisl. gr. 20, 75 n. 6
 Coisl. gr. 31, 5, 5 n. 27
 Coisl. gr. 79, 87 n. 31
 Coisl. gr. 213, 37 n. 19
 gr. 9, 5
 gr. 64, 75 n. 6, 76 n. 7
 gr. 70, 75 n. 6
 gr. 74, 16, 17, 18, 19, 20, 23, 24, 36
 gr. 189, 93–94, 96, 97, Figs. 55, 56
 gr. 278, 5
 gr. 479, 37 n. 24, 38, 87 n. 29
 gr. 510, 6 n. 32, 7, 87 n. 31
 gr. 550, 97
 gr. 580, 75 n. 4
 gr. 784, 37
 gr. 2832, 75 n. 1
 nouv. acq. lat. 1203, 10 n. 67
 suppl. gr. 27, 10, 16, 17, 19, 20, 21, 22, 24, 27, 28
 suppl. gr. 384, 75 n. 1
 suppl. gr. 1096, 10 n. 67, 37 n. 21
 suppl. gr. 1155, 4 n. 16, 5 n. 19
Paris, Société biblique française, unnumbered lectionary (Aland l 351), 9
Paschal Chronicle, 44
Passion reading(s), 22, 25, 27, 28, 83, 84, 85
Patmos, monastery of Saint John, 36–37
 inventory, 3 n. 13, 9
 library:
  cod. 33, 25 n. 21
  cod. 70, 11
  cod. 221, 37 n. 20
  cod. 245, 37 n. 14
patriarch of Constantinople, 4 n. 17, 9, 41, 91
patron(age), 7, 9, 11, 26, 27, 29, 40, 42, 71 n. 17, 72, 76, 87–88, 91
Paul the Silentiary, 6 n. 35
Pentecost, 2, 7, 19, 27, 28, 78, 83
Pentecost, represented, 19
pericope, 2, 3, 42, 70, 72
Peter, of the Chalkoprateia School, 10 n. 67
Pilate, 23, Fig. 33
Pliny the Younger, 1
Presentation in the Temple, 7, Fig. 39
priest, 6, 8
Princeton, University Library:
 Garrett MS 1, 11, 76
 Garrett MS 2, 75 n. 6
 Garrett MS 3, 76 n. 8
 Garrett MS 6, 10 n. 67, 71 n. 19
 Scheide MS 1, 75 n. 6
Proklos, Patriarch, 44
psalter, 4 n. 18, 22, 26, 71, 79

quire. *See* gathering

Rahlfs, Alfred, 43
Riddle, Donald W., 42, 69
Rigopoulos, George, 14
Rome, Biblioteca Apostolica Vaticana:
 Barb. gr. 372, 22 n. 15, 87 n. 31
 Ottob. gr. 175, 4 n. 17
 Pal. gr. 24, 79
 Pal. gr. 189, 76 n. 8
 Reg. gr. 1, 75 n. 4
 Urb. gr. 2, 75 n. 6
 gr. 351, 5, 5 n. 27, 7
 gr. 364, 75 n. 6
 gr. 463, 37–38, 40 n. 35, 76 n. 8
 gr. 756, 11 n. 70, 71 n. 19
 gr. 1156, 9, 10, 23, 81
 gr. 1162, 92 n. 5, 97 n. 24
 gr. 1522, 5, 10 n. 65
 gr. 1613 (Basil Menologium), 38, 87 n. 31
rubrics, significance, 28–29

sabbatokuriakon, 3 n. 13
Saint Andrew, 17
Saint Athanasios, 37
Saint Basil, sermons, 37, 38
Saint Demetrios, 24, 27, Fig. 37
Saint Gall, Stiftsbibliothek, cod. 908, 7 n. 39
Saint John the Baptist, 10, 17, 82, 96, 98 n. 27, Fig. 5
Saint John, at Crucifixion, 23, Fig. 34
Saint Joseph, 24, Fig. 39
Saint Niketas, 24, 27, Fig. 35
Saint Peter of Monabata, 5, 10, 98 n. 27
Saint Peter, 17, 83, 96, Fig. 60
 betrayal, 11, 21, 83, 85, 92, 93
 runs to Christ's tomb, 16, 27, 28, 82, 96, Fig. 4
 weeping, 22, 40, Figs. 25, 54
Saint Symeon Stylites, 22, 27, 32, Fig. 29
Saint Theodore Tiron, 21, 83, Fig. 21
Saints of Dumbarton Oaks Lectionary, 84. *See also* individual saints
Saints of New York Lectionary, 59–64. *See also* individual saints
Saturday-Sunday lectionary, 3 n. 13, 28
scribe(s), 2, 4, 7, 29, 31–33, 37, 38, 39, 40, 68, 69, 72, 75, 79, 82, 84, 91
scriptorium, 36, 37
Scrivener, Frederick H., 77
Serres, Prodromos monastery, cod. 17, 25 n. 20
Simias, "Axe," 75
single leaves, 15
sketch, 33–34, 35, 36
skevophylax, 25, 41, 71
Smyrna, Evangelike Schole (Evangelical School), cod. A.1 (Smyrna Octateuch), 38
Sotheby's, 81
stichararion, 37
Strategos, priest and scribe, 37
Symeon Metaphrastes, 8
Symeon, 24, Fig. 39
Symeon, monk and scribe of the Galakrenai monastery, 37
synaxarion, 2, 10, 15, 25, 27, 28, 70, 72, 81
Synaxarion, Constantinople, 69

tetraevangelion, 3
Theocritus(?), "Pipes," 75
Theodore, Abbot, Galakrenai monastery, 37, 38
Theodore the Studite, 37
Theodosius, Emperor, 44
Theophilus, Emperor, 6 n. 37
Timothy, monk, 41

Index

Trajan, Emperor, 1
Transfiguration, 7, Fig. 40
Turin, Biblioteca Nazionale Universitaria, cod. C.I.6, 38 n. 27
typikon(a), 41, 71
typology, 23–24, 27

underdrawing. *See* sketch

Venice, Biblioteca Nazionale di San Marco:
  cod. gr. 1.18 (=1276), 75 nn. 5, 6
  cod. lat. cl. 1, 87 n. 30

cod. Z 540 (=557), 11 n. 70
Venice, Greek Institute of Byzantine and Post-Byzantine Studies, cod. 2 (Aland l 279), 9, 11 n. 69, 22, 27
Venice, San Giorgio dei Greci, lect. 1 (Aland l 279). *See* Venice, Greek Institute of Byzantine and Post-Byzantine Studies
vermilion, 14 n. 5, 19, 21, 22, 34
Vienna, Nationalbibliothek:
  theol. gr. 126, 81, 81 n. 23
  theol. gr. 154, 2, 80
  theol. gr. 336, 71 n. 16
Virgin:
  Annunciation, 7, 27

  birth of, 7
  and Christ (image), 8, 10, 70–71
  at Crucifixion, 23
  Dormition, 7, 27
  veneration, 71

Walter, Christopher, 22
Washington, D.C., Dumbarton Oaks Collection:
  cod. 1, 28, 40, 81–86, 96–97, Figs. 60, 61
  cod. 3, 71 n. 16
Weitzmann, Kurt, 8, 70

Illustrations

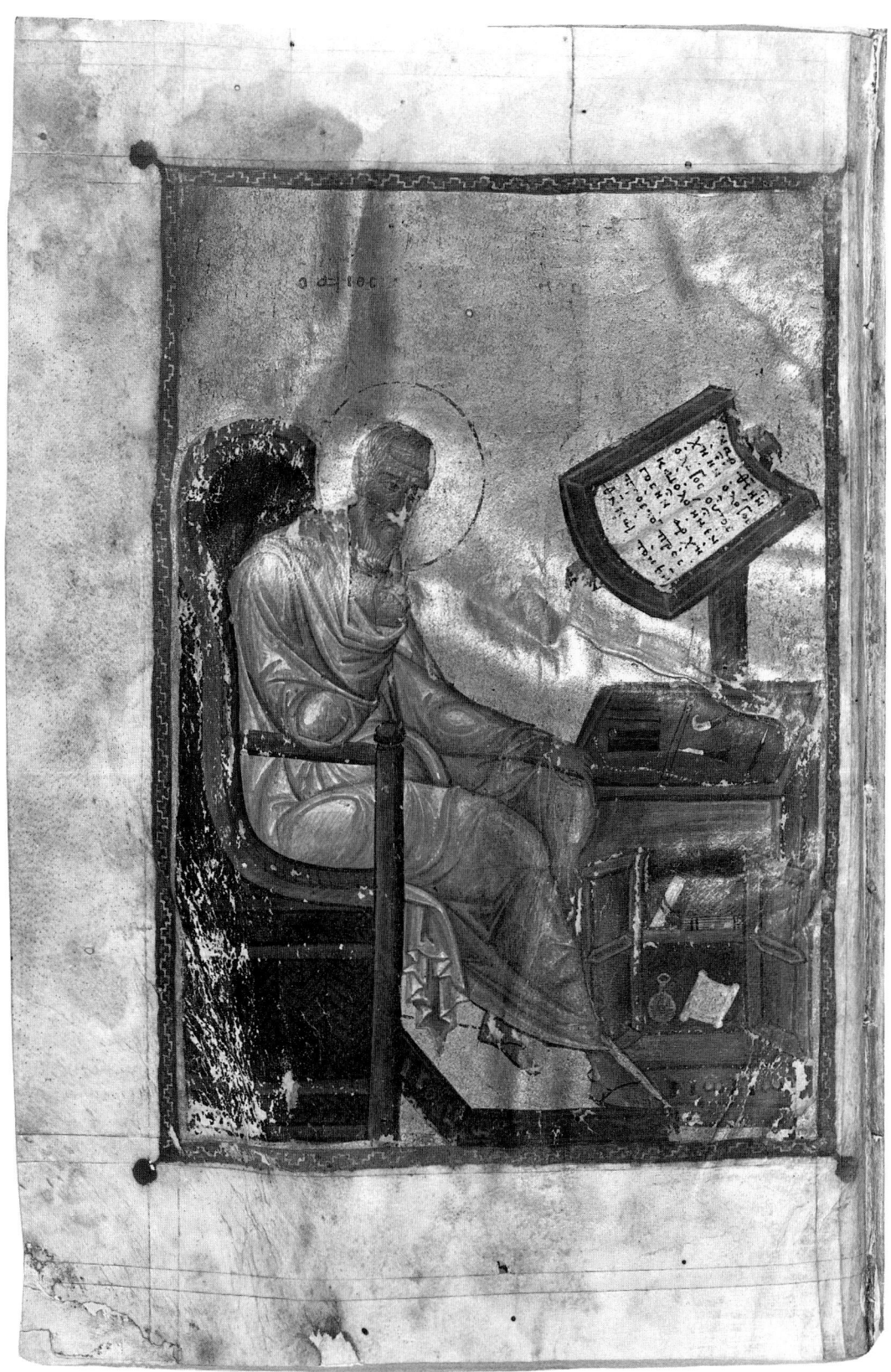

Fig. 1. New York, Morgan Library, MS 692, fol. 1v: Saint John the Evangelist

Fig. 2. New York, Morgan Library, MS 692, fol. 2: Title page of the Easter and John readings

Fig. 3. New York, Morgan Library, MS 692, fol. 2v: John the Evangelist writing

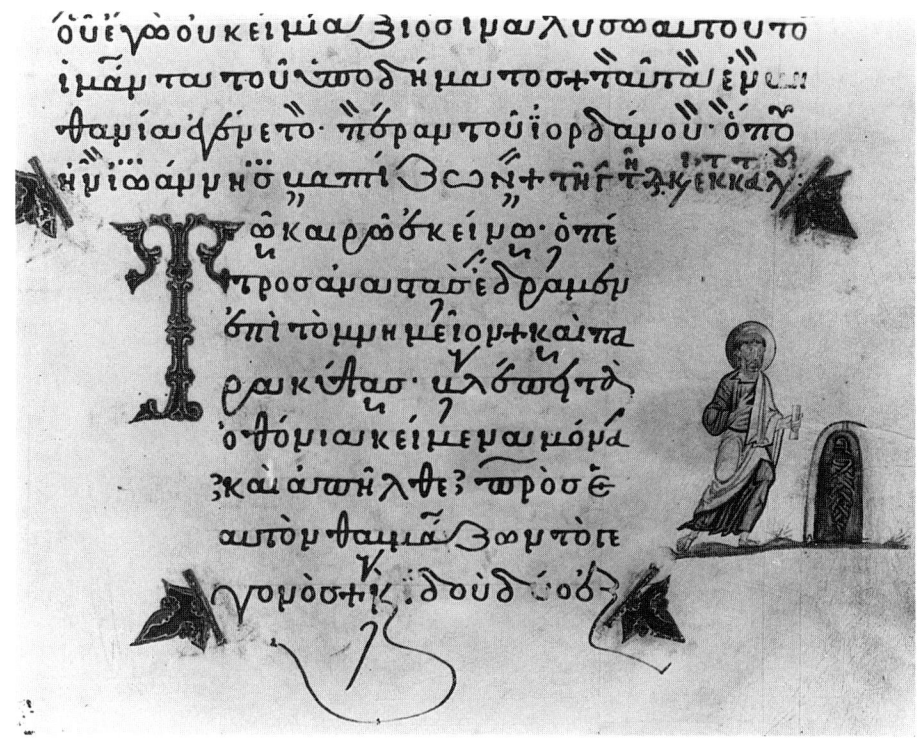

Fig. 4. New York, Morgan Library, MS 692, fol. 4: Saint Peter runs to Christ's tomb

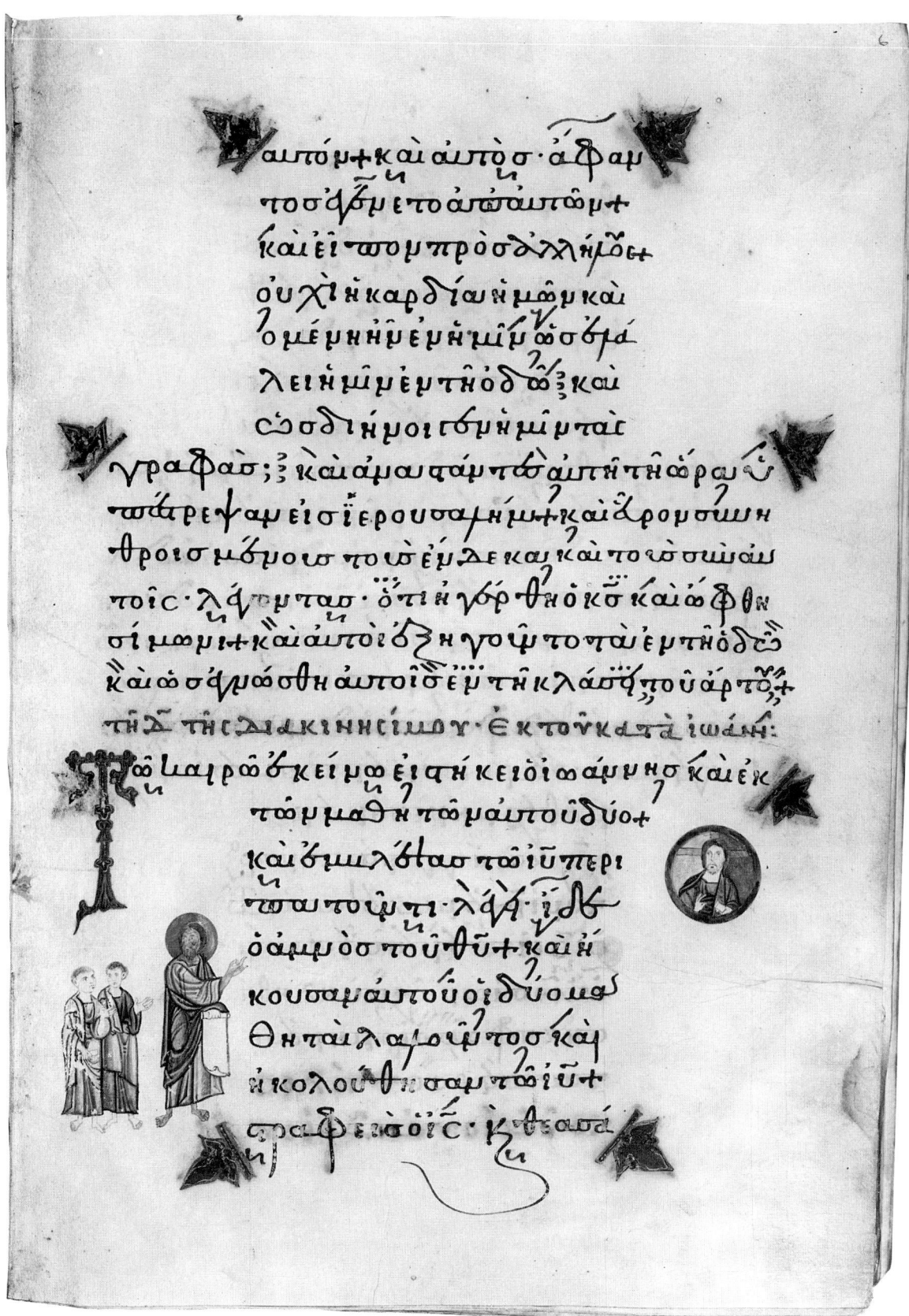

Fig. 5. New York, Morgan Library, MS 692, fol. 6: John the Baptist speaks of Christ to his disciples

Fig. 6. New York, Morgan Library, MS 692, fol. 10v: Christ appears to the Disciples

Fig. 7. New York, Morgan Library, MS 692, fol. 11: Christ speaks to Thomas and the Disciples

Fig. 8. New York, Morgan Library, MS 692, fol. 22v: Miracle at the pool of Bethesda

Fig. 9a. New York, Morgan Library, MS 692, fol. 23 (top): Christ and the Paralytic

Fig. 9b. New York, Morgan Library, MS 692, fol. 23 (bottom): The Jews and the Paralytic

Fig. 10. New York, Morgan Library, MS 692, fol. 25v: Christ in the temple at Capernaum

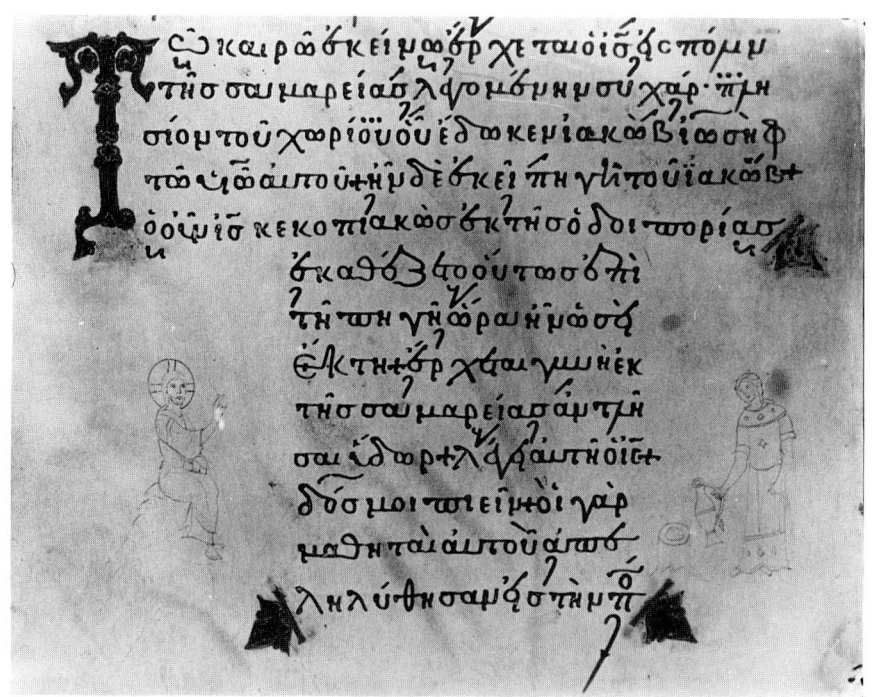

Fig. 11. New York, Morgan Library, MS 692, fol. 29v: Christ and the Woman at the Well

Fig. 12. New York, Morgan Library, MS 692, fol. 38: Christ and the Blind Youth

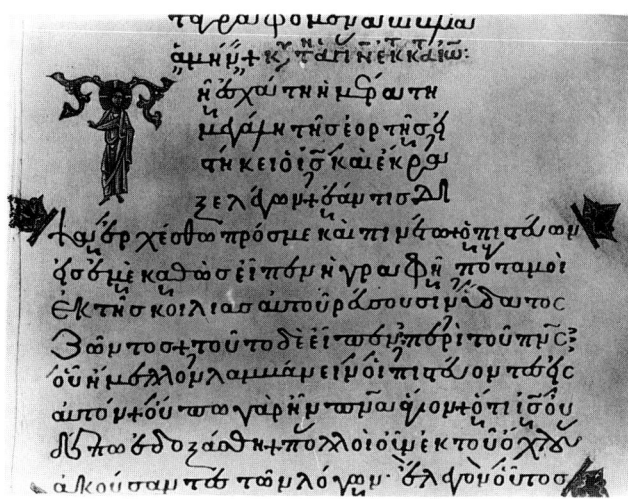

Fig. 13. New York, Morgan Library, MS 692, fol. 56: Christ Teaching

Fig. 15. New York, Morgan Library, MS 692, fol. 64v: The Healing at Gadara

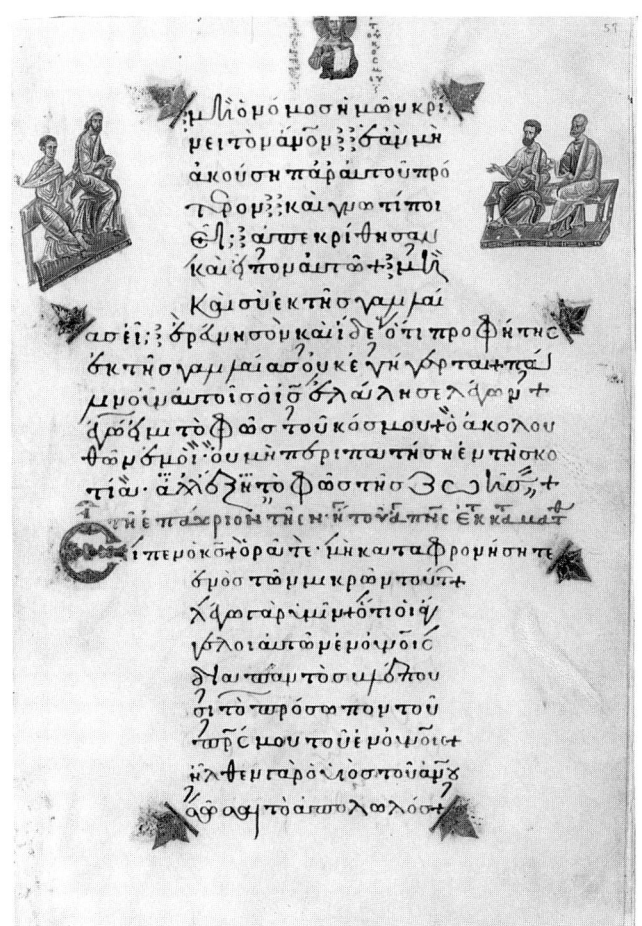

Fig. 14. New York, Morgan Library, MS 692, fol. 57: Christ, the Priests, and the Pharisees

Fig. 16. New York, Morgan Library, MS 692, fol. 87: Title page: Beginning of the new year and the readings from Luke

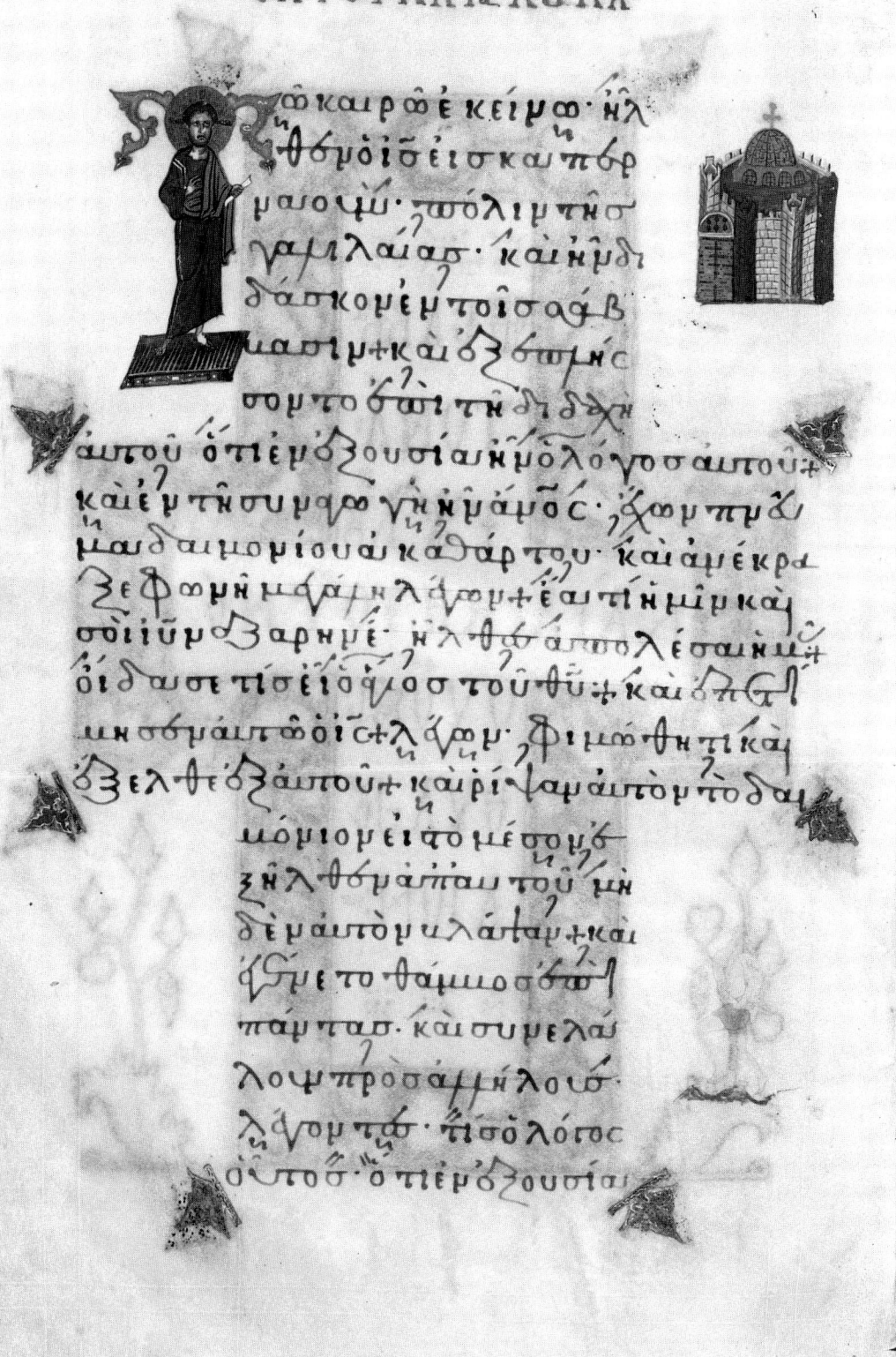

Fig. 17. New York, Morgan Library, MS 692, fol. 87v: Christ teaching at Capernaum, and the Man Possessed

Fig. 18. New York, Morgan Library, MS 692, fol. 91: Christ raises the son of the Widow of Nain

Fig. 19. New York, Morgan Library, MS 692, fol. 94v: Christ and the Rich Man

Fig. 20. New York, Morgan Library, MS 692, fol. 123v: Saint Mark the Evangelist

Fig. 21. New York, Morgan Library, MS 692, fol. 124: Title page of the first Sunday of Lent, and the beginning of the Mark readings; portrait of Saint Theodore Tiron

Fig. 22. New York, Morgan Library, MS 692, fol. 135v: Christ on the Mount of Olives and Jerusalem

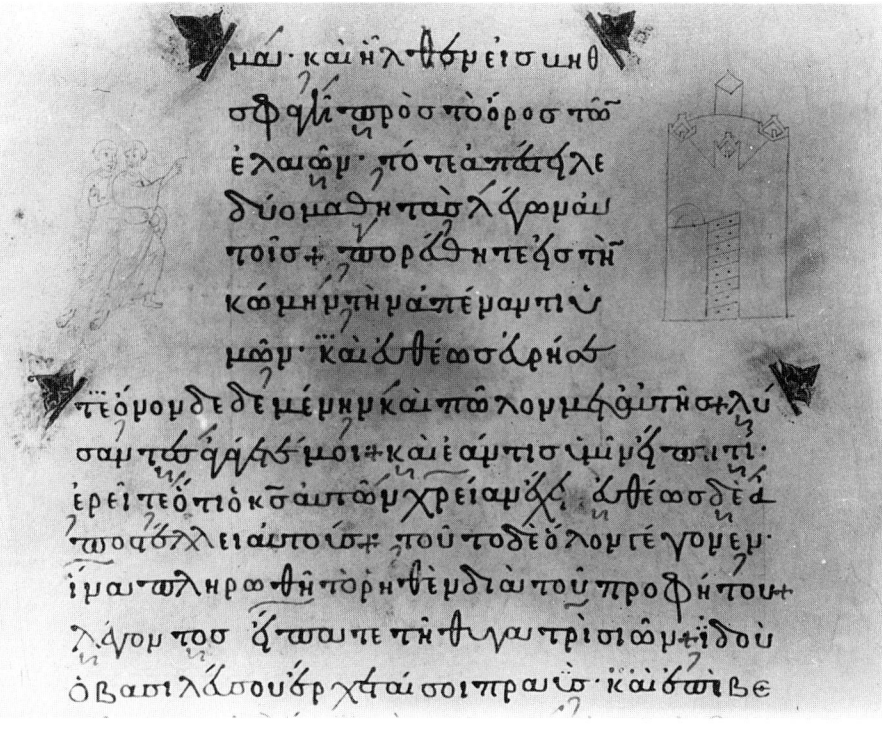

Fig. 23. New York, Morgan Library, MS 692, fol. 136: The Disciples go to Jerusalem

Fig. 24. New York, Morgan Library, MS 692, fol. 159v: Crowing rooster

Fig. 25. New York, Morgan Library, MS 692, fol. 167v: Saint Peter weeps as rooster crows

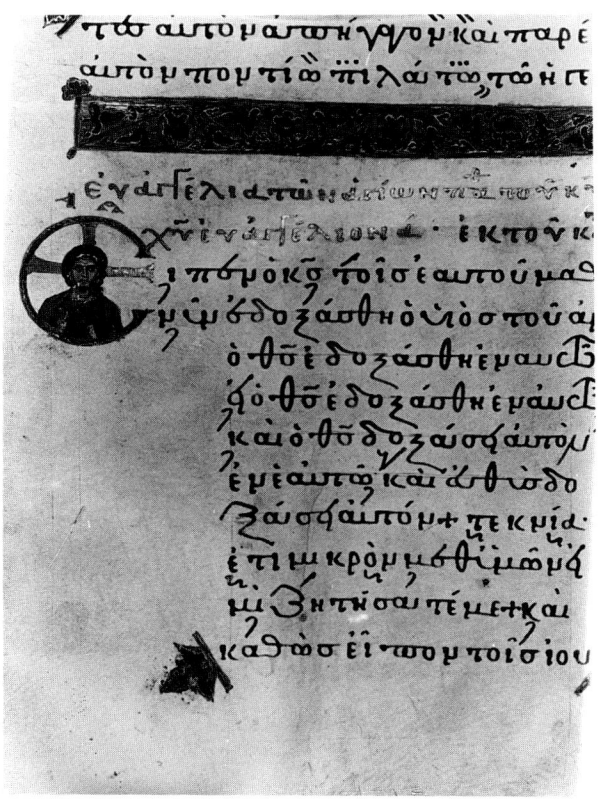

Fig. 26. New York, Morgan Library, MS 692, fol. 168: Portrait of Christ

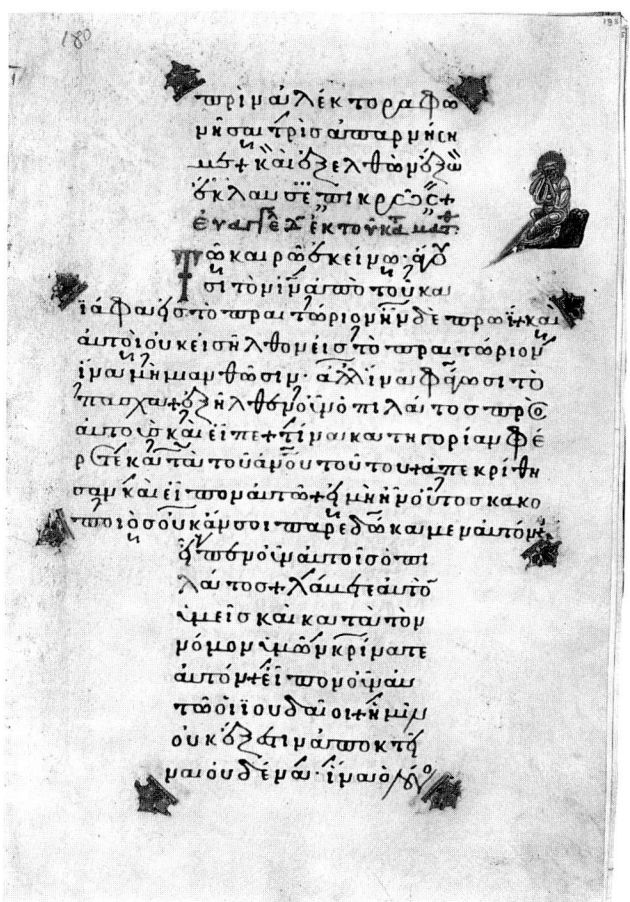

Fig. 28. New York, Morgan Library, MS 692, fol. 183: Saint Peter weeping

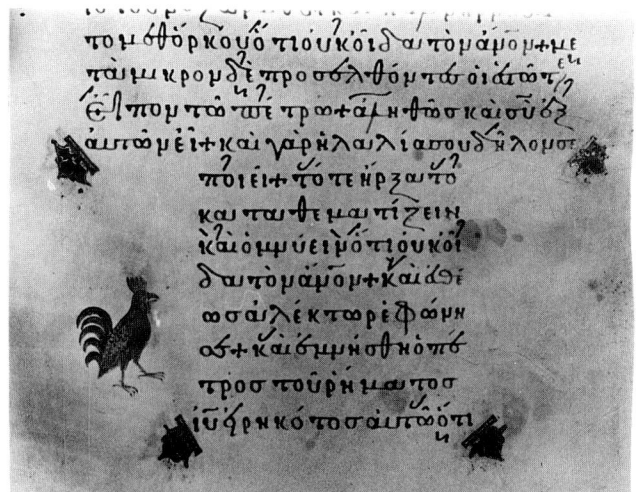

Fig. 27. New York, Morgan Library, MS 692, fol. 182v: Crowing rooster

Fig. 29. New York, Morgan Library, MS 692, fol. 214: Title page of the Menologion; portrait of Saint Symeon Stylites

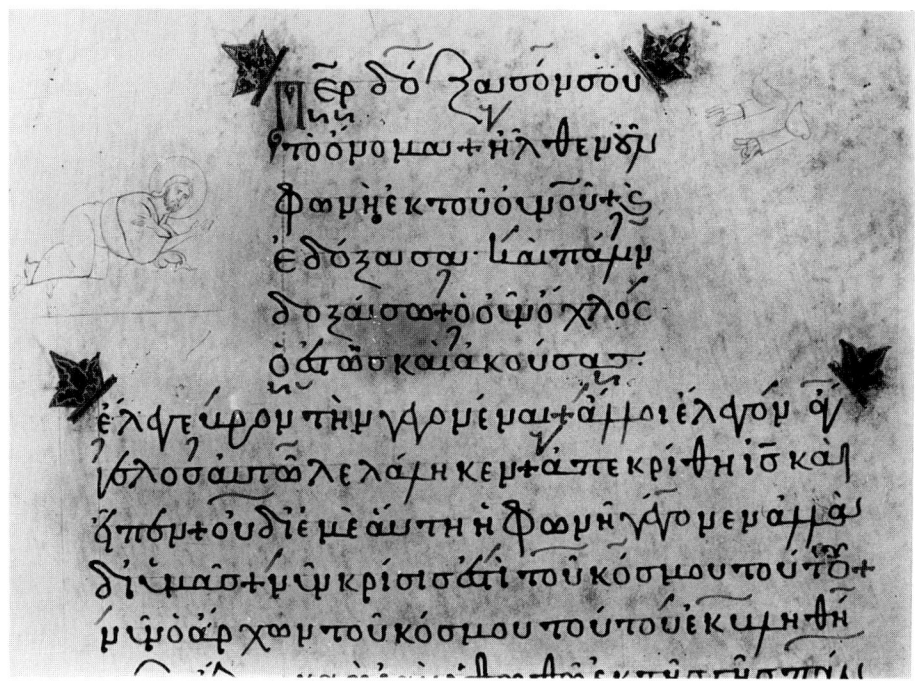

Fig. 30a. New York, Morgan Library, MS 692, fol. 221v (top): Christ kneels before the hand of God

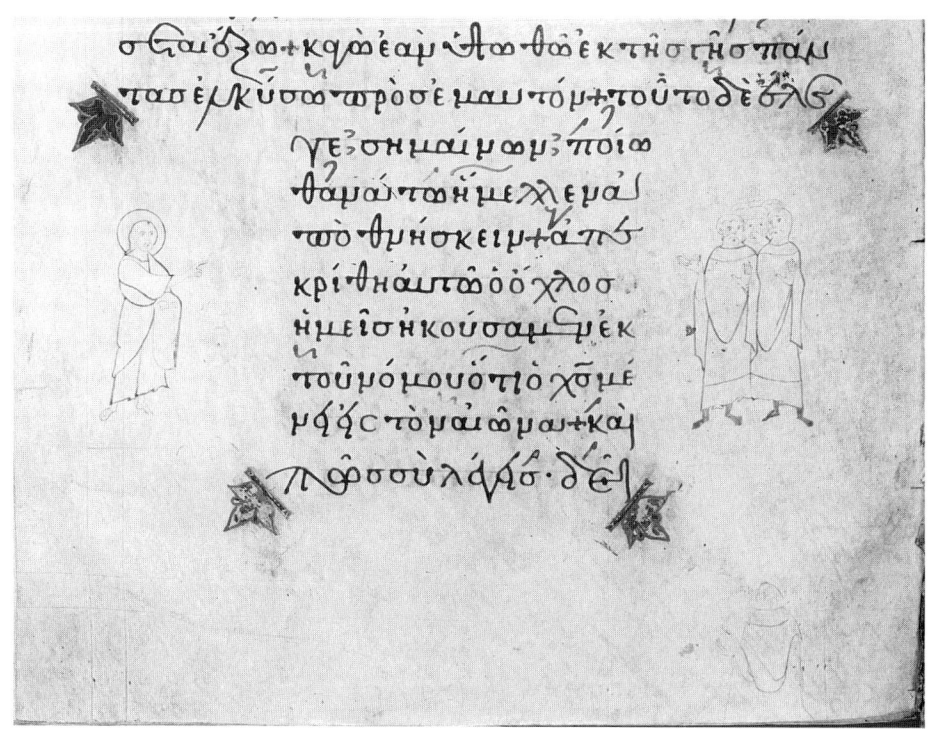

Fig. 30b. New York, Morgan Library, MS 692, fol. 221v (bottom): Christ explains the voice from heaven

Fig. 31a. New York, Morgan Library, MS 692, fol. 222 (top): Crosses on Calvary

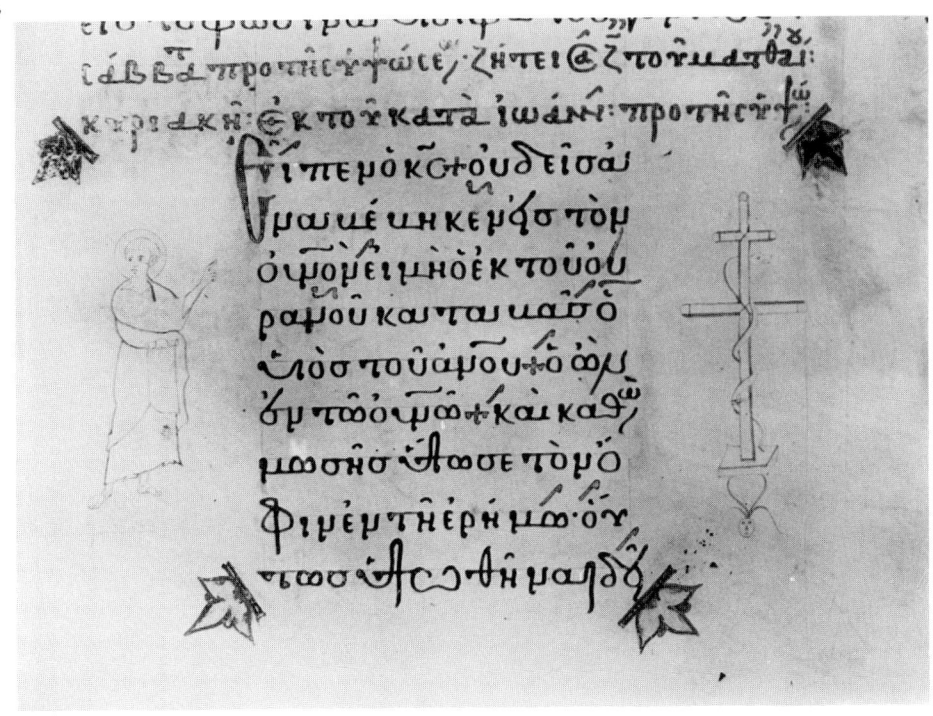

Fig. 31b. New York, Morgan Library, MS 692, fol. 222 (bottom): Moses and cross with serpent

Fig. 32. New York, Morgan Library, MS 692, fol. 222v: Priests plotting Christ's death

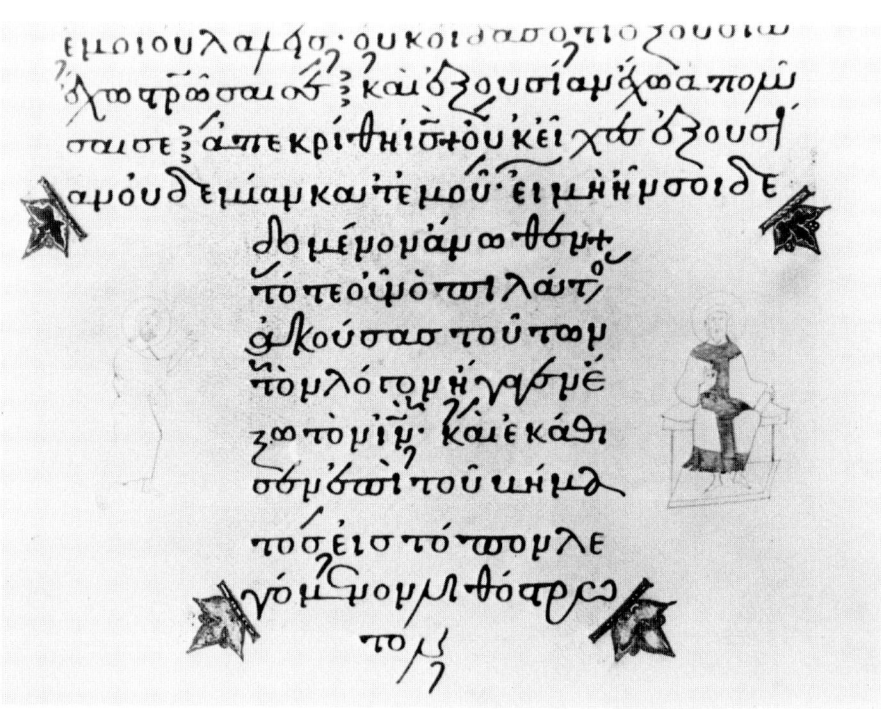

Fig. 33. New York, Morgan Library, MS 692, fol. 223: Christ and Pilate

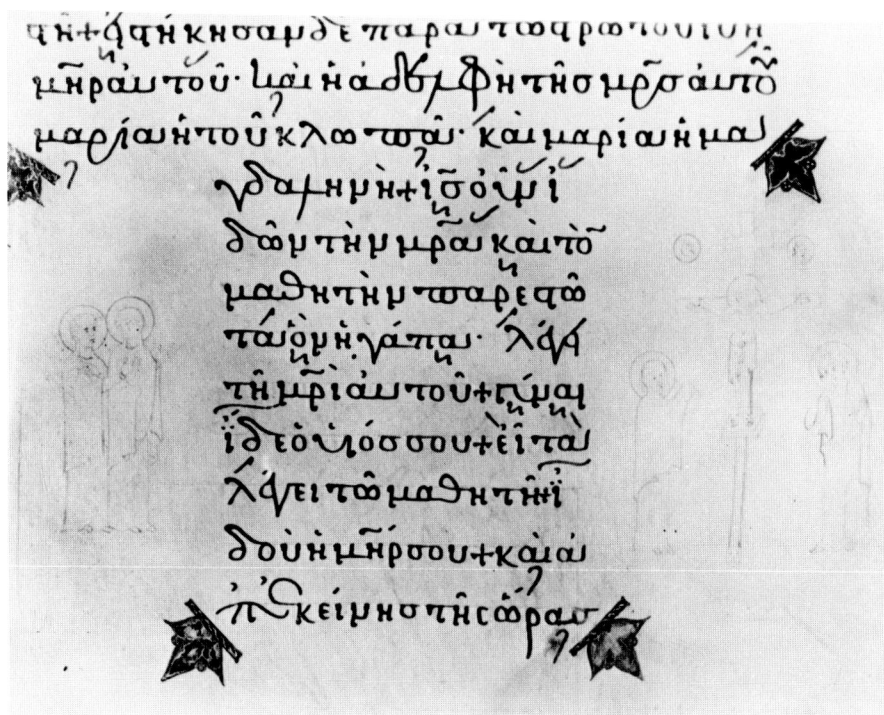

Fig. 34. New York, Morgan Library, MS 692, fol. 224: The Crucifixion

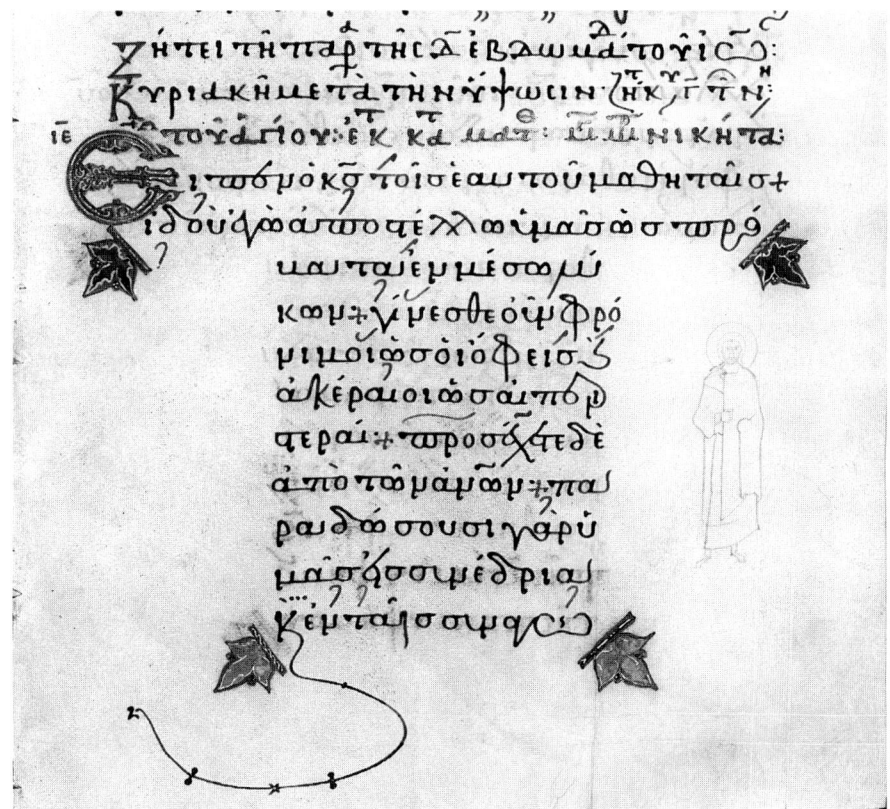

Fig. 35. New York, Morgan Library, MS 692, fol. 225: Saint Niketas

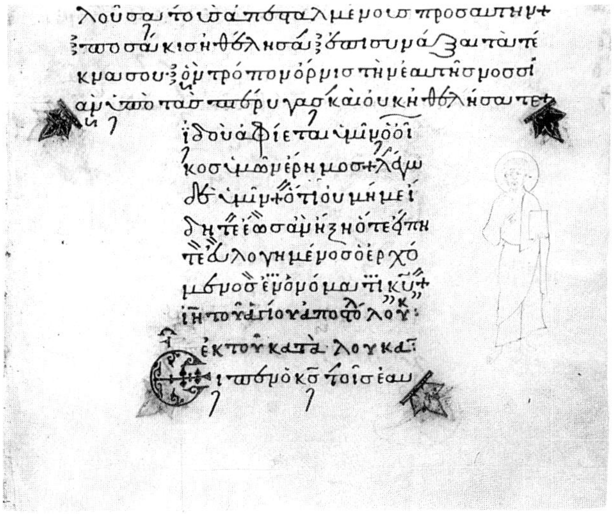

Fig. 36. New York, Morgan Library, MS 692, fol. 235: Saint Luke

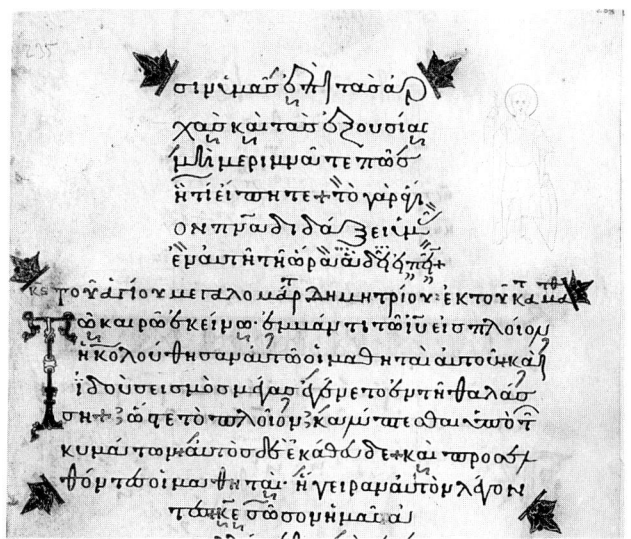

Fig. 37. New York, Morgan Library, MS 692, fol. 238: Saint Demetrios

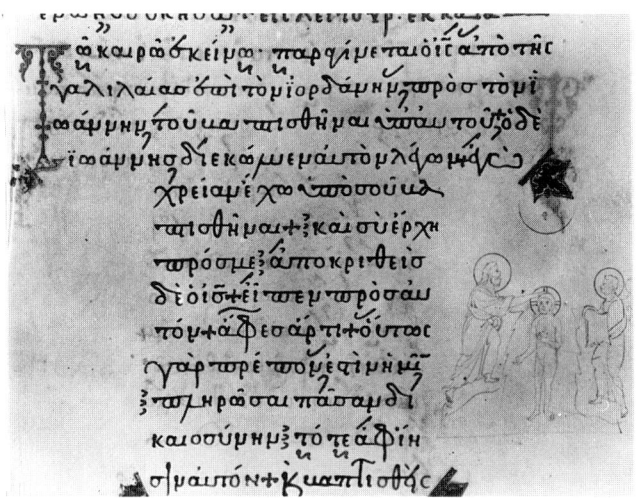

Fig. 38. New York, Morgan Library, MS 692, fol. 260: The Baptism of Christ

Fig. 39. New York, Morgan Library, MS 692, fol. 264: Presentation of Christ in the Temple

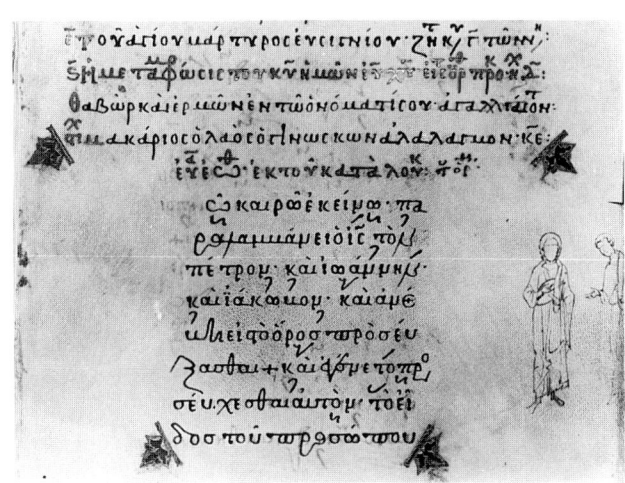

Fig. 40. New York, Morgan Library, MS 692, fol. 284: The Transfiguration

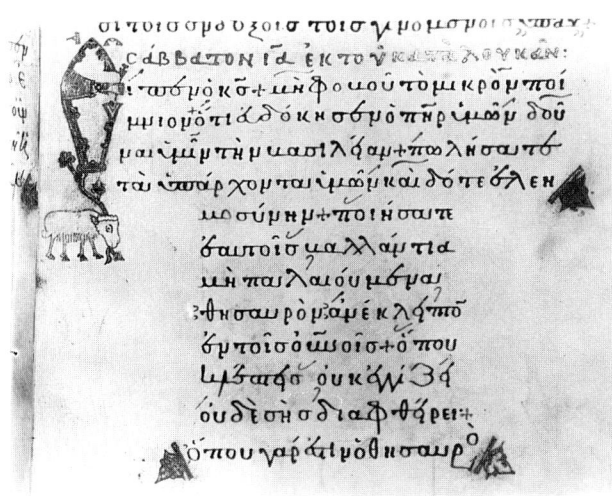

Fig. 41. New York, Morgan Library, MS 692, fol. 104: Initial *epsilon*

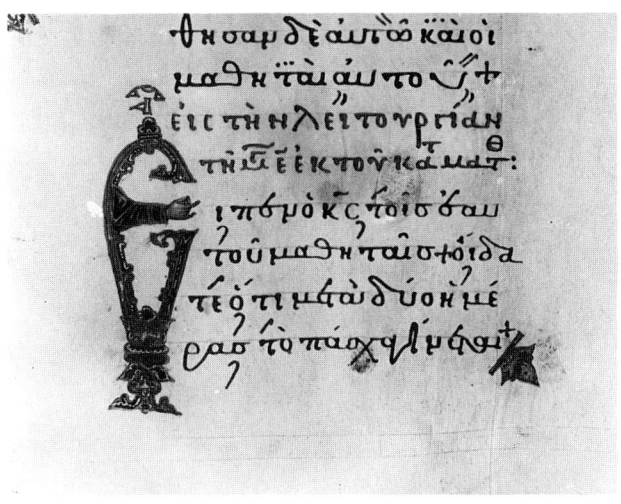

Fig. 42. New York, Morgan Library, MS 692, fol. 160: Initial *epsilon*

Fig. 43. London, British Library, Add. MS 39,603, fol. 1: Title page of the Easter and John readings

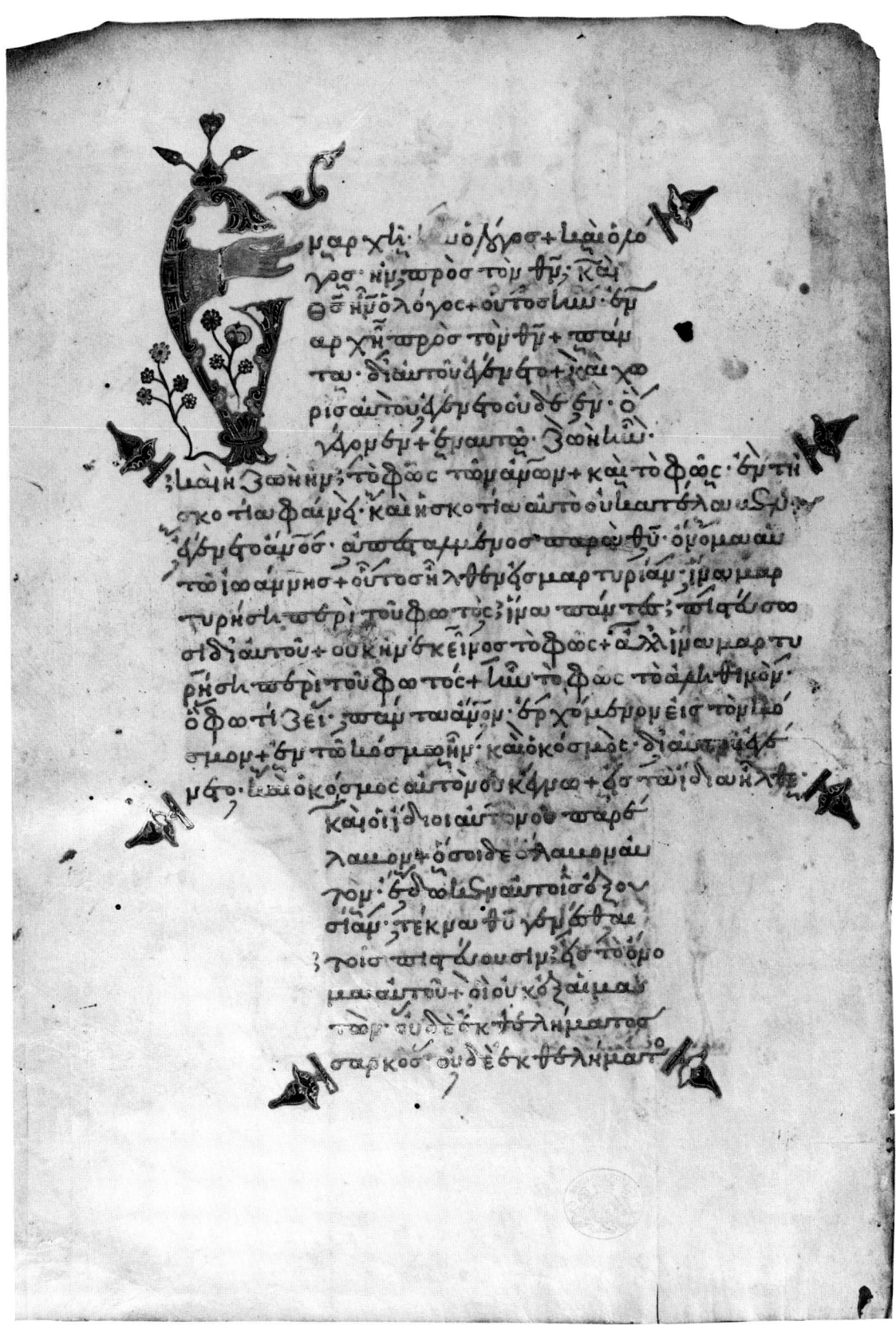

Fig. 44. London, British Library, Add. MS 39,603, fol. 1v: Initial *epsilon*

Fig. 45. London, British Library, Add. MS 39,603, fol. 42: Title page of the Matthew readings

Fig. 46. London, British Library, Add. MS 39,603, fol. 112: Title page of the Luke readings

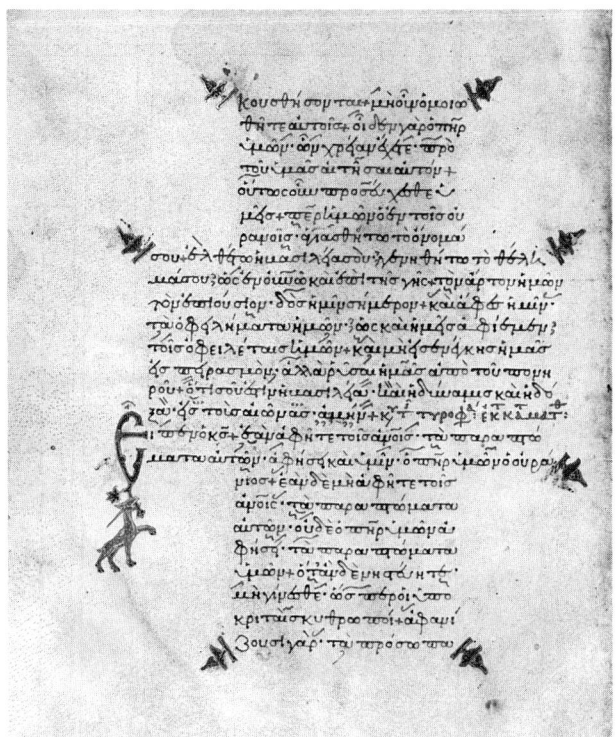

Fig. 47. London, British Library, Add. MS 39,603, fol. 195v: Initial *epsilon*

Fig. 48. Mount Athos, Iviron Monastery unnumbered lectionary, fol. 1: Title page of the Easter and John readings

Fig. 49. Mount Athos, Iviron Monastery unnumbered lectionary, fol. 100: Title page of the Luke readings

Fig. 50. Mount Athos, Iviron Monastery unnumbered lectionary, fol. 135: Title page of the Lenten and Mark readings

Fig. 51. Mount Athos, Iviron Monastery unnumbered lectionary, fol. 281: Title page of the Menologion

Fig. 52. Washington, D.C., Dumbarton Oaks Collection, MS 1, fol. 22: Christ and the Woman at the Well

Fig. 53. Washington, D.C., Dumbarton Oaks Collection, MS 1, fol. 65: Title page of the Luke readings

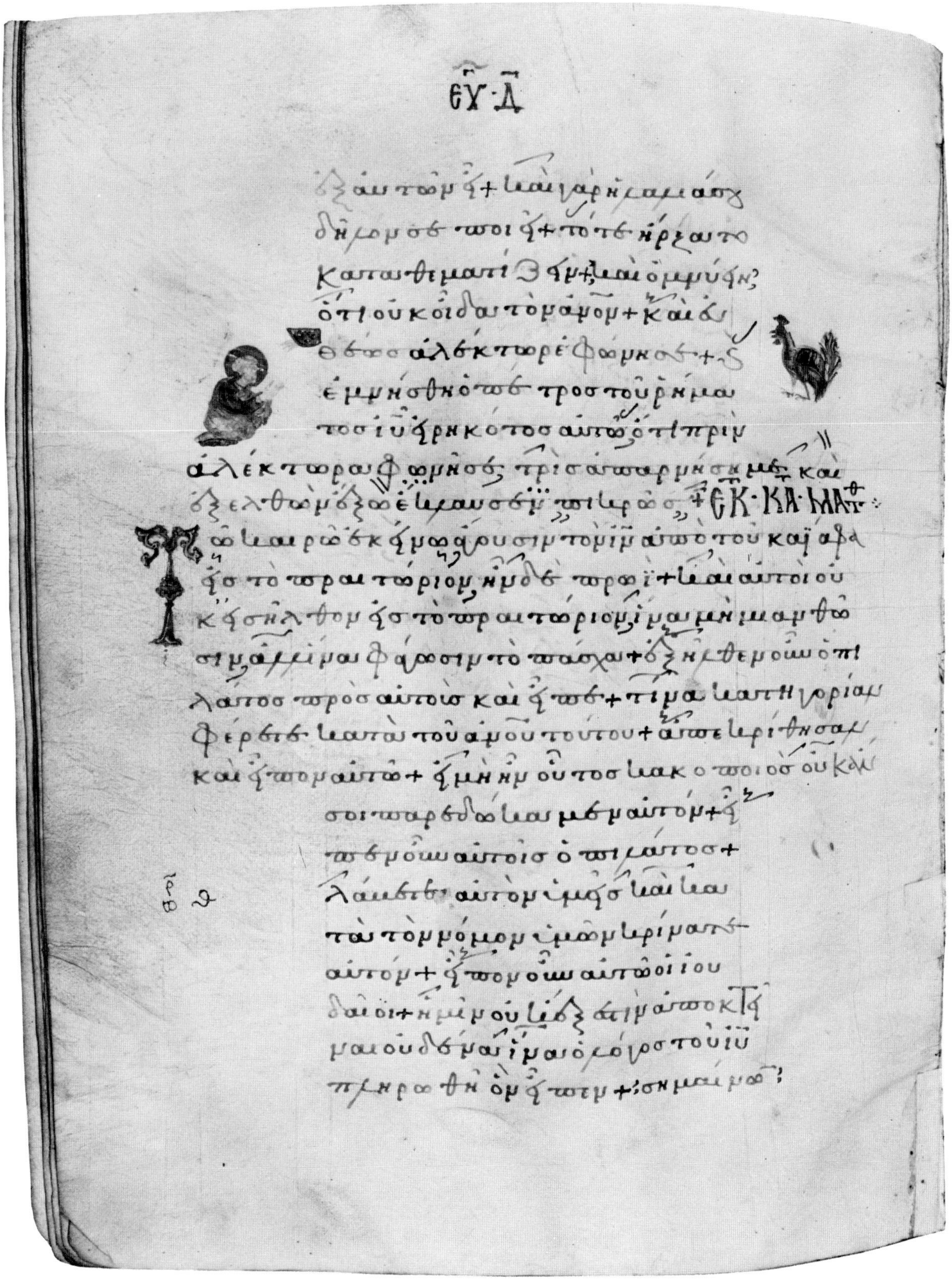

εὐ. Δ

Fig. 54. Washington, D.C., Dumbarton Oaks Collection, MS 1, fol. 122v: Saint Peter weeps as the rooster crows

Fig. 55. Paris, Bibliothèque Nationale, gr. 189, fol. 315v: Saint Mark the Evangelist

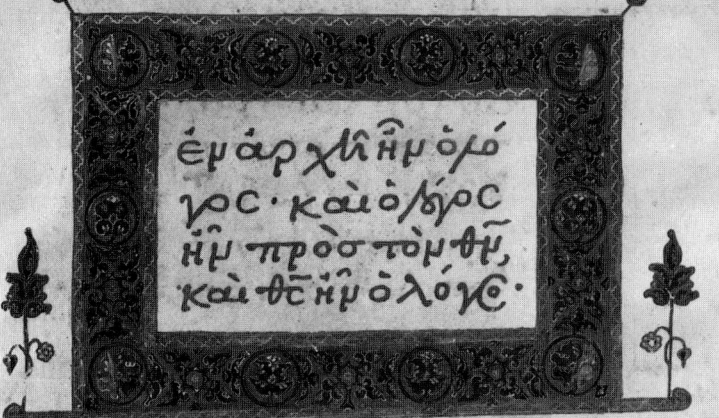

Fig. 56. Paris, Bibliothèque Nationale, gr. 189, fol. 2: Beginning of the Gospel of John

Fig. 57. Mount Athos, Panteleimon Monastery, cod. 2, fol. 115v: Saint Mark the Evangelist

Fig. 58. Mount Athos, Panteleimon Monastery, cod. 2, fol. 40v: Christ heals the Blind Youth

Fig. 59. Mount Athos, Panteleimon Monastery, cod. 2, fol. 63: The healing at Gadara

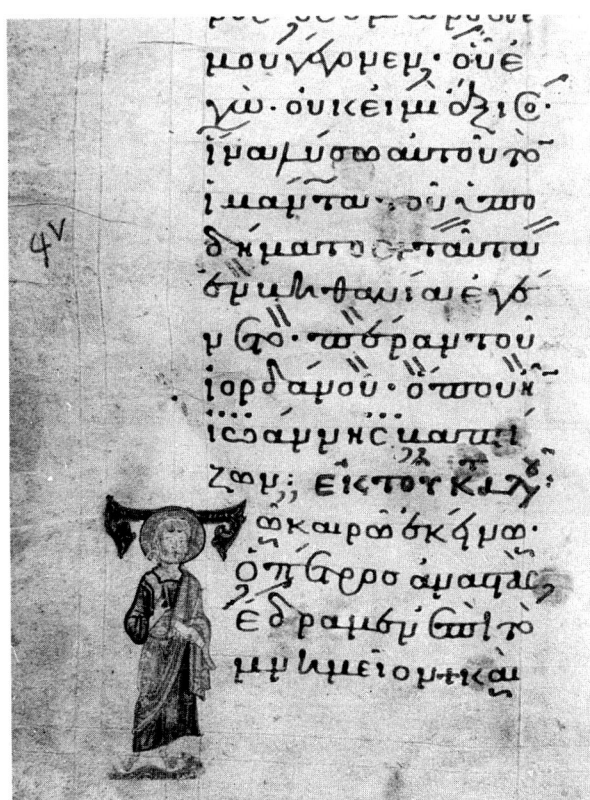

Fig. 60. Athens, National Library, cod. 190, fol. 2v: Saint Peter

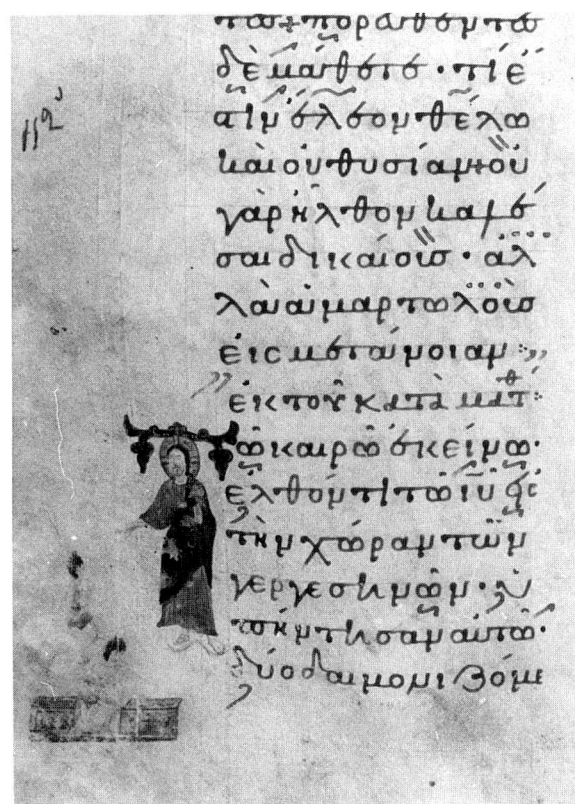

Fig. 61. Athens, National Library, cod. 190, fol. 56v: The healing at Gadara

Fig. 62. Mount Athos, Gregoriou Monastery, cod. 157, fol. 79: Moses teaching

Fig. 63. Istanbul, Topkapı Sarayı, cod. 8, fol. 203: Miracle of the Quail and Manna

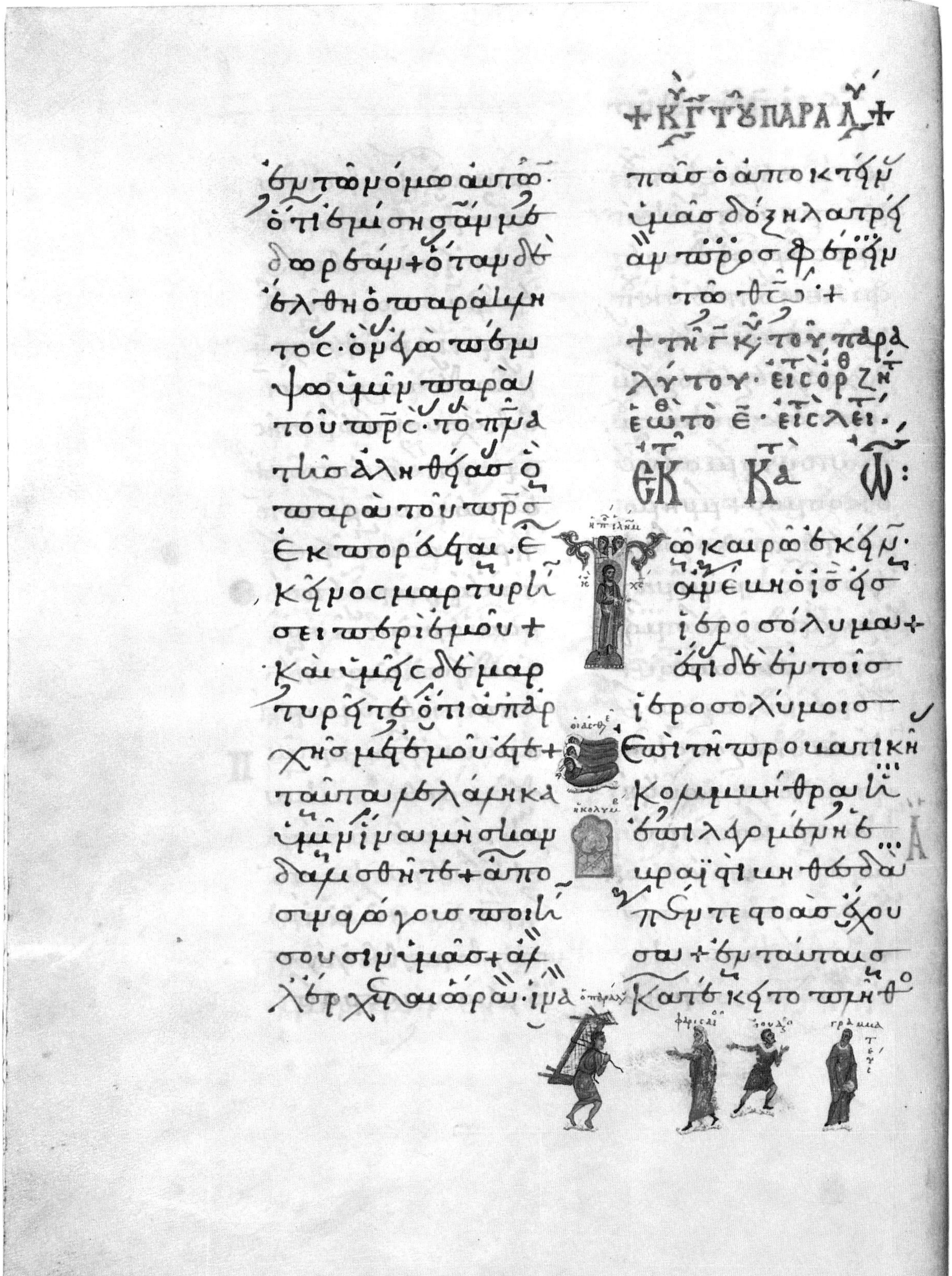

Fig. 64. New York, Morgan Library, MS 639, fol. 19v: Miracle at Bethesda